A SHEARWATER BOOK

The New
Economy
of Nature

The New Economy of Nature

The Quest to Make
Conservation Profitable

With sustainably good wishes!
Kath Ell

Gretchen C. Daily
and
Katherine Ellison

Island Press / SHEARWATER BOOKS
Washington • Covelo • London

Library of Congress Cataloging-in-Publication Data

Daily, Gretchen C.
The new economy of nature : the quest to make conservation
profitable / Gretchen C. Daily and Katherine Ellison
p. cm.
Includes bibliographical references (p.).
ISBN 1-55963-945-8 (cloth: alk. paper)
1. Nature conservation—Economic aspects.
I. Ellison, Katherine. II. Title.
QH75 .D345 2002
333.7'2—dc21   2001008713

British Cataloguing-in-Publication Data available.

For Gideon,
and for
Jack, Joe, and Joshua,
with love.

CONTENTS

The New
Economy
of Nature

The Wealth of Nature

"Nature's first green is gold."

—*Robert Frost*

W<small>HEN</small> <small>THREE-YEAR-OLD</small> Becky Furmann got the "poopies" and became dehydrated, her doctor urged her to drink water. He had no way of knowing that water had caused the rare illness that would kill her. As the chubby blond child grew thin and pale, her sufferings were finally confirmed as the ravages of *Cryptosporidium parvum,* a parasite almost unheard of until April 1993, when it slipped through one of the two modern filtration plants in Milwaukee, Wisconsin, and entered the city's water supply. Becky had been born with human immunodeficiency virus (HIV), which weakened her immune system, yet she had seemed otherwise healthy until then. Cryptosporidiosis sealed her fate. "She tries to ask us to kiss it and make it better, and we can't," said her father, near the end.

In all, Milwaukee's cryptosporidiosis epidemic led to more than 100 deaths and 400,000 illnesses. The victims had been betrayed by their water—and by their faith in the technology keeping it safe. What's more, they had plenty of company throughout the world.

With the start of the twenty-first century, every year more than 3 million people were dying of diseases spread by water, and another 1 billion were at risk, lacking access to water suitable to drink. As Milwaukee's disaster showed, the problem wasn't limited to developing countries. Some 36 million Americans were drinking water from systems violating United States Environmental Protection Agency (EPA) standards. One million Americans were getting sick every year from the contamination, and as many as 900 were dying from it. Fecal bacteria, heavy metals, arsenic, and pesticides had become familiar ingredients in many U.S. water supplies, and, as happened in Milwaukee, sometimes the highest-technology methods couldn't keep the contaminants out. Breakdowns were becoming a serious problem as mechanical systems aged and many strapped local governments deferred maintenance, to the point that the American Water Works Association estimated it would cost $325 billion to rehabilitate the country's dilapidated mechanical systems to ensure safe drinking water for everyone.

This crisis, and particularly this specter of expense, led the city of New York in 1997 to embark on a bold experiment that would reveal the value of what had been a mostly hidden but huge gift of Nature. With billions of dollars and the drinking water of nearly 10 million people at stake, planners weighed the costs and benefits of two alternative solutions to their water problem—constructing a filtration plant or repairing the largely natural filtration system that had been purifying the city's water all along. Nature won. And in a turn of events that would have global implications, it won on economic grounds.

The battlefield on which this victory was achieved is the Catskill/Delaware Watershed, the heart of New York's purification and delivery system, named after the two major rivers flowing from it. The rural landscape is famed as a scene of great beauty, with sun-struck slopes, glistening streams, and trees that explode in color each fall. Less well known is that it's also a highly efficient and valuable machine.

The cogs are 2,000 square miles of crop-filled valleys and mountains blanketed in forest, all connected by meandering streams feeding into an extensive system of nineteen reservoirs. For nearly a century, the complex natural system has been delivering water of exceptional purity to the people of New York City and several upstate counties. In recent years, it has produced as much as 1.8 billion gallons per day, serving New Yorkers with a healthy drink whose taste and clarity have been the envy of mayors throughout the United States. And unlike the case in most other large U.S. cities, New York's tap water has never passed through a filtration plant.

Instead, the water, born as rain and melted snow on mountaintops as far as 125 miles away from those who will ultimately drink it, is naturally cleansed as it makes its way downhill toward the reservoirs. Beneath the forest floor, soil and fine roots filter the water and hidden microorganisms break down contaminants. In the streams, plants absorb as much as half of the surplus nutrients running into the waterway, such as nitrogen from automobile emissions and fertilizer and manure used on nearby farms. In open stretches, wetlands continue the filtering as cattails and other plants voraciously take up nutrients while trapping sediment and heavy metals. After reaching the reservoirs, the water is further cleansed as it sits and waits. Dead algae, floating branches and leaves, and remaining particles of grit slowly sink to the bottom. Some pathogens left in the water may bind to the grit and settle, too.

This mostly natural process—supplemented by small doses of chlorine and fluoride at the end of the water's journey—worked beautifully for most of the twentieth century. But then signs appeared of some mechanical failures. The trouble was relentless new development: roads, subdivisions, and second homes were popping up all over the watershed, most of which is privately owned. Failing septic systems were leaking raw sewage into streams. Farming and forestry were also taking a toll, with lawn chemicals, fertilizers, pesticides, and manure all being washed into the reservoirs at an unprecedented rate.

By 1989, these problems could no longer be ignored. The United

States Congress that year amended the Safe Drinking Water Act, putting into motion a major review of the country's drinking water systems. New York City was faced with the potentially enormous cost of an artificial water filtration plant, estimated at as much as $6–$8 billion, plus yearly maintenance expenses amounting to $300–$500 million. That price tag meant potential catastrophe for New York's budget, and city officials were determined to avoid it. With vigorous lobbying, they won agreement from federal regulators to try the alternative of a watershed protection program capable of guaranteeing water quality indefinitely. Rather than pay for the costly new filtration plant, the city would spend the much smaller amount of about $1.5 billion to protect the upstate watershed, including buying tracts of land as buffers and upgrading polluting sewage treatment plants. The EPA, in turn, would grant a five-year reprieve of its order, with the possibility of renewal.

The scheme was seriously challenged from the start. Powerful developers filed suit, claiming that property values would plummet as the city imposed restrictions on new construction. Environmentalists criticized the city's efforts as too weak. Nonetheless, the unprecedented agreement was a milestone in a world in which Nature's labor has too long been taken for granted. A major government body had acted as if an ecosystem—the watershed—were worth protecting in its natural state for the economic benefits it gives society. And it had invested in its restoration as if it were in fact a precious piece of infrastructure.

New York City planners had joined a new and diverse movement of prospectors for "green gold." Like the miners of yore, they were out to extract value from Nature and were in a rush to do so against competing forces. But rather than aiming pickaxes and dynamite at a nonliving, finite trove of gold, they wielded scientific studies and restoration projects, for the assets they sought were alive and renewable and would, if managed properly, continue to yield wealth for many years to come.

For most people who were paying attention, this came as a reve-

Forests, for example, not only help purify water but also reduce potential harm from flooding, drought, and mudslides. They shelter people from winter storms and summer heat and provide homes for many of Earth's other living inhabitants. Most dramatically, they help stabilize climate by absorbing heat-trapping carbon dioxide (CO_2) from the atmosphere.

Wetlands provide a similar range of valuable services. Along river floodplains, they slow and diminish the flow of water, protecting homes and roads from flood damage. In the process, they also purify the water. Along coastlines, wetlands and similar habitats nurture young fish, oysters, and other seafood. Coral reefs offer stunning beauty and recreational opportunities while supplying people with 10 percent of the fish consumed globally.

In farming regions, hedgerows and remaining native habitats support bees and other insects that pollinate crops. All told, the harvest of about one in three food crops worldwide—from alfalfa to watermelons—is possible thanks to the work of pollinators. And finally, all ecosystems foster genetic diversity, maintaining a "library" of genes with values yet to be discovered for future medical and industrial products.

Just as it makes human life possible, the work of ecosystems helps make life worth living. Forests, beaches, and wide-open spaces nourish our spirits and culture in ways we're only beginning to understand. Research suggests that communion with natural landscapes, plants, and animals can not only soothe and restore but even heal. In one study, for instance, hospital patients were randomly assigned to one of two types of room. Some looked out on a natural setting—a modest stand of trees—and others looked out at a building wall. The study, which controlled for health-related factors such as sex, weight, and tobacco use, showed that patients who looked out on a natural setting fared much better than did those with the view of a wall.

Historically, all these labors of Nature have been thought of as free. And with the exception of the production of a few specific goods, such as farm crops and timber, the use of Nature's services is

lation. Conservation could *save* money—a lot of money
example, could be worth something more than timber,
financial value for the gifts they give while standing and
healthy, functioning forest. Land could have financial va
from its potential to have something mined from it or
farmed on it. The labor of ecosystems previously regarded a
might even be quantified in some way, recorded on balance
and formally considered in decision making.

Around the world, in city offices and university conference
among small groups of community activists and at the World Ban
entists, legal scholars, bureaucrats, and professional environmen
debated the implications of New York's experiment. Could it pos
work? Did scientists know enough about the mechanics of watersh
to give reliable advice on their management? And assuming
approach turned out to be justified, how widely could it be replicate

In fact, without clear answers to these questions, and in man
cases without knowing much about New York, governments aroun
the world—in Curitiba, Brazil; in Quito, Ecuador; and in more than
140 U.S. municipalities, from Seattle, Washington, to Dade County,
Florida—were starting to calculate the costs of conserving watersheds and compare them with the costs of building mechanical
plants. In a bold departure from business as usual, they were taking
stock of their natural capital. In the process, they were learning how
ecosystems—environments of interacting plants, animals, and
microbes, from coastal tide pools to Loire Valley vineyards to
expanses of Amazonian rain forest—can be seen as capital assets, supplying human beings with a stream of services that sustain and
enhance our lives. These "ecosystem services" provide not only food
and wine but also cleansing of Earth's air and water, protection from
the elements, and refreshment and serenity for human spirits.

As the saying goes, a woman's work is never done—nor fairly
compensated—and this is nowhere truer than in the case of Mother
Nature. Much of Nature's labor has enormous and obvious value,
which has failed to win respect in the marketplace until recently.

actually quite startlingly unregulated. Despite our assiduous watch over other forms of capital—physical (homes, cars, factories), financial (cash, savings accounts, corporate stocks), and human (skills and knowledge)—we haven't even taken measure of the ecosystem capital stocks that produce these most vital of labors. We lack a formal system of appraising or monitoring the value of natural assets, and we have few means of insuring them against damage or loss.

Although governments have negotiated a wide array of global and regional agreements to protect certain ecosystems from degradation and extinction—such as the Ramsar Convention on Wetlands, the Convention on Biological Diversity, and the Convention on the Law of the Sea—these agreements are mostly weak, lacking the participation, resources, and systems of incentives and enforcement they need to be effective.

Even more striking is how rarely investments in ecosystem capital are rewarded economically. Typically, property owners are not compensated for the services the natural assets on their land provide to society. With rare exception, owners of coastal wetlands are not paid for the abundance of seafood the wetlands nurture, nor are owners of tropical forests compensated for that ecosystem's contribution to the pharmaceutical industry and climate stability. As a result, many crucial types of ecosystem capital are undergoing rapid degradation and depletion. Compounding the problem is that the importance of ecosystem services is often widely appreciated only upon their loss.

The source of this predicament is easy to comprehend. For most of humankind's experience on Earth, ecosystem capital was available in sufficient abundance, and human activities were sufficiently limited, that it was reasonable to think of ecosystem services as free. Yet today, Nature everywhere is under siege. Each year the world loses some 30 million acres of tropical forest, an area slightly larger than Pennsylvania. At this rate, the last rain-forest tree will bow out—dead on arrival at a sawmill or in a puff of smoke—around the middle of the twenty-first century. Biodiversity—short for biological diversity, the amazing variety of life on Earth—is being reduced to the lowest levels in human history. *Homo sapiens* has already wiped out one-quarter of all bird species, and an estimated 11 percent more are on the path to extinction, along with 24 percent of mammal and 11 percent of plant species. One-quarter of the world's coral reefs have been destroyed, with many others undergoing serious decline. To top it off, we're taking fish out of the sea for consumption faster than they can reproduce. Dramatic as they are, these global statistics mask the accelerating loss of local populations of species—the individual trees that help keep water pure, the individual bees that pollinate our crops.

An overriding force behind this liquidation of ecosystem capital is the tremendous human demand for food and fiber—wheat, rice, cotton, timber, and so on. To produce these commodities, people already have dramatically transformed half of the planet's ice-free land surface, from natural landscapes to farmland, ranchland, and tree plantations. In many parts of the world, these activities are undermining the very resources that support them, depleting soil fertility and water supplies. Yet pressures are enormous to expand and intensify this production, despite its obvious toll.

The twenty-first century began with a growing sense among scientists that crucial thresholds had been reached and time to fix things was running out. We were operating beyond the limits of what Nature could sustain, conscious that we couldn't keep it up, but with no plan under way to change our course. As Stanford University biologist Peter Vitousek has said, "we're the first generation with tools to understand changes in the earth's system caused by human activity, and the last with the opportunity to influence the course of many of the changes now rapidly under way."

This increasingly apparent deadline has begun to inspire a shift in thinking for many scholars, most notably economists. To be sure, economists have long been concerned with issues of resource scarcity and limits to human activities. That's why their field was dubbed "the dismal science." Yet throughout the 1960s, 1970s, and 1980s, most economists clashed with ecologists. Economists accused ecologists of being alarmist about adverse human effects on Earth and of proposing costly and unnecessary measures of protection. Meanwhile, ecologists charged economists with promoting "growth" at any price and misusing partial indicators of well-being, such as the gross national product, that are blind to wear and tear on the planet.

This conflict began to ease in the late 1980s, however, with efforts to forge a new discipline integrating ecology and economics. An early participant in this movement was Stanford professor and Nobel laureate Kenneth Arrow, who for decades has been disturbed by the way economics dismisses "externalities," activities of which there are two types. Positive externalities are activities that benefit people who don't pay for them; negative externalities harm people who don't receive compensation.

An example of a positive externality is modern Costa Rica's careful stewardship of its forests—a striking turnabout from the rampant deforestation that lasted into the 1980s. The new conservation policies contribute to sustainable development in the region while also helping to stabilize the global climate and maintain biodiversity. Yet for the most part, only Costa Ricans pay to preserve these widely enjoyed benefits. In contrast, a negative externality occurs when Americans drive gas guzzlers. This activity contributes to air pollution, potential climate change, and the risk of the U.S. government being drawn into foreign conflicts over oil. Yet even though these negative consequences affect large numbers of people, the drivers— since U.S. gas is cheap and relatively untaxed—don't pay the costs.

"Internalization" of such externalities—enactment of a system of fair pricing and fair payment—is badly needed, but it will not be simple. Arrow has tried to meet the challenge in part by joining other economists and ecologists in a growing effort to "rethink economics," a process fortified by their yearly meetings on the island of Askö in the Stockholm Archipelago.

Another major player in these meetings has been Cambridge University professor Partha Dasgupta, the recent president of both the British and the European economics associations. Born in India,

Dasgupta has devoted much of his career to studying the interplay of overpopulation, poverty, and environmental degradation. He remembers being stunned, at a United Nations meeting in 1981, when economists from developing countries stood up one by one and told him they couldn't afford to protect their environments. The encounter, he later said, gave him "some measure of how far we had yet to go. We must stop viewing the environment as an amenity, a luxury the poor can't afford." Quite to the contrary, Dasgupta is convinced that the local environment is often the greatest asset for poor families because they have few alternatives for income if it fails. The rich, by contrast, have a global reach for all sorts of ecosystem goods and services, as revealed by their dinner tables laden with fresh fruit, fish, spring water, and flowers from all over the planet. Ultimately, though, the rich are also vulnerable to faltering ecosystem services and the social instability that can arise as a result.

Important as they clearly are to rich and poor alike, ecosystem services typically carry little or no formally recognized economic value. As Columbia University economist Geoffrey Heal points out, economics is concerned more with prices than with values or importance. "The price of a good"—say, a loaf of bread or a car or piece of jewelry—"does not reflect its importance in any overall social or philosophical sense," says Heal. "Very unimportant goods can be valued more highly by the market—have higher prices—than very important goods."

This contradiction isn't new. Economists throughout the eighteenth and nineteenth centuries were perplexed by the paradox of diamonds and water. Why do diamonds command a much higher price than water, when water is obviously so much more key to human survival? The answer, proposed by Englishman Alfred Marshall, is now common knowledge: price is set by supply and demand. In the case of water, the supply (at least in Marshall's England) "was so large as to exceed the amount that could possibly be demanded at any price," Heal explains. "Consequently the price was zero; water was free. Now, of course, the demand for water has increased greatly as a result of population growth and rising prosperity, while the supply has remained roughly constant, so that water is no longer free." Diamonds, by contrast, started out scarce: the desire for ownership always exceeded their supply. Their market price was thus high—set by rich people competing for the few diamonds available.

Ecosystem assets have the importance of water and are gradually acquiring the scarcity of diamonds as the human population and its aspirations grow. As they become more like diamonds, they take on increasing potential value in economic terms. But major innovations to our economic and social institutions are needed to capture this value and incorporate it into day-to-day decision making.

The main challenge in the pursuit of this goal is that most ecosystem services are currently treated as "public goods," which if provided for one are provided for all, no matter who pays. An example is air quality: if a government spends on reducing pollution, it helps taxpayers and nontaxpayers alike. That leads to a problem of "free riders," in which some people benefit without charge from services paid for by others. And this is particularly true with the services provided by Nature. Although we've engineered a financial system so sophisticated as to include market values for feng shui masters and interest rate derivatives, we've not yet managed to establish them for such vital and everyday services as water purification and flood protection.

The big challenge now—and a major concern of this book—is how to measure, capture, and protect these newly discovered values before they are lost. There's been an urgent flurry of calls to do just that since the late 1990s, yet the quest to realize the value of Nature's services is anything but new. Even Plato drew attention to the links between the clearing of forests in Attica and the drying of local springs. And in the 1860s, U.S. statesman George Perkins Marsh lamented how "rivers famous in history and song have shrunk to humble brooklets" in the deforested lands of the once powerful Roman Empire.

Still, not until New York made its historic decision to invest in its watershed did it seem possible that big governments would catch on, supporting the concrete results of Nature's work with cash on the table. Replicating that endeavor to any great extent, by conserving not only watersheds for water purity but also wetlands for flood control and forests for climate stabilization and biodiversity conservation, would require a tremendous amount of new scientific understanding of ecosystems—of their functioning, of their susceptibility to adverse human effects and their amenability to repair, and of the pros and cons of replacing them with technological substitutes. More important, it would require a willingness to look at the world's economy in an entirely different way, starting with the assumption that ecosystems are assets whose output has concrete financial worth.

It's not that we don't value these services *at all*. It's clear that we're willing to pay. We buy costly water bottled from faraway, pristine springs, send checks to support endangered species, pay premiums for homes next to preserved "open space," and part with outlandish sums to travel to places where we can still catch glimpses of untrammeled Nature. All the same, we still think of conservation basically as something to do for moral or aesthetic reasons—not for survival and certainly not for profit.

Nevertheless, the record clearly shows that conservation can't succeed by charity alone. It has a fighting chance, however, with well-designed appeals to self-interest. The challenge now is to change the rules of the game so as to produce new incentives for environmental protection, geared to both society's long-term well-being and individuals' self-interest.

One way to do this is with taxes and subsidies targeting major environmental externalities, tools widely employed in Europe. A tax on consumption of fossil fuels, for instance, makes users of a shared resource—in this case, the sky, being used as a dumping ground—reduce their consumption and the damage it causes. It also makes higher-priced alternative energy sources (with lower environmental costs) more attractive financially. Consumption taxes such as this can be offset by reductions in income tax rates. In the United States, however, such taxes have been virtually impossible to pass through Congress.

Another tactic, sometimes more politically feasible, is to establish ownership of ecosystem assets and services. This can avert the famous "tragedy of the commons" that often occurs when there is open access to a natural resource. It happens because each individual has more to gain by, say, launching another fishing boat than to lose as the fishery is depleted. But when ownership rights to Nature's goods and services are assigned, the new owners—be they private citizens, communities, corporations, interest groups, or governments—face unshared risk of those rights diminishing in value. Thus, as explained by economist and Nobel laureate Ronald Coase, they are motivated to fight for the asset's protection.

In other words, establishing ownership of natural capital and services allows bargaining between those affected by an externality and those causing it. Creating a place where people can get together to bargain—a market, whether in the town square or on the Internet—is an old approach being newly applied to capture the value of ecosystem assets. A premier example is the evolving legal concept of "carbon rights"—ownership of the capacity of forests to stabilize climate by absorbing CO_2. Efforts are under way to establish such rights and develop international markets for the purchase and sale of this forest ecosystem service, which in turn would establish a "market value," or price.

"Without prices being set, Nature becomes like an all-you-can-eat buffet—and I don't know anyone who doesn't overeat at a buffet," says Richard Sandor, an environmentally minded financial innovator based in Chicago. Sandor, who has been experimenting with ways of mass-marketing New Age environmental commodities, including permits to pollute, has been a leading member of the "green gold" prospectors looking at the problem of our dwindling resources in a striking new way. This group has also begun to act, launching bold initiatives to find financial incentives for environmental conservation.

This book seeks to document that promise. We began working together on it in the winter of 1999, when the two of us met at Stanford University. One of us, Katherine, a longtime foreign correspondent, was studying environmental science on a John S. Knight journalism fellowship. The other, Gretchen, was Stanford's Bing Interdisciplinary Research Scientist, weaving together a network of scholars and businesspeople in search of innovative approaches to solving environmental problems. Gretchen wove Katherine into that net, and we made several trips together, chiefly from April 2000 to April 2001, to explore the promising signs of change under way.

As it happened, that year was a formative time for this new paradigm, featuring diverse efforts to bring the abstract theory about ecosystem services down to Earth, harmonizing economic activity and environmental protection. The efforts we describe in the pages that follow differ greatly in the type of ecosystem capital involved, in the geographic and cultural context of that capital, and in the incentives employed to protect it. What they have in common is that each offers insights into a prosperous, sustainable future. In just the twelve months in which we traveled together, we witnessed these developments:

- In Boston, the Hancock Natural Resource Group, a $3 billion division of John Hancock Financial Services, prepared a revolutionary fund to invest in newly planted forests that would be carefully—"sustainably"—managed in order to preserve them for future generations. Contributors to the fund would receive two types of return: dividends based on revenues from selective timber harvests and credits for the amount of CO_2 absorbed by the new trees as they grew. Under anticipated new laws that might restrict corporate CO_2 emissions, such credits could become valuable as "offsets" to substitute for actual reductions in emissions.

- In Adelaide, Australia, environmentalist John Wamsley listed his conservation company on the national stock exchange, saying it was the first of its kind to go public. Wamsley's venture, Earth Sanctuaries, buys degraded farmland and turns it into ecotourist attractions by restoring it with native plants and restocking it with native animals threatened with decline or extinction. Wamsley calls his turn to the market "trading in biodiversity" and aims to use his business model to restore and protect vast regions—amounting to fully 1 percent—of Australia.

- In Napa, California, a city plagued for decades by floods, work began on an innovative effort to free the Napa River from its levees and dams and allow it to spill over onto its historical floodplain, providing natural flood protection. The U.S. Army Corps of Engineers, famous for pouring concrete, began tearing it out, removing dams and levees along a seven-mile stretch. Napa residents, who had voted to raise their own taxes to pay for the plan, saw immediate paybacks, with property values soaring in expectation of an enticing new waterfront district and a dry downtown.

- In Costa Rica, the government expanded its pioneering program of paying private landowners to maintain functioning forests and other ecosystems, giving individuals an incentive to work for the common good. Under its auspices, property owners who conserve or regenerate forest on their land can receive compensation for the resulting flow of services, including carbon sequestration (for climate stability), watershed protection (for safe drinking water and low-sediment hydropower supplies), biodiversity conservation (for pharmaceutical and other uses), and provision of scenic beauty (for ecotourism and other aesthetic enjoyment).

- In Bilthoven, The Netherlands, ninety-five of the world's top-ranking scientists met to launch the Millennium Ecosystem Assessment, the first comprehensive review of the state of Earth's ecosystem assets, with a historically unique focus on the goods and services they render. The aim of this effort is to supply decision makers worldwide with the information needed to incorporate ecosystem assets into business plans and policy development.

Most of the experiments we discuss are controversial in some way, not least in their blunt appeal to self-interest. The approaches we describe have attracted prospectors with widely diverse motivations along the spectrum from environmental protection to pure financial gain. A great unanswered question is whether the drive for profits, which has done so much harm to the planet, can possibly be harnessed to save it.

One thing is clear: private enterprise cannot substitute for governments, particularly in view of the increasing risk of climate change, a global problem requiring global cooperation if it's not to override all other environmental *and* economic worries in a matter of decades. We strongly believe that government regulation is called for to kick-start and supervise the profound economic transformation needed to ward off this and other environmental threats. Yet we also believe this transformation can be speeded with the use of market mechanisms and other financial incentives, tactics that have been glaringly underemployed.

We wrote this book as both advocates and critics, but chiefly as pragmatists. Financial motives and markets aren't going away anytime soon. And whether they appeal to us or not, experiments in finding market values for such essential gifts of Nature as clean water and fresh air are well under way. Understanding them is key to making the best of them and, as the eminent biologist Edward O. Wilson has urged, to giving economist Adam Smith's "invisible hand" a green thumb.

We therefore set out to tell the stories of some of the dedicated, innovative people implementing this new approach. In the following pages, you'll meet, among others, John Wamsley, amid the wombats and wallabies in his Adelaide sanctuary; Karen Rippey, the tall, strapping former welder who helped convince the voters in her town to raise taxes to pay to let the Napa River run free; and David Brand, the Johnny Appleseed of the new "green" investments and pioneer of the Hancock Natural Resource Group's New Forests Fund. You'll also hear the stories of Claire Kremen, the Stanford biologist who is patiently documenting the economic value of wild pollinators, and Daniel Janzen, the award-winning ecologist who is restoring a tropical forest in Costa Rica while also putting it to work in several ways, including, briefly, as a waste disposal system for a local orange juice firm.

Each story that follows illustrates different combinations of hope and controversy, potential and problems. At the same time, each shows some necessary history in the making. In his or her own way, with small and large contributions, each of these people is facing up to the greatest test put to humankind: the challenge of making our daily living from Earth's resources without compromising our children's prospects for doing so in the future. As the tragedy of Becky Furmann and all the other victims of the Milwaukee disaster shows, this challenge is real and urgent.

In his classic poem contemplating the loss of innocence, Robert Frost mourned the inevitable changes in Nature, concluding, "Nothing gold can stay." With apologies to the poet, we'd like to argue that Nature's gold *can* stay, as long as it is recognized as such, and that this new vision, evoked in the discoveries by the prospectors you'll read of in the following pages, is the key to a new economy.

Katoomba and the Stratosphere

"Under the general name of Commodity, I rank all those advantages which our senses owe to nature. This, of course, is a benefit which is temporary and mediate, not ultimate, like its service to the soul. Yet although low, it is perfect in kind, and is the only use of nature which all men apprehend."

—*Ralph Waldo Emerson*

ADAM DAVIS STRODE PAST the doily-covered parlor sofas at Lilianfels Blue Mountains, an elegant hotel in the New South Wales resort city of Katoomba. He'd arrived in Sydney two days earlier from San Francisco and was still jet-lagged, but you couldn't tell that from looking at him. Davis had the laser gaze of a gambler, and the grin of a man who feels the odds are with him.

This was doubly impressive, considering the wager. Davis was out to save the world from environmental catastrophe, and to make some money in the bargain. The son of an impassioned wilderness photographer and the product of a highly liberal education (bachelor of arts, cum laude, in Africana Studies, Cornell University, 1983), he was also the child of a peculiar place and time: the fringe of California's

Silicon Valley in April 2000. The Nasdaq Stock Market was flirting with its 5,000 peak, and the romance of financial innovation was never keener nor more widely shared. Davis was zealous in his quest to rescue Nature, but unlike his mother, back in Baltimore, he didn't think the Audubon Society could do the job. He wanted, instead, to give Wall Street a shot.

After a stint in an Ithaca, New York, commune, Davis had an epiphany while working for a compost company. He was thrilled by the idea of turning waste into something useful, creating value where none existed before. He went on to make his career in waste management, rising high in the recycling ranks before starting his own firm to counsel corporations on their environmental policies and marketing. He was skilled at writing business plans and had been working furiously on a particularly bold one in recent months, in the hours he could spare from his clients. He carried several copies of it, printed on recycled paper, in the canvas briefcase slung over his shoulder.

He called his plan The Conservation Exchange. Although it remained little more than a theory, Davis was sure it would eventually have global ramifications. He'd made the long trip to Australia that week to see whether he could create a buzz.

The occasion was an extraordinary conference sponsored by a Washington, D.C., think tank called Forest Trends. It brought together from four continents about 150 economists, scientists, investors, and professional conservationists who shared an interest in creating new financial incentives for conservation. The meeting opened with a series of lectures at Sydney's Taronga Zoo, after which a select group of four dozen conference-goers took a bus to Katoomba, in the stunning, 250-million-year-old Blue Mountains. There, they'd spend two days contemplating ways to transform the world's economy to support the increasingly urgent needs of the besieged environment. Davis thought Katoomba the perfect venue to debut his Conservation Exchange. He networked with a vengeance, beginning the night he arrived in Sydney, when he held forth to a small group of conference-goers at an open-air wharfside café.

"Some $600 billion changes hands each year in international gambling," he said, running a hand over his close-cropped, graying hair. "We have to add some of that excitement, some of that gaming element, to conservation."

Davis spoke fast and with assurance, outlining his plan. The Conservation Exchange would be a World Wide Web site that people all over the world could visit, logging on to trade new commodities called ecosystem service units. The ESUs, as Davis called them, would be different from any stocks ever sold. They'd be based not on products of humankind or Nature but rather on Nature's work. Each ESU would represent a precisely measured quantity of a vital environmental service. Included would be the manner in which water is purified by watersheds, the way forests help regulate the climate by absorbing—or, in scientists' lingo, becoming "sinks" for—heat-trapping carbon dioxide, and even the way healthy ecosystems provide habitats and preserve biodiversity. Scientists would help certify the ESUs, and accountants would parcel them out for sale.

The sellers, at the start, would be landowners marketing the rights to services from their property. The initial values of the ESUs would be partly determined by perceived supply and demand: the rarity of the ecosystem type involved, be it rain forest, desert, savanna, or wetland, and the demand for services from such ecosystems.

Buyers of the shares might at first include businesses trying to find ways to comply with environmental regulations. Already, some rules in the United States allowed companies to "trade" in habitat. In wetlands mitigation banking, for instance, a "bank" of wetland habitat is established, consisting of newly created or restored wetlands. Property developers who are required to make amends for wetlands they destroy may then pay money to fund or enlarge the bank. Davis' plan would simply extend that concept.

Initial purchasers might also include wealthy conservation organizations. They might buy environmental conservation from a private landowner, as spelled out in a contract, without actually buying the land, thus saving money. Yet in time, Davis felt certain, speculators would enter the market and investors would trade ESUs just like shares in Amazon.com or Cisco Systems.

He realized the scheme was audacious. He also knew "green" purists might challenge him for having the anthropocentric nerve to try to commercialize Earth's basic life-support systems. But Davis was sure of his own good intentions. As far as he was concerned, he was as devoted an environmentalist as any member of Greenpeace. Profits and glitz were just the means to a worthy end. The time was ripe for thinking outside the box about Nature and markets. Besides, he had come to believe—along with a number of mainstream economists of various political persuasions—that establishing property rights to ecosystem services and a market for trading in them was the way to create financial value where none existed before. He'd seen the instant creation of value in Silicon Valley with Netscape's stunning initial public offering and the skyrocketing stock values of JDS Uniphase Corporation and other telecommunications companies. If all this were possible, why shouldn't people be able to trade in the perceived worth of Nature's labors, which, after all, were more precious than diamonds, given that human life depended on them?

His six-page business plan explained the reasoning, with liberal use of italics. Just like the "new-economy" stocks, his ESUs would be valued less on current earnings than on future potential. In the case of the ESUs, it was a simple question of supply and demand, something people had never truly applied to Nature because Nature's bounty had generally been just that—bountiful. Yet as the scale of the human enterprise grew, with more people crowding Earth and greater levels of consumption per person, the supply of "free" services, such as natural detoxification and recycling of wastes, would inevitably dwindle just as demand for them reached historic peaks. Market forces would have to apply.

"The key to understanding The Conservation Exchange is understanding that these services were once free and unlimited *in relation to human population,*" read the executive summary of Davis' plan. "As human population doubles and doubles again, the flow of services provided by intact ecosystems *becomes increasingly scarce in both absolute terms and even more so in per capita terms.*" It was inevitable, he was convinced, that the scarcity would cause a major shift in people's perceptions about Earth's assets. In time—in a short time—people would simply have to recognize their intrinsic worth.

"I *know* these things are valuable," Davis said, talking eagerly at the café between bites of angel hair pasta. "Ecosystem services are valuable. Not tree-hugging valuable but *economically* valuable."

Overhead, in the balmy subtropical night air, a fruit bat abruptly relieved itself, soiling the white shirt of a foundation executive who was listening in. Davis kept right on talking. His intensity, combined with the truly astonishing nature of his plan, was mesmerizing.

There was quite a lot of work still to do, he conceded. Fundamental was the effort to figure out how to quantify these new commodities. How would he parcel off an "ecosystem service flow"? And how would he quantify biodiversity? These questions were unanswered in his business plan, though Davis noted he intended to address them by hiring "top-notch credible scientific talent" with recourse to "satellite and air observation, direct measurement and peer-reviewed publications."

The plan, in fact, was meant to raise money for such research and recruitment, as well as the "spectacular high-speed graphics and state-of-the-art information presentation features" Davis wanted for his Web site. Yet even with so much to be done, he assured his small audience at the café that he'd have the site up and running within the next six months. The Conservation Exchange, his plan said, would then be marketed "with a major national splash, aimed square at the heart of Wall Street."

Davis had learned about the Australia meeting just two weeks earlier in California, when he first met Michael Jenkins, the director of Forest Trends. Jenkins' think tank was dedicated to finding market-based ways to save imperiled timberlands, and in the course of his work, Jenkins had heard of Davis' new consulting firm, Natural Strategies, which was dealing more and more with corporate purchases from certified sustainable forests—forests in which selective harvesting is practiced to ensure that they will yield timber into the future. The two men ended up having lunch at a Palo Alto book-store-café, after which Davis drove Jenkins to the airport. On the way, Davis broached the subject of his Conservation Exchange.

Jenkins was taken by Davis' energy. But his first impression of the Conservation Exchange was that it was "too stratospheric and dot-com." Jenkins didn't move in dot-com circles. His milieu was the much more reserved world of East Coast philanthropy. He'd grown up a Foreign Service brat, born in Bangkok and reared in Moscow and Caracas, and he'd chosen a career that kept him close to the developing world, with its burden of poverty and debt.

He'd loved trees ever since spending childhood afternoons play-ing in the Russian countryside and the woodsy hills behind his home in Venezuela. But it wasn't until later, while living for three years in northwestern Haiti and working for a private philanthropy called Appropriate Technology International, that Jenkins dedicated his career to forests. Haiti is one of the world's poorest and most heav-ily deforested countries—two characteristics Jenkins came to see as inextricably linked. Most of the world's remaining tropical forests are found in developing countries, inhabited by the world's poorest peo-ple. In Haiti, as in other impoverished areas, trees were a precious but easily squandered wealth. And it was useless to try to save them with-out helping the people who lived in their shadows. You couldn't blame people for cutting down forests if they had no alternative income.

If financial markets could offer a solution to this dilemma, Jenk-ins certainly wanted to hear it. Still, he felt uneasy with Davis' emphasis on profits. Flush with enthusiasm, Davis was constantly say-ing things like "There's a huge opportunity for somebody to make a ton of money off this stuff!"

Jenkins, in contrast, feared the profit motive was to blame for most of the world's environmental degradation to date. He didn't believe markets could ever seek social welfare; left alone, they'd simply make rich people richer. All the same, he sensed he needed pragmatic, dogged people like Davis to take some of the creative ideas about Nature and finance that had been floating around for the past few years and make them real. Davis clearly knew how the business world worked. And Jenkins had come to share the view that it was time to try to harness people's self-interest in the quest for environmental protection. "Envy trumps guilt," as Davis liked to say. Regulations hadn't worked, nor had moral appeals. So Davis may have been in the stratosphere, but Jenkins was now ready to admit he wanted to follow the same path.

It had been barely a year since Jenkins, then forty-five, founded Forest Trends with the help of some like-minded friends from the World Bank and the Rainforest Action Network. Before that, he'd spent ten years at the John D. and Catherine T. MacArthur Foundation, growing ever more frustrated. For each of those years, he had helped choose recipients for millions of dollars in forest program grants. Yet each year, he had watched forest destruction around the world accelerate. It came down to a question of values, he decided. Cut timber was worth money. Standing forests weren't. Global markets were rewarding short-term more than long-term returns, with the result that the world's largest ecosystems had been reduced to being providers of a single commodity whose price was falling. There was every incentive to clear-cut timberlands and sell the land for other uses, but it was all but impossible financially to engage in sustainable forestry, which preserves the asset of the forest itself. As Jenkins would warn in his welcoming speech at the zoo, people were missing the forest for the trees.

Even so, Jenkins could see there were all sorts of interesting ideas bubbling up in academic circles about how to use financial incentives to spur conservation, despite the fact that precious few of them were being put to use. It was all ecologists talking to ecologists about theoretical solutions that were never really tested. Jenkins decided his role should be that of a matchmaker, bringing together experts of diverse talents with potential financiers to work on crafting actual deals. He envisioned what he called a "skunk works" project—a focused effort to solve a specific problem—in which a team of eggheads would work in isolation and with minimal supervision on a common, urgent mission. His plan was to convene at least four high-intensity meetings over two years, in different cities around the world, during which participants would be charged with coming up with concrete products, including a new "green" mutual fund.

Jenkins had taken much care with the guest list for that first meeting in Katoomba, calling on his long-cultivated international network of colleagues and acquaintances and emphasizing diversity. Thus it was that at Lilianfels, a trader from Sumitomo Mitsui Banking Corporation would be found having cocktails with a Greenpeace activist and a World Resources Institute analyst. All would come to refer to themselves as the Katoomba Group in the months to come. Most remarkable of all, however, was that Jenkins had managed to secure cosponsorship from the Sydney Futures Exchange, the clearest sign that major money might be poised to flow into the contemplated conservation projects. A few brave executives at that institution thought they recognized lucrative opportunities in some potential new "green" products, and that year they were trying to promote the exchange as a global nexus for "green trading."

Their main source of inspiration was an innovative young market in pollution permits then flourishing in the United States. It was in fact the same market that had engendered Davis' grand dream of a Conservation Exchange.

Since the early 1990s, U.S. businesses and individuals had been buying and selling rights to emit sulfur dioxide (SO_2), a contributor to acid rain. The trade was made possible by the 1990 Amendments to the Clean Air Act, signed by President George Herbert Walker Bush, and it got under way in earnest five years later in annual auctions at the Chicago Board of Trade. The United States Environmental Protection Agency (EPA) unleashed the market by giving electrical utilities across the country permits to emit SO_2 in their combined operations (in other words, a property right to SO_2 emissions) and the ability to trade these permits with other utilities. The cleaner, more efficient companies could meet their targets inexpensively, but others, with older equipment, would have to pay a lot more. This motivated the efficient companies to reduce emissions below their targets so that they could sell their unused permits. The less efficient firms found it more economical to buy permits than to replace older equipment with a lot of life left in it. Eventually the permits were being traded much like pork bellies, with speculators entering the market to bet on future prices.

The theory was that in this way a given cut in overall emissions could be achieved at the lowest cost—and by that spring of 2000, the theory seemed sound. The market in pollution permits had grown to nearly $3 billion, with the utilities as a group even going beyond EPA demands in reducing SO_2 emissions. Even more exciting for the firms involved, they had achieved their pollution reductions at about one-tenth of the predicted cost. This success owed largely to the flexibility of market mechanisms: utilities had an incentive to experiment with a wide range of innovative emission reduction options, from new fuel mixes to instruments, such as options and swaps, that reduced risks.

The whole system was known as "cap and trade," with the cap, or emissions limit, motivating the trade. Its success was so celebrated that, by the time of the Katoomba conference, several efforts were under way around the world to copy it with CO_2, the leading "greenhouse gas" responsible for climate change. In fact, the Kyoto Protocol to the United Nations Framework Convention on Climate Change—the draft treaty in which industrialized countries agreed to cap their greenhouse gas emissions—already included provisions promising to allow trade in a strange new commodity that would be come to be known as a carbon credit, though the rules for how to do so hadn't yet been worked out. Even so, the mere idea was eliciting a frenzy of interest among the environmental-product brokers who'd cut their teeth on the SO_2 trade. That market was mostly regional, at best national. But a carbon-emissions trade would be global, and analysts were predicting it could eventually amount to more than \$100 billion. Carbon credits could become one of the world's top commodities.

To implement the treaty, each country's major sources and sinks of CO_2 would be quantified. Most significantly for conservationists, the Kyoto Protocol specified that land-use activities, such as planting of forests, would earn points in the accounting scheme. That meant that investments in forests, which absorb CO_2 and thus sequester carbon as they grow, might generate carbon credits. This promise at the time was still vague, yet it was enough to dazzle people, such as Jenkins, who'd despaired of finding arms against the disastrous scale of deforestation around the world. Suddenly, forests had a new cachet. Some of the billions of dollars generated by the carbon market, as nations and individual firms moved to reduce CO_2 emissions, might find their way to reforestation of degraded land. Farmers might earn extra income by "growing carbon" alongside traditional commodities such as rice and wool. Even imperiled rain forests might finally win protection, due to the economic consequences of allowing rampant fires to release the carbon they had stored. This was by far the most evolved case of potential money to be made by "monetizing" an ecosystem service. It was also the bright green hope behind the Sydney Futures Exchange's cosponsorship of the Katoomba conference.

The New South Wales state government enthusiastically supported the Katoomba conference as well, sending officials (though no cash) to the Taronga Zoo kickoff. The state's leaders recognized their special opportunity to profit from any global climate treaty that would include credit for forest investments. They had a lot to gain because of how much they had lost: in the previous fifty years, nearly half of Australia's forests had been felled, mostly as a result of an ill-advised government policy of granting title to land to the farmers who cleared it. Much of the land had been unsuitable for agriculture to begin with because most of Australia is plagued by fragile, nutrient-poor soil, and quite a lot of land that could maintain crops was badly managed and becoming degraded.

Over the previous few years, Australian officials had begun to realize that their crisis was truly grave. Without deep-rooted vegetation
to draw out excess groundwater, the water table had risen in some
areas, as if in a bathtub, from ninety feet or more below ground level
to near the surface. With it came salts that devastated crops and even
eroded roads and bridges. Australia's breadbasket, the Murray-Darling
river basin, was at particular risk in what the environment minister
had called the most significant environmental issue the country
faced. A farmers' group had estimated it could cost $37 billion to fix
the problem. A government report in 2001 predicted that crop-
killing salt could gobble up more than 65,000 square miles by 2050,
the bulk of it some of the country's most fertile land. "Basically, we're
buggered," was the way a Commonwealth Bank of Australia executive summarized the situation. Yet New South Wales officials hoped
they'd found a way out. With massive planting of new trees in plantations and forests, they could solve their agricultural problems and
in the process become a major carbon-farming center.

The New South Wales state legislature had taken an aggressive
step to forward this vision in November 1998, adopting the world's
first law establishing "carbon rights." These could be sold by forest
owners, separately from land titles and similar to timber rights. With
the stroke of a pen, they gave standing forests unprecedented new
value. And by the time of the Katoomba conference, the potential
rewards looked promising. Just a couple of months earlier, the Tokyo
Electric Power Company had agreed to invest in establishing as
much as 16,000 acres of new forest over a ten-year period, in return
for the carbon rights. This voluntary investment gave the firm early
experience with the carbon market and helped insure against higher
future costs should carbon offsets be legally required.

On the heels of this achievement, the Sydney Futures Exchange
was preparing to take the next big step and launch an international
trade in carbon rights. Stuart Beil, a slim, brash senior analyst who
hadn't yet turned thirty, was at the forefront of that effort, and if
Adam Davis had a soul mate at the Katoomba conference, Beil was
the man. They spoke the same strange language with the same

boundless confidence. Beil assured Davis that he'd worked out his concern about measurements, at least for carbon sequestration. "Lawyers have told us what we can trade, and it's one ton of carbon absorbed by a forest for a year," he said. Beil predicted that carbon trading would be launched in Sydney by that year's end. The market, he said, would soon grow to hundreds of billions of dollars, and "mums and dads" in no time would have carbon credits in their retirement portfolios.

Underscoring Beil's exuberance throughout the conference were signs of money, and lots of it, in the wings. It was evident from the first reception, on the Sunday before opening day, when workshop invitees were taken on a catered cruise of Sydney's harbor. For three hours, as the yacht passed the city's famed opera house and then drifted by immaculate suburban mansions and the gleaming, futuristic downtown, white-jacketed waiters circulated with wine, champagne, and plates of barbecued octopus, lamb, and shrimp. The next evening, after the lectures, the special guests were whisked away on a luxury bus to Lilianfels, where more comforts awaited in the form of cocktails, feather beds, gourmet jelly beans, and two types of chocolate mousse at dinner. The final morning featured a guided walk through the canyons of the Blue Mountains with a wildlife expert who played a didgeridoo. For several of the scientists and nongovernmental organization members involved, it was remarkably unlike their normal run of conferences, held in drab meeting rooms in university towns. They'd entered the beguiling world of high finance, where an "invisible hand" was sparing no expense.

"This is the first conference I've gone to which my father-in-law has respected," said Sara Scherr, a University of Maryland agroforestry expert who spent months on end involved in field research with impoverished Central American peasants. "He said, 'The Sydney Futures Exchange! Wow!'"

Nor was the Sydney Futures Exchange the only rich uncle at the conference. In recent years, some environmental groups had grown tremendously in clout and resources and were spending fortunes to protect land and sponsor research in environmental issues. Chief among these groups was the Virginia-based Nature Conservancy, which had become the world's largest international conservation agency, with some $700 million in annual income.

On arriving in Katoomba, the career environmentalists were treated to primers on financial concepts such as options and futures. Many were novices in this realm, but Adam Davis was starting to feel more in his element. He was impressed with Stuart Beil, but even more so with a burly Canadian named David Brand, a transplant to Australia who as deputy chief executive officer of State Forests of New South Wales, Australia, a government-sponsored trading enterprise, was cosponsoring the conference. Brand, who had a doctorate in forest ecology and three books on forestry issues to his credit, had been a major force behind most of the innovative experiments launched by New South Wales' government. As manager of State Forests, with 5.3 million acres of timberland under its control, Brand had quickly learned how to turn a profit. He had seen the potential for carbon as a commodity years earlier and had been working closely with the Sydney Futures Exchange on its trading plan.

Along with Beil and Davis, Brand spoke of the carbon market to come with boyish excitement. "One atmosphere, one product. It's huge," he said. And like Davis, Brand didn't stop at carbon. In his PowerPoint presentation to the Katoomba Group, he described the forest of the future as similar to a hospital: offering a variety of services bringing in varied revenue streams. The income from carbon alone wouldn't be enough to make sustainable forestry truly profitable. Brand pictured forest owners one day selling carbon rights, water purification services, and biodiversity credits, all from the same property. The credits could be marketed in a variety of ways, but as one example, he said, developers who destroyed biodiversity in one area could purchase credits to protect it in another. Governments would maintain "banks" of biodiversity credits and sell them as needed.

Chatting with Brand over beers in the Lilianfels parlor, Davis was amazed to see how closely their thinking coincided. It was thrilling to have worked so long alone, on something everyone back home had seemed to think was nuts, only to discover so many people around the world thinking the same thoughts. He was particularly impressed to learn that carbon-trading exchanges were being contemplated not just in Australia but also in Great Britain, Norway, and Sweden.

Davis quickly ran out of copies of his Conservation Exchange business plan, having handed them out to business executives, environmental organization representatives, philanthropic investors, and a journalist from *Time* magazine. By now, he not only wanted feedback but also wanted to make sure that as many people as possible would associate him personally with the ideas. He was suddenly worried about losing his intellectual capital. The markets were moving that fast.

The Katoomba participants all seemed to share a sense of history in the making. Discussions began before 8:00 A.M. and lasted, with few breaks, into the evening. In the large, windowless conference room, everyone was anxious to describe his or her projects, from the insurance executive looking into ways to cover the new carbon deals to the socially responsible investment specialist searching for relevant funds. Business cards were exchanged, e-mail addresses scribbled. At meals, the scientists and businesspeople huddled together, still talking over the mechanics of the markets. At times, the normally sober scientists seemed downright dreamy. "I've never sat down with people like this," marveled University of Florida botanist Jack Putz. "There's some beautiful language floating around, like 'price discovery.'"

"I've become more excited the more I've learned," said Scherr, the Maryland agroforestry expert. "These ideas have enormous potential for poverty reduction, since they're creating new income sources and may improve land productivity." Scherr envisioned markets for ecosystem services offering poor farmers new ways to earn income from certain types of land, such as steep slopes, not well suited to intensive agricultural production but ideally suited to, say, carbon sequestration or flood control.

At the same time, both the risks and the limitations of the brave new ideas were evident. Despite hours of discussion, for instance, on the second day in Katoomba, workshop members failed to come up with any market-based ideas for coping with the urgent problem of out-of-control fires set to clear Brazil's vanishing Amazon rain forest. Dan Nepstad, a forestry expert who worked half the year in Brazil and who had called for ideas, quietly voiced his skepticism. "I'm leery of turning everything over to the markets," he said. "I think there must still be a strong role for governments."

He wasn't alone. On the first day, back in Sydney, Brian Walker, a veteran scientist representing an Australian government research center, pointed out that carbon trading, the most evolved of the ideas being discussed, could ultimately amount to a lot of sound and fury that would have little real effect on climate change. Even the most optimistic projections of trading levels seemed to come up short, considering the dramatic reductions in greenhouse gas concentrations that might actually be needed to avert climate disaster.

There were other issues. If forests were to become like hospitals, would everyone be entitled to their environmental benefits, or only those who could pay? Is profit what hospitals, or forests, should be about? Could the profit motive, applied to forest conservation, really enhance environmental protection?

Scherr, the agroforester, worried that the new opportunities might end up hurting the poor, that peasants lacking title to their land might be evicted if carbon and biodiversity credits suddenly made the land more valuable. It has been said that water flows toward money and power—why wouldn't the same be true of ecosystem services?

Adam Davis didn't share any of these fears. Traditional conservation approaches were obviously not up to their task, he believed, and there was no time to waste in trying something new. Back in Sydney again, a few days before he headed home, he hiked the trail above Bondi Beach, barely pausing for breath in his excitement. He spoke with new hope of finding "angel" investors soon for his Conservation Exchange, which of course would be followed by leagues of traders. "It's like having the first fax machine," he said. "It's useless unless a lot of other people have fax machines. But once they've got them—once enough people are thinking along the same lines— you're in business." It all made him more eager than ever to get his Web site up and running that year. Even if it couldn't handle trades right away, the site might start as something else. Perhaps a game: an Internet game that would teach people in an engaging way how to think of the planet's ecosystems as assets. "Even if you *only* did a game, with people betting on the value of scarce resources—and forgot about the actual Exchange—you would have a powerful tool for education," Davis said.

Alternatively, he saw The Conservation Exchange as a way of making environmental philanthropy more efficient, allowing donations to be targeted to specific ecosystem service units that would render specific returns. He called it venture philanthropy. "Listen," Davis asked, grinning again, "if it ends up as just a sophisticated way of channeling millions of dollars into environmental projects, what am I, a loser?"

In fact, in the year that followed that first meeting in Katoomba, Davis wouldn't lose at all from his financial gamble on Nature. His winnings wouldn't be of the kind he originally imagined, nor of the amount of which he dreamed. But the wild ideas that brought him to Katoomba would in a short time come to be accepted in ways that even he would find surprising.

How to Make Carbon Charismatic

"Don't wait to touch bottom before you start swimming."

—Luis Gámez, advisor to Costa Rica's
Ministry of Environment and Energy

DAVID BRAND, the Canadian forester, was every bit as much the gambler as Adam Davis, though he held his cards closer to his chest. He spoke softly, weighing his words, yet still managed to let anyone listening know of his faith that the world was in the midst of a sea change in its view of the value of Nature, and that he personally was helping to lead the way. Indeed, by the time of the first Katoomba Group meeting, Brand, who was then forty-three years old, with slicked-back hair turning white at the temples and wary pale blue eyes, had already achieved more than anyone else at the conference in making the common dream a reality. And he would soon go much further in realizing his plans.

Part of Brand's success was simply being in the right place at a time when enthusiasm about the nontimber value of forests was catching on as never before. He'd chosen to study forestry mostly because he loved being outdoors, and he'd ended up working in government jobs in Canada and Australia just as both countries had become ready, under great pressure, to transform their forestry policies. But Brand also had a knack for getting through to public and corporate officials about their own self-interest in seeking environmentally sustainable paths. In time, that skill would help make him a kind of Johnny Appleseed of forest finance, raising fortunes for the purpose of restoring timberlands in Australia and, later, the United States.

Nearly a year to the day following the Katoomba conference, in late March 2001, Brand was deploying his networking talents at another extraordinary meeting, this time in Beverly Hills, California. Its host was Michael Milken, the notorious former junk-bond dealer who had served nearly two years in prison for white-collar crimes in the early 1990s. Since then, Milken, a longtime donor to such causes as research and education to combat acquired immunodeficiency syndrome (AIDS), had branched out to fund studies on global economics and the environment. His new organization, the Milken Institute, was striving, similarly to the Katoomba Group, to develop a for-profit approach to conservation by devising financial instruments to capture the value of ecosystem services such as carbon sequestration, water purification, and flood protection. Milken's researchers had been working with The Nature Conservancy, which had a strong practical motive for its involvement, being by then the second largest private landowner in the United States, after television mogul Ted Turner. The nonprofit environmental group was establishing an International Center for Innovative Conservation Finance and was keen to connect conservation biologists with Wall Street financiers. The meeting in March, a roundtable called "Financing Our Global Environmental Future," was a way for the two groups to seek input from potential investors. At the same time, its guest list hinted at the tremendous odyssey that some of the world's largest and most powerful industries were making in reimagining the value of Nature.

Slim and dapper, Milken made his backslapping way through a dark-suited crowd that included executives from the Bank of America, Tokai Asia, the giant reinsurance firm Swiss Re, and, as a particularly striking presence, a representative of the Ohio-based American Electric Power, one of the world's biggest energy suppliers and the largest U.S. consumer of coal. As presentations began, Brand sat in the front row, nervously jiggling his knee, alongside Davis, who was furiously taking notes.

Business executives such as those in the audience that day were showing increasing interest in the environment, mostly for one reason. It had finally become clear that Nature's response to decades of abuse was threatening not only their world but also their bottom lines. They could no longer read the daily news and not comprehend that some of Earth's ecosystems were breaking down, unable to keep up with the demands of the global economy. The flow of services to humankind from Nature was thinning to a trickle in some parts of the world or simply ceasing, causing a great deal of pain and costing a lot of money.

In the Gulf of Mexico, a gargantuan, oxygen-sucking bloom of algae, fed by farm fertilizer carried from the Mississippi River basin, had created a "dead zone" the size of New Jersey that was killing off fish and threatening a $5 billion commercial and sport industry that employed 200,000 people and provided one-quarter of the U.S. catch. In China, recent floods on the Yangtze River, aggravated by loss of forests that once helped absorb heavy rains, had taken 2,100 lives and cost an estimated $30 billion. Throughout the United States, even in the rainy Pacific Northwest, water shortages were growing serious, in part because suburban sprawl was covering the land, compromising the sponge effect that helps replenish reservoirs.

Overshadowing such gathering storms was the most alarming fact of the planet's steady warming, which mainstream scientists agreed was partly due to cars and industries burning fossil fuels—coal, gas, and oil—which spewed heat-trapping greenhouse gases into the air. It was the climate change threat above all else that brought so many executives to the Milken meeting. Most saw in it another, more immediate threat, that of more government regulations and imposed costs. Yet the most adventurous and informed of them also sensed potential profits. In fact, the world's mounting concern over global warming was already inspiring unprecedented changes in the way many governments, corporations, and philanthropies looked at the economic value of the work of ecosystems. These shifts in view promised to give forests in particular a new lease on life, marshalling millions, and perhaps in time billions, of dollars to support their labor in storing carbon dioxide (CO_2), the most abundant of the greenhouse gases. This was Brand's dream and the focus of his career.

Concern about greenhouse gases wasn't really new. The Swedish scientist Svante Arrhenius, in 1896, was the first to propose that industrial CO_2 emissions might produce what was later dubbed global warming. From elementary physics, he knew that CO_2 and an array of other natural gases functioned as a heat-trapping blanket over the planet: without them, Earth's average surface temperature would be about 60°F cooler than it is, or around 0°F. Arrhenius reasoned that industrial activities might increase the concentration of some of these gases sufficiently to change the global climate system. More than sixty years later, U.S. researchers in Mauna Loa, Hawaii, began collecting samples of atmospheric CO_2 in little handblown glass globes. Within five more years, they would show conclusively that the levels of the gas were indeed rising. There followed a rising drumbeat of alerts from environmental scientists about the dangers of changing the content of the air around us.

These warnings went mostly unheeded until the scorching summer of 1988, when forests in the United States were in flames and news of global warming finally landed on the front pages of U.S. newspapers. But editorial concern died down as the seasons turned. By the late 1990s, humanity was annually spewing an estimated 6 billion tons of CO_2 and other greenhouse gases into the sky, and the atmospheric concentration of CO_2 had increased by 30 percent over preindustrial levels. Complacency was shattered once again in early 2001 when the Intergovernmental Panel on Climate Change (IPCC), a United Nations–sponsored group of top scientists from around the world, predicted that continuing business as usual could raise Earth's average surface temperature by as much as 11°F over 1990 levels. In just a few decades, the world might heat more than it had since the depths of the last ice age, with the threat of more frequent catastrophic storms, hurricanes, and droughts; floods due to rising sea levels; and epidemics borne by mosquitoes migrating to previously inhospitable climes.

In the hopes of averting climate catastrophe, representatives of industrialized countries meeting in Kyoto, Japan, in 1997 had agreed to individual targets meant to lower net greenhouse gas emissions by an average of 5.2 percent from 1990 levels by 2012. (The U.S. target was a 7 percent cut.) Yet even those modest targets promised to be costly if they were all achieved by cutting emissions at their source. This led to consideration of a more economical way to work toward the targets—that is, allow companies to earn credits for reducing their net carbon emissions by investing in forests and soil, which store carbon and thus are known as "carbon sinks."

Forests, together with all of Earth's plants, play a key role in the way CO_2 cycles around the planet. Each time a plant sprouts and grows, it absorbs the gas, which it transforms chemically through photosynthesis. It uses the carbon to build its roots, stem, branches, leaves, and flowers, and releases the oxygen, supporting other life-forms. When the plant dies, some of the carbon returns to the atmosphere and some is bound in the soil. The storing of carbon in plants and in the earth is called carbon sequestration.

To be sure, all this was far from David Brand's thoughts when he started out in forestry at the age of eighteen, a restless maverick in a family of bankers. Trees were the backdrop of his canoeing and camping expeditions in Ontario; CO_2 was the fizz in his soda pop. Global warming wasn't on his radar screen. He worked one summer plotting roads into the boreal forest of northern Saskatchewan so that the trees might be logged for newspaper pulp. He wasn't thinking then about the bulldozer that would follow. But as he learned more about forests, he became intrigued with their complex powers—how a tree can lift water 300 feet from its roots to its leaves, how timber-lands revive themselves in the wake of sweeping fires. His fascination led to commitment. A few years later, after witnessing a camp boss, just for spite, bulldoze an old-growth knoll along the scenic Toba River, Brand left private enterprise and joined the Canadian Forest Service.

By the late 1980s, Brand's attachment to forests had been strengthened by his sense of their peril. The price of logs was falling, along with the prices of other commodities. Sustainable forestry was nowhere near economically viable. And in the Tropics, every year an area of forest the size of Tennessee was being cleared.

None of the vital services that sustainably managed forests provide, from sequestering carbon to preventing soil erosion to purifying water or providing habitats, were then visible parts of any country's gross national product (GNP). Yet the omissions were finally starting to be questioned and, in parts of the world, even addressed. At the time, Brand was trying to tackle the problem in Ottawa, having risen in the Forest Service to become its director of environment. He was also watching efforts elsewhere around the world to derive financial value from standing forests. Most were bold experiments in the terra incognita of environmental finance, launched with funding more solid than their footing. One of the most ambitious of these forays took place in the denuded highlands of Guatemala in October 1988.

In the wake of that year's blazing summer, when global warming was still topic A in the news, the AES Corporation, a global power company, was building a new 180-megawatt plant in the city of Uncasville, Connecticut. The environmental toll was predicted to be 15 million tons of carbon released into the air over the estimated forty-year life of the plant. To live up to the company's widely acclaimed values of social responsibility, AES officers decided to mitigate, or "offset," this pollution voluntarily by contributing $2 million to a major reforestation effort. AES' chief, Roger Sant, who later became chairman of the World Wildlife Fund–U.S., intended for the investment in ecosystem capital to sequester as much CO_2, or more than, the plant would emit. The new trees wouldn't do that work alone, however: AES' carbon calculations included the labor done by trees already standing, which were to be protected from land-hungry farmers and loggers.

After looking at investment options in several other countries, AES chose Guatemala as the most promising site. Half of the country's original forests had been cleared in the previous thirty-five years for fuel, timber, and farms. Deforestation had led to soil erosion, which in turn was reducing farm productivity, creating a vicious circle in which peasants were driven to cut down more trees. The mitigation project's total cost, about $14 million, was shared by AES, the Guatemala forestry service, the U.S. Agency for International Development, CARE, and the Peace Corps. The idea was not only to pay for the planting and care of new trees but also to train farmers to use their land more efficiently so that they wouldn't continue to expand their activities into existing forests.

A few years later and a little farther south, in Costa Rica, environmental entrepreneurs took the idea of offsetting carbon emissions a bold step further, inventing a way in which credits for such offsets could be traded like commodities. Richard Sandor, a Chicago-based financial investor and avid environmentalist who'd been active in the sulfur dioxide (SO_2) market, helped Costa Rica's government officials package credits from carbon sequestration by forests. Sandor called these credits certified tradable offsets, or CTOs, because their purchase would make up for, or offset, CO_2 emissions in lieu of corporations reducing them outright. Now investors wouldn't have to be tied to a particular forest, as in the AES venture, with all the risks and lack of liquidity that entailed.

The AES investment and the Costa Rican CTOs were some of the first of what would later be called flexibility measures, inventive ways of meeting possible future commitments to a global climate agreement. They included investments in both carbon sequestration and cleaner technology; in the latter option, a developed country might, for instance, buy China a gas power plant to replace a coal-fired plant on the drawing boards. Because such investments were not yet legally required, however, the CTOs drew little interest, other than from the governments of Norway, Holland, Switzerland, and Finland, which were experimenting philanthropically with a system that only *might* eventually become law. Still, Brand recognized their potential.

As negotiations leading to the climate pact signed in Kyoto got under way, it seemed clear to Brand, among many others, that some kind of credits for forest-based offsets would be involved. After all, a working group of the IPCC had declared that by protecting existing forests and planting new ones, countries could sop up as much as 20 percent of the CO_2 expected to be emitted by human travel and industry over the next half century. So after Brand left Canada in 1995, lured by the offer of a job managing millions of acres of forests for State Forests of New South Wales, Australia, he started looking for ways his new employer could exploit the new market. "I think this one's got legs," he told his boss.

Several U.S. and European firms came to agree. In the next few years, companies including British Petroleum (BP), American Electric Power, Cinergy Corporation, PacifiCorp, and Wisconsin Electric Power began making investments similar to AES' Guatemala project. By 1999, the total spent on such deals would approach $75 million. Most of these transactions took place in Latin America, where there was still relatively abundant and cheap forestland for sale, and most were brokered by The Nature Conservancy. Each represented a cumbersome triumph over government and corporate bureaucracies and a show of good faith in a radically new way of looking at Nature.

None of the idiosyncratic deals could be called typical, but one with features common to them all was a $5.4 million investment by Central and South West Corporation, a Dallas-based power firm that later merged with American Electric Power, the one utility represented at the Milken conference. The Texas company passed the money to a Brazilian environmental organization, which would buy, own, and reforest about 17,000 acres of pasture in Brazil's southern state of Paraná. The deal's philanthropic and public relations value was high because the land was near the largest remnant of the extremely endangered Atlantic rain forest and home to at least fifteen species of threatened birds, in addition to a rare primate species, the black-faced lion tamarin, only recently discovered by scientists. But the company also had its eye on the price of the carbon that would be stored: just $5.40 per ton—a bargain considering that Sandor, in Chicago, was predicting that the price of a permit to emit a ton of carbon would soon rise to $20, and other analysts were forecasting even higher amounts.

In press releases, investor corporations declared that they had purchased carbon rights, or credits—even though no laws in the United States or elsewhere had established such rights at the time. Without the ease of CTOs, each arrangement had to be laboriously negotiated, with projections of carbon sequestration left to outside auditing firms (part of a burgeoning cottage industry), and the actual purchase and management of land assigned to local groups, to avoid domestic restrictions on foreign ownership.

But Brand, who'd been intrigued by Costa Rica's CTOs, thought he saw an answer to this problem. With his Australian bosses' go-ahead, he helped create the world's first official carbon rights. These were a kind of forestry right, like timber or grazing rights, but pertaining to carbon sequestration, which could be bought and sold independently of the land itself. Brand helped write the legislation, which the state parliament approved in 1998. "Everyone just went nuts," he later recalled. The story was front-page news in national papers, Brand added, and "the government loved it."

The kudos continued as Brand and his team packaged the rights to newly planted forests on state-owned cattle pasture and offered them for sale to power firms. In 1999, State Forests was able to announce the biggest climate change investment thus far. The Tokyo Electric Power Company, the world's largest power firm, had signed up for the carbon rights from new pine and eucalyptus forests expected to absorb 200,000 to 800,000 metric tons of CO_2 per year, offsetting the company's emissions in Japan. Two years later at the Milken conference, Brand described this sale as the start of a future in which forestry would become mainly a business of environmental services, with timber and energy as by-products.

Following the Tokyo firm's investment, Brand started pushing the envelope, aiming to market a variety of services from a single ecosystem. That was the Holy Grail, he believed, because it was likely that no one service alone could pay for effective conservation. In addition to selling carbon rights, he planned to market "salinity control" credits, derived from the labor of deep-rooted vegetation in drawing water from the soil and evaporating, or transpiring, it through its leaves, lowering the rising salty water table. In Australia, where salinization of agricultural soil was widely viewed as the country's most urgent problem, finding buyers for salinity control credits was easy. With the eager participation of farmers' groups, Brand launched a pilot project in which State Forests leased upstream land from property owners and planted trees on it. Downstream cotton farmers paid a monthly rate based on the amount of transpiration delivered by the new trees, which would eventually restore the water table's natural level. This was the stuff of the Katoomba Group's dreams: users of an environmental service were paying a fixed rate for Nature's labor. Furthermore, it was a bargain for the farmers, who paid only a fraction of the cost of the reforestation, since State Forests owned and managed the trees in return for revenues from the transpiration credits. Meanwhile, the upstream landowners got a steady revenue from leasing property to the state agency. Brand hoped in the future to add biodiversity credits, from the same trees, to the mix, with the value of the credits based on the quality of habitat they provided to native animals. He envisioned himself one day packaging "bios" and selling them on an Internet auction site such as eBay.

With Australia and Latin America competing to sell fledgling carbon credits, California jumped into the fray, touting what Andrea Tuttle, the optimistic director of the state's Department of Forestry and Fire Protection, called its "*charismatic* carbon." The state, as the century turned, was plagued by energy shortfalls and power outages and thus was planning to develop a slew of new gas-fired power plants. The plants would boost power supplies, of course, but would also add to net greenhouse gas emissions. Even though California at the time had no requirement for investments in offsets, Tuttle hoped to whip up enthusiasm for purchases of carbon rights from redwood forests. Redwoods, she pointed out in meetings with potential buyers, were champions of carbon storage, growing taller and living much longer than most other trees. They also offered the public relations cachet of being a particularly beautiful state icon. By the summer of 2001, Tuttle had yet to close a redwood deal, but she believed it would be only a matter of time.

There were plenty of would-be carbon sellers by the century's turn, but without question the most eager vendors were U.S. farmers, walloped by falling commodity prices and desperate for aid. Many were excited about the notion of carbon sinks in their soil; it raised the idea that they could be subsidized simply for switching to tilling methods that minimized disturbance of the soil, thus maximizing carbon storage. In effect, they might be paid more for doing less. "We've run through a lot of ideas, including food stamps, income supplements, and export enhancements, but I'm thinking this global warming issue could be a real political consensus engine," said agricultural economist Steve Griffin, who brokered the first such deal.

In October 1999, Griffin was sure he could see the engine leaving the station. As vice president of IGF Insurance Company, a provider of crop insurance, he helped sign up a group of Iowa farmers who promised to sell 2.8 million metric tons of greenhouse gas reductions and options to the Greenhouse Emissions Management Consortium (GEMCo), a group of energy companies based in Vancouver, British Columbia. The farmers agreed to reduce plowing on 2.5 million acres in return for a few dollars per acre per year. That wasn't going to make them rich, Griffin acknowledged, but it did bring some collateral benefits, such as an ability to make do with much less fertilizer.

The Canadian investors were acting with a mix of strategic motives. Unlike other industrialized countries, Canada couldn't easily reduce emissions by switching from coal to natural gas because it was already burning natural gas from its abundant domestic supplies. Furthermore, Canada's vast forests and agricultural lands provided huge potential sinks, a tremendous asset if sinks were made part of the Kyoto plan. Canada was hoping to get U.S. support for the carbon-sink tactic, and GEMCo executives apparently thought it wouldn't hurt to show U.S. farmers the money—or at least the potential for future earnings.

The deal was the first significant carbon sale by farmers anywhere and was announced with fanfare and great expectations. "Canada's biggest power companies are paying farmers in Iowa $5–10/acre to park their ploughs this spring," began an article in *Farmers Weekly,* which exaggerated the payment. It quoted a happy maize farmer as saying: "It's a good source of income for doing nothing. It's a gift." New research encouraged this optimism. Rattan Lal, director of the Carbon Management and Sequestration Program at Ohio State University, maintained that better management practices on crops, on grazing land, and in forests could help sequester as much as 270 million tons of carbon in U.S. soils. Yet as the GEMCo deal would eventually, and somewhat painfully, reveal, the gap between theory and results in carbon sequestration by soil remained enormous.

Joining the farmers and foresters climbing on the carbon-sink bandwagon were some even more unlikely travelers. Major U.S. energy companies whose chiefs had once dismissed the idea of global warming as a tree-huggers' fantasy were finally facing up to the danger of climate change. While some were joining the trek to Latin America to purchase carbon credits, others were voluntarily making much greater economic sacrifices to adapt.

Well into the 1990s, this scenario might have seemed as likely as a band of Fortune 500 executives trying to sweet-talk the Internal

Revenue Service into making them pay more taxes. Back then, even in the face of mounting evidence of the seriousness of climate change, most of the biggest greenhouse gas–belching multinational companies simply balked. American industry leaders such as DuPont, the Royal Dutch/Shell Group of Companies, American Electric Power, and Ford Motor Company belonged to the Global Climate Coalition, which spent millions of dollars to downplay the threat of global warming. The allied Global Climate Information Project spent $13 million in 1997, just before the Kyoto Protocol was signed, on a scare campaign including television advertisements designed by the same agency that created the ads in which "Harry and Louise" attacked President Bill Clinton's health-care reform plan. The ads claimed, without any clear basis for doing so, that the price of gasoline would rise by $0.50 per gallon if the Kyoto Protocol were ratified. Meanwhile, a few prominent climate change "skeptics," scientists who often turned out to be funded by the oil and coal industries, appeared regularly in the press and before the United States Congress, for years managing to give the false impression that the mainstream scientific community was divided as to whether climate change was a serious issue.

In 1995, however, things started to change, quite rapidly. The evidence by then had become overwhelming that humanity had reached the limit of its ability to treat the atmosphere as a sewer without risking catastrophic consequences. Climate change was a time bomb, becoming ever harder to ignore. The watershed event that year was the second IPCC report, which stated with unprecedented certainty that the global warming of the twentieth century could be attributed at least in part to the burning of fossil fuels. Dale Heydlauff, environmental chief for American Electric Power, called it "a wake-up call we didn't feel we could ignore. For the first time, some of the major uncertainties were beginning to be settled."

Then, in May 1997, several months before the Kyoto conference, came the first major break in the naysayers' ranks. Speaking at Stanford University, John Browne, the chief executive officer of BP, declared that to ignore climate change concerns "would be unwise and potentially dangerous." He called for "change and for a rethinking of corporate responsibility," and he backed up his words with action. BP soon afterward promised $1 billion in investments in solar energy and vowed to reduce its net greenhouse gas emissions by 10 percent below 1990 levels by 2010—exceeding the U.S. target, agreed to in Kyoto, of a 7 percent cutback by 2012.

Browne's defection seemed similar to the break in ranks in the tobacco industry that occurred the same year when the Liggett Group acknowledged that smoking causes cancer and heart disease. Tobacco firms and major CO_2 emitters had tacitly enforced similar codes of silence. In the BP case, however, the break set off a much more dramatic shift in corporate attitude. By the century's turn, a rash of defections had made the Global Climate Coalition a shadow of its former self as its erstwhile stalwarts tried to outdo one another in slashing greenhouse gas emissions. DuPont, once infamous for making chemicals that thin Earth's protective ozone shield, had by 2001 cut its carbon emissions to a stunning 45 percent below its 1990 levels. Shell promised to follow BP in a 10 percent cut by 2010, and United Technologies Corporation vowed to reduce its carbon emissions by 25 percent before 2007.

Corporate leaders had staked out their previous positions in an atmosphere of tremendous uncertainty about the economic costs of adapting to laws that might limit greenhouse gas emissions, but with a fair idea that adapting wouldn't be cheap. A 1998 report by the Energy Information Administration (an arm of the U.S. Department of Energy) had offered the absurdly wide range of $13–$397 billion as an estimate of potential losses to the U.S. gross domestic product were the United States to keep the promise it made in Kyoto. The slipperiness of the Department of Energy's estimate had mostly to do with continuing confusion over what kinds of flexibility measures might be allowed.

At the same time, some firms were discovering that when they set their sights on reducing wastes, including fossil fuel emissions, they made gains in efficiency that helped their bottom line. DuPont is the company most often held up as an example of this kind of success. In just one of its strategies for cutting waste and saving money, the firm slashed its energy use by one-third at its 1,450-acre Chamber Works facility in New Jersey, saving $17 million per year on power and reducing greenhouse gas pollution per pound of product by nearly one-half.

Were carbon-emissions reductions to be made obligatory, flexibility measures, including the sinks and emissions-trading schemes embraced from Katoomba to Beverly Hills, could obviously make a huge difference in reducing the overall pain of adjustment. But back in 1997, the point seemed destined to remain obscure—that is, until Eileen Claussen, a former assistant U.S. secretary of state with a wisecracking smile and a steely will, came along to spread the word and build a powerful counterweight to the Global Climate Coalition.

Claussen had quit her government job just a few months before the Kyoto Protocol was signed, out of frustration with what she saw as the Clinton administration's failure to lead on climate change. In this, to be sure, U.S. politicians were simply reflecting their constituencies' great ambivalence. As late as March 2001, a Time/CNN poll showed that although 75 percent of Americans thought global warming was a serious problem, only 48 percent would be willing to pay an extra $0.25 per gallon of gasoline to combat it. Legislators balked at inviting real-time economic pain in order to benefit generations to come, long after they'd left office.

Claussen noted this problem in a speech she made in London just before she left her post. Chief executive officers, she pointed out, were better equipped than politicians to meet the long-term global warming challenge because they look beyond four- and six-year periods. Some make investments that must last for decades. "I said I thought governments were really hopeless on this issue, and it was up to business," she later recalled. "Having made this speech, I convinced myself this was correct."

She went on to convince the purse-string holders at The Pew Charitable Trusts, which in early 1998 made her director of its new Pew Center on Global Climate Change. There, she created the Business Environmental Leadership Council, convincing hitherto infamous polluters to sign up with promises of full-page glossy ads sponsored by the Trusts extolling their new "green" accomplishments, as well as special access to her Rolodex file of high-level international government officials. "If Eileen didn't exist, we'd have had to invent her," said Stephen Schneider, a leading climate change expert at Stanford University. "She came around and made it safer for corporations to get involved."

As a condition of joining the council, executives had to sign a list of principles that, in stark contrast to the Global Climate Coalition's message, declared that climate change was a serious threat, that determined action was necessary, and that the Kyoto Protocol "represents a first step in the international process." That last part, tepidly worded as it was, constituted the highest hurdle for companies that had so recently reacted to the protocol with the subtlety and goodwill of a cornered beast. Many executives turned Claussen down, but within six weeks she'd recruited thirteen big firms, several of them former members of the Global Climate Coalition. Their immediate reward was an editorial in the *Washington Post* praising them for having had the "courage to step out from the crowd of stone-throwers." It was titled "A Few Brave Firms." "They just loved being called that," Claussen said.

By 2001, Claussen's council had grown to thirty-three members and was meeting four times a year to share insights on preparations for what they all were becoming convinced was an inevitable transition from coal and gas to hydrogen power. As she was fond of pointing out, they had combined annual sales of more than $800 billion— were the group a country, it would rank eleventh in the world in terms of GNP. Her mantra, in press interviews and meetings with White House officials, was that Kyoto's dictates aren't draconian, as conservative opponents insist, but rather "replete with the kind of market mechanisms and flexible approaches that Republicans usually applaud."

Claussen's vision was certainly far-reaching, yet it wasn't unique. In Chicago, Richard Sandor, the financier who helped Costa Rica invent CTOs, also believed that enlightened corporations could change the government's course on global warming, and he was pursuing an equally imaginative path to prove it. Using the SO_2 trade as a model and with support from the wealthy Joyce Foundation, Sandor had set out to design the United States' first trading exchange in greenhouse gases. His plan was to help firms gain direct experience in cutting their greenhouse gas emissions while giving the rest of the world a glimpse of the strategy's potential.

The son of a former vaudeville singer, Sandor shared Claussen's strong will and boundless energy. "Have you ever had someone come in a revolving door behind you and go out in front of you? That's him," said one acquaintance. He was set to launch his Chicago Climate Exchange at the end of 2001, having won commitments to participate in the market-design phase from twenty-five companies and nonprofit organizations. Among those signing on were Ford, DuPont, Suncor Energy, International Paper, and PG&E National Energy Group. Were the Kyoto Protocol to become law, these firms would have gained valuable expertise and possibly even carbon credits they could use to ease the weight of regulation. The protocol, of course, looked unlikely to become law anytime soon, but Sandor and his staff weren't deterred. By 2004, he predicted, firms from all over the world would be trading permits in carbon emissions on his exchange, pushing governments to fall in line. "The private sector will lead the public sector, and the public sector will end up ratifying private sector practices," Sandor said.

This sentiment had become the guiding conviction of the earnest environmentalists and executives coming to meetings like the ones in Katoomba and Beverly Hills. Although few big transitions come without pain, the U.S. executives participating hoped to minimize their losses on the road to environmental sustainability. They'd decided, in the phrase used by Costa Rica's Luis Gámez to describe his government's turnaround from environmental apathy, that they didn't want to wait to touch bottom before starting to swim.

For one thing, whenever they traveled outside U.S. boundaries, they saw evidence that they'd better start preparing for a world with climate change rules. The United Kingdom was about to enact a climate change levy, a modest tax on energy use by businesses, to take effect in 2001. And the European Union (EU) as a whole was considering committing to an EU-wide emissions-trading scheme by 2005.

Back home, meanwhile, some two dozen climate change bills, including greenhouse gas regulations and credit for early voluntary action, were making their way through Congress. Although it often seemed as if the glaciers would melt entirely before any of the bills were passed, smart businesspeople knew that the pace of change might quicken dramatically. A single sufficiently freakish weather event could lead to an overnight surge of political will and a belated rush to regulate. Such a quickly turning tide could drown firms without good strategies in place.

Making this point at the Milken conference and elsewhere that same year were analysts from a recently established New York brokerage firm, Innovest Strategic Value Advisors, which had begun making predictions for its investor clients about what a tax on CO_2 emissions might do to leading firms' bottom lines. It called the risk "carbon exposure," warning that some companies' profits might fall by as much as 30 percent if such a tax were levied. Innovest and other researchers also called attention to something many multinationals' executives already knew: that Japan and Europe were moving well ahead of the United States on climate change strategies, forcing their companies to become more energy efficient and, as a result, more globally competitive.

At home, U.S. corporate chiefs were also starting to recognize that it pays to pay attention to the environment because, increasingly, customers and shareholders are doing so. Firms were under the spotlight as never before for their environmental decisions, with their brand names' worth boosted or weakened by consumers' sense of their "green" goodwill.

A burgeoning industry of "socially responsible" investment firms and analysts had begun tracking companies' "triple bottom lines": not just their financial performance but also their social and environmental performance. This field was quickly maturing from a quaint niche market to a sophisticated mainstream force, with billions of dollars in investments screened to eliminate holdings in tobacco, guns, and, increasingly, firms with a poor environmental record. Geeta Aiyer, president of Walden Asset Management, told the Milken meeting's audience that her company went beyond screening to negotiate directly with firms in which it invests, on topics ranging from energy and water use to the companies' contribution to urban sprawl. "It's very much a blue-suit-to-blue-suit affair—no placard-waving protesters," she said. "Our attitude is [that] we own this stock and we want to see it go up."

Of course, other environmentalists were conveying their concerns more vocally. As the Milken invitees met in the Beverly Hilton ballroom, a group of celebrities in England, including Bianca Jagger and pop star Annie Lennox, were joining in a boycott against Exxon Mobil gasoline stations. Unlike most other U.S. power firms, the company was still lobbying against U.S. participation in the Kyoto climate change plan and publishing opinion pieces raising questions about the seriousness of global warming. About the same time, in a development that sent a chill up the spines of at least some utility executives who heard about it, the environmental group Greenpeace began looking into filing a tobacco industry–type suit against big greenhouse gas emitters for their liability in global warming.

Yet while power firms grew nervous about global warming as the millennium turned, the insurance industry became absolutely terrified by it. Insurers had the most to lose—indeed, many executives feared they were already losing as mounting claims from some extraordinary weather events depleted their coffers. The Worldwatch

Institute found that insurance firms worldwide had paid almost $92 billion in losses from weather-related natural disasters in the 1990s—nearly four times the cost of similar claims in the 1980s. Although at least some of the higher amounts were due to more properties being insured for more money, the payments also coincided with the warmest decade in recorded history. Officials at the giant reinsurance firm Munich Re publicly worried about whether their industry was headed for bankruptcy. They predicted that claims resulting from more frequent tropical cyclones, rising sea levels, and damage to fishing stocks, agriculture, and water supplies could cost as much as $30 billion per year.

Some insurance firms, most notably Swiss Re, the world's biggest catastrophic loss enterprise, resolved to meet this challenge head-on by seeing what they could do to minimize their costs. They had a lot at stake: not only property they insured but also enormous assets in which they'd invested worldwide, on whose long-term value their survival depended. "We have to look at a 100-year horizon," explained William Romero, a jovial, bow tie–wearing Swiss Re executive who came to the Milken conference. To do so, he said, his company relies on scenarios generated in part by its 600 in-house executives with Ph.D. degrees. "We're geekorama!" Romero boasted. "The executives worship knowledge."

All those Swiss Re geeks hadn't found a smoking gun linking the slew of costly weather-related claims and global warming, Romero acknowledged. But it looked as if nailing down that connection would be just a matter of time. Masters of risk, they knew that the *odds* of climate-linked disasters were increasing. Rising temperatures meant more energy and moisture in the atmosphere, and that energy and moisture had to go someplace. "We believe climate change will increase the frequency of natural disasters, particularly weather-related ones, so we've dedicated ourselves to acting responsibly and trying to be proactive," Romero said.

The concerns eventually led Swiss Re to team up with the Milken Institute in its efforts to mine the value of ecosystem services. Numerous scientific studies suggested that intact ecosystems help reduce potential damage from extreme weather events such as floods and droughts.

With this in mind, Swiss Re had started to let its corporate imagination run free on the topic of twenty-first-century premium management. It was looking for ways to put a price on the risk-mitigating services of ecosystems by offering lower premiums to property owners who took care of the soil and trees on their land. In addition, it was contemplating whether to start issuing insurance coverage for "offset" projects such as forests grown specifically to absorb CO_2. Insurance firms already had experience in covering forests for timber losses, Romero noted. Guaranteeing the benefits of CO_2 storage would be but a modest step forward.

While Swiss Re was stretching its corporate imagination, other, smaller entrepreneurs were being much more daring as they grabbed for shares of the emerging greenhouse gas market. Even without resolution as to what, if anything, might eventually be accepted as a global carbon credit under the Kyoto Protocol or other rules, a lively industry of carbon traders was springing up around the world. It included newly specialized greenhouse gas brokers at big, established U.S. firms such as Cantor Fitzgerald (later to suffer disastrous losses in the September 11, 2001, terrorist attack on the World Trade Center) and ambitious rookies such as corn farmer Andrew AcMoody and antique stove salesman Ed Semmelroth, who seized Carbonfarming.com as an Internet domain name and put up a World Wide Web site from their rented office in the tiny town of Tekonsha, Michigan.

At London Luton Airport, travelers were being asked to pay a voluntary $4.25 fee to offset the carbon emissions of their flights, with the money to be invested in forest conservation. In New York, an environmental brokerage firm, Natsource, was selling certificates over the Internet for carbon-emissions reductions. These papers had no legal value and were being purchased mostly for symbolic value by students and activists. They represented "credits" marketed by a

Washington, D.C., group called CO2OL-USA, based on a sustainably managed forest in Panama. The forest was monitored by an independent Costa Rican agency and followed strict guidelines in its treatment of local workers, leading CO2OL-USA's founder, Keegan Eisenstadt, to boast, "Ours is the Rolls Royce of carbon."

Yet with all the hype about charisma, cars, and a carbon market that some analysts predicted could eventually be worth billions, many nagging questions remained about carbon credits. To start with, there was still great doubt that the Kyoto Protocol, the best hope to set off worldwide trading, would become law anytime soon. No major nation had ratified it by late 2001, and controversy besieged it in the United States, the source of a full one-fourth of the world's greenhouse gas emissions. Although a declining number of critics were still questioning whether climate change was a serious threat, many challenged the protocol as unfair because it held industrialized countries, but not developing countries—not even future heavy greenhouse gas emitters such as China—to targets. And even had the Kyoto Protocol seemed bound for worldwide acceptance, it remained to be decided what kinds of carbon sequestration would get credit. No one knew then whether protection of standing forests, which would avert emissions resulting from their clearance, would count. Nor was it certain that projects to store carbon in soil would be included.

Further questions were raised by strong opposition to the idea of sinks and trading on the part of major environmental groups, including the Sierra Club, Greenpeace, and the World Wildlife Fund, not to mention European governments, which were lobbying hard against them at the turn of the new century. Many environmentalists loathe the concept of "pollution permits," arguing that they encourage polluters to keep on polluting as long as they find it advantageous to pay for the permits instead. (Supporters argue, however, that pollution permit schemes ensure lower levels of pollution by imposing a cap on emissions when the permits are allocated; they also serve to make the reductions less costly for both corporations and consumers.)

There were countless other fears and doubts, large and small. Some analysts contended, for instance, that trading and sinks are dangerous distractions from the deep, hard changes the world must start making soon—"like offering a manicure to a cancer patient," as author Ross Gelbspan once characterized it. Others worried whether acceptance of sinks would encourage landowners to plant genetically modified tree plantations, which would earn more carbon credits but sacrifice biodiversity. Some scientists even feared that a warming world would kill off old and new forests alike, converting the proposed sinks into grasslands and other ecosystems with lower carbon-storage capacity, and emitting a lot of CO_2 in the process.

As the global push to expand trading in pollution permits continued, it mirrored the messy birth of great exchanges in Amsterdam and New York, where soaring initial expectations periodically soured. After all, even the poster child of pollution trading, the SO_2 market, so widely praised for its low-cost emissions reductions, can be seen as a textbook argument as to why markets can't substitute for strong governments. Ecosystem scientist Gene Likens, who has studied sulfur emissions in the northeastern United States since 1963, said that although there's no doubt that net SO_2 emissions have been reduced cheaply, "I don't think anyone knows for sure" whether acid rain itself has diminished. That's because when Congress put a cap on SO_2 emissions, launching the trading, it failed to put equally strong controls on nitrogen oxides, also a contributor to acid rain. Many regulated companies ended up buying cheap, low-sulfur coal, which produced just as much nitrogen oxides as did the high-sulfur coal. (Besides, even if there have been net reductions in acid rain throughout the United States, Likens points to evidence that the problem is as bad as ever in New England, where it's damaging particularly sensitive forests.)

A closer look at the fate of the AES Corporation's pioneering carbon investment in Guatemala also yields a somewhat disappointing result. The firm's expectation in 1988 was that the project would sequester nearly 28 million tons of carbon during a forty-year period. Thirteen years later, however, that sanguine estimate had been sharply revised. Guatemalan peasants and CARE ended up planting 40 million trees, not the 52 million originally planned, and of those, 10 percent were lost through disease, highland frosts, and incursions by people seeking firewood. Furthermore, AES' initial estimates were made long before the Kyoto Protocol came into existence and assumed that "avoided emissions," such as protection of standing trees, would eventually count as carbon offsets. In 2001, however, avoided emissions were not credited in the official reporting scheme. What all this meant was that in the project's first ten years, by prevailing standards of accounting, it had sequestered just 1 million tons of carbon, well short of the initial estimates. Still, against great odds of poverty and political instability, the pilot project had achieved remarkable success. AES officials said that most of the trees were thriving and the farmers trained in agroforestry had stopped clearing the forest, halting at least temporarily the prevailing vicious circle of deforestation and land degradation. AES continues to support the project with interest from the endowment set up in 1988.

Finally, dashing the hopes of U.S. farmers who'd fantasized about "growing carbon," the touted carbon-sink deal between Canada and Iowa had been dramatically deflated. In the end, no farmers would be paid to park their plows. Carbon stored in the soil wouldn't be part of the deal because too many problems had cropped up with the plan. The scientific basis was, as Steve Griffin said, too "iffy," though research was continuing. Farmers were reluctant to trust the low-till scheme, and the whole process was nearly impossible to insure. In the end, the deal was ramped down to a sale of 500,000 tons of greenhouse gas reductions to be made by about 100 hog farmers who planned to improve their waste storage and treatment practices. Rather than follow the common practice of pumping the hog's excrement into ponds, where it would decompose under water, deprived of oxygen, and thus release considerable amounts of methane, nitrous oxide, and CO_2, the farmers would invest in concrete holding tanks, from which the manure could be injected into the soil or spread on crops as fertilizer. It would thus decompose *with* oxygen, cutting down on greenhouse gas emissions. Compliance would be much easier to monitor in this case; Griffin had developed a precise formula for the amount of manure that would decompose into methane and nitrous oxide per 150-pound hog, per day, in open-air lagoons versus pits. "These hog tons are pretty good," Griffin said. "They're about as sterling quality as any carbon tons out there. Which I guess is pretty funny, since they're based on hog manure and not as pristine an image as a forest or tree farm."

As David Brand watched the fits and starts of the emerging carbon trade, he worried about the cost of runaway expectations and setbacks brought about with the best and worst of intentions. "I see this market starting to get crowded with cowboys," he fretted during a rare downbeat moment before his upbeat talk at the Milken conference. He was particularly haunted by the memory of young traders at the Sydney Futures Exchange, drinking beer out of milkshake cups as they launched their initial public offerings, screaming, "Let's light this candle!"—referring to the setting off of Roman candle fireworks. What havoc might they wreak on forests whose carbon credits were put up for sale?

"It's a new market, with all sorts of weird and wonderful entrepreneurs," Brand said. "Some of them don't know what they're doing, don't worry about the fact that maybe in this particular forest they're going to cut the trees in ten years, and, oops! Someone had bought the carbon credits."

Still, Brand was convinced that the general trend was in the right direction. *Not* to include forests in any global climate change accord would be reckless, he believed. A full 25 percent of the world's yearly CO_2 emissions came from deforestation. At its best, the carbon-sink approach addressed the devastating loss of timberlands and biodiversity as well as climate change. At the least, it was a transitional tool, buying time for companies to adjust to the more painful changes required.

What gave Brand even more faith, as he flew between conferences and meetings in the first years of the new millennium, was hearing captains of industry ask questions about climate change and photosynthesis and debate the values of carbon credits. There was no doubt in Brand's mind that the deeper changes Earth so desperately needs were already in motion as people gradually awakened to the state of the environment. The entire global system was now threatened by climate change, water scarcity, biodiversity loss, and desertification. Whole regions, including Australia's Murray-Darling river basin and sub-Saharan Africa, might collapse in coming decades from land degradation. At some point, people would simply have to start behaving as if the natural environment is our most valuable asset, not just in spiritual terms but also in hard commercial terms. The conquistadores melted down Aztec artifacts for their gold because they saw no value in the art; generations passed before Europeans came to see the art as priceless. Brand felt sure the same shift was happening with forests: carbon sequestration, biodiversity, and other vital services would become the art. The world wasn't quite there yet, he conceded. Give it ten more years.

New York: How to Put a Watershed to Work

"We all live downstream."

—Environmentalists' motto

EVERY FEW DAYS, Arthur Ashendorff's assistant walks into his sunny twentieth-floor office in Queens and drops a long sheet of paper with a bar graph on his desk. The graph displays patterns in sales of drugs to treat stomach upsets and diarrhea, comparing recent purchases of Pepto-Bismol and Imodium in nearly forty stores throughout New York City with patterns established over the previous four years. It immediately alerts this sixty-year-old civil engineer, New York's deputy director of drinking water quality, to any sharp increases in sales. Every once in a while he'll see an uptick, which invariably makes him peer through his rimless granny glasses with alarm.

In the past, random episodes of food poisoning or special store sales of the drugs have accounted for all such increases. But Ashendorff is on alert for something quite different: an outbreak of disease caused by a single-celled parasite such as *Giardia lamblia* or *Cryptosporidium parvum* traveling through New York City's water supply.

The city has not had a major outbreak of a waterborne disease since 1832, when cholera killed thousands of residents. But its leaders have reason to be wary: the watershed system on which the city depends is the largest surface water supply in all of the United States that is not mechanically filtered. Through their innovative and internationally praised watershed protection program, New Yorkers trust Nature to do that job—but they're not trusting blindly. Disaster too easily could follow in the wake of the tiny travelers.

Both *Giardia* and *Cryptosporidium* are thought to originate in the bowels of wild or domestic animals (*Giardia* was once known as "beaver fever"), and both move easily through water. But whereas *Giardia* causes, at most, painful cramps, the more recently discovered *Cryptosporidium* can be devastating. Swallowing just one cyst can lead to severe illness or death for people with weak immune systems—including babies, old people, and HIV and cancer patients. Before 1976, cryptosporidiosis, or "crypto," as it's called, was not known to have taken a single human life, but since then it appears to have become more resistant to chlorination, and it has begun to kill. Dispatched from the guts of a cow, it can travel for long distances as hard-shelled spores that, once embedded in a human intestine, break open and reproduce at a violently rapid rate. In its worst toll to date, in Milwaukee in 1993, this parasite made 400,000 people sick and cost 103 lives. (Crypto outbreaks have also occurred in Nevada, Oregon, and Georgia.)

Large as Milwaukee's outbreak was, Ashendorff knows it could have been much worse had public health officials not caught it when they did. Waterborne illnesses such as crypto can easily remain unidentified for a long time, chiefly because relatively few infected people ever seek a doctor's care. All but those with the most agonizing stomach complaints tend instead to treat themselves with over-the-counter drugs and wait it out. Of those who do end up seeing a doctor, only a much smaller number submit to a parasite test, establishing a medical record. In Milwaukee, it was only thanks to a vigilant druggist, who noticed Imodium flying off the shelves, that officials had reasonable time to warn city residents to start boiling their water. Word of that lucky break gave Ashendorff the idea for his diarrhea vigil.

His weekly information is supplied by secret agreement (because sales figures are normally treated as propriety information) with a high-ranking sales employee of a major drug chain. The store survey supplements an extensive program of daily on-site water quality sampling in the reservoirs, but, as Ashendorff likes to say: "This is New York City. We have belts and suspenders. You can't be too careful."

There's much more at stake, of course, than local pride. With his shirtsleeves rolled up and the Manhattan skyline laid out across the window before him, Ashendorff at his desk is positioned as if atop a dike, with an eye out for a potential double disaster. A major crypto outbreak would surely mean a human tragedy for New York City and its environs, where 9.5 million people depend on the water flowing from three upstate reservoir systems. (If it happened in proportion to Milwaukee's epidemic, millions would get sick and hundreds would die.) At the same time, such an outbreak would mean failure for the city's watershed conservation program, which has already spared New York billions of dollars in expense.

With its more than $1.5 billion price tag, New York's watershed project may well be the largest investment on record in the strategy of letting Nature pay for its own conservation. It's the fruit of a bottom-line calculation showing trees winning out over technology, and it has also been one of the most successful realizations of David Brand's vision of a forest as a kind of hospital, providing a stream of services besides producing timber. At a time when carbon credits were still lingering on the drawing board, the watershed investment, managed by more than 900 city workers, was rendering major savings.

Environmental protection became an irresistible option for New York City in 1989, when officials were faced with an order from the United States Environmental Protection Agency (EPA) to build a filtration plant that might have cost $6–$8 billion, a budget-breaking amount. Instead, planners chose to gamble a fraction of that amount on protecting their natural asset, the 2,000-square-mile upstate watershed, which they're legally authorized to manage. Through the watershed conservation program, administered by the New York City Department of Environmental Protection (DEP), city residents have become acutely conscious of where their water comes from, the threats to its purity, and the extra benefits, apart from water purification, that derive from maintaining a healthy watershed—benefits such as habitat for fish and birds, carbon sequestration, and landscapes refreshing to the spirits. In launching their experiment, New Yorkers were prospecting for one specific treasure but potentially gaining many more.

New York's water predicament is as huge and unique as the city itself. Yet its response, and the success of its actions so far, has compelling relevance for thousands of other communities around the world facing similar problems. In the United States, 180 million people—two-thirds of the population—depend on surface drinking water systems, such as lakes and reservoirs, rather than groundwater. Most of the largest cities in that position have already built filtration plants, yet even in those cases it's clear that a relatively natural watershed will still provide an extra measure of drinking water safety.

The loss of natural water purification services is just now sneaking up on many urban communities, especially those that take their water from uplands where, until recently, people were few and their activities not terribly disruptive. The rapid growth of urban sprawl in such places has worsened water pollution, making those who live downstream take a hard second look at the value of keeping that upstream land as natural as possible. In fact, one expert, Walter Reid of the Millennium Ecosystem Assessment, estimates that there might be an economic justification for conserving—that is, managing in a relatively natural condition—some 12 percent of the entire U.S. land area (in the contiguous forty-eight states), with protection of water quality as a major goal.

In the years since New York City initiated its upland watershed investment, more than 140 U.S. cities have studied a similar approach, with several having launched their own experiments, according to research published by the Katoomba Group. In Boston, water officials escaped an EPA order to filter their water by enacting a comprehensive watershed program similar to the New York scheme, including land acquisitions, wildlife control, and regulation of development along tributaries. In Ocean County, New Jersey, voters approved a property tax providing nearly $4 million annually to buy land seen as critical in protecting water supplies. In Rochester, Minnesota, city officials have been paying farmers to establish buffer zones, where land is left free from development, along key water bodies. Meanwhile, more dramatic developments were taking place outside the United States. The European Union in 2001 began formally requiring watershed protection in order to ensure drinking water quality. And in Costa Rica, the Ministry of Environment and Energy, inspired by New York City's efforts, began charging more than 20,000 water consumers near the capital city of San José a few cents more on their monthly bills to fund payments to upper watershed farmers who had agreed to maintain and restore forests.

There's also at least one case of a big corporation financing watershed conservation to help an ecosystem do its job. In northeastern France, the bottled water firm Perrier Vittel has been practicing watershed maintenance since the late 1980s, predating New York's efforts. Company officials had started to fear that contaminants, including pesticides and fertilizers from farms in the Rhine-Meuse watershed, were compromising the quality of their prestigious, pricey water. (That fear was painfully confirmed in 1990, when Perrier water was temporarily pulled off the shelves after it was found to contain benzene, a carcinogen that is a component of gasoline.) Rather than simply relocate to other springs, as water firms have done in the past, executives chose to invest. They spent $9 million to buy 600 acres of farmland around the springs and went on to sign eighteen- to thirty-year contracts with farmers who agreed to switch to more environmentally benign practices on an additional 4,000 acres of strategically important land.

In the midst of these proliferating experiments, New York's program remains the leading model of how watershed conservation can pay off. Yet conversations with city officials, activists, scientists, and farmers, beginning over a few brilliant fall days in upstate New York in October 2000, revealed that a sticky mix of political, legal, and financial complications was threatening the project's survival.

WATER IS URBAN BLOOD, sustaining life and permitting growth. Ancient Rome, which tapped local wells and springs and the Tiber River for nearly five centuries, finally flourished after slaves built its famous aqueducts, which drew water from distant rivers and lakes. Los Angeles was set on the road to greatness, in the first years of the twentieth century, after its water company officials secretly wrangled the rights to the Owens River, 250 miles away in the Sierra Nevada. For New York, the turning point arrived on the heels of a catastrophe: the epidemic of Asiatic cholera in 1832, which killed nearly one in fifty inhabitants and prompted more than half the population to flee. The cholera outbreak fired political will in the city and state to start construction of a major upstate reservoir system.

This ambition was the most dramatic extension to date of a pattern that had slowly developed after Dutch settlers founded New York on the southern tip of Manhattan Island in the early 1600s. As the population grew and the city expanded, residents simply reached farther beyond their borders for clean water. Initially, New York depended for its drinking supplies on local springs and wells, and a city collection pond, periodically replenished by storm water, carried sewage off the streets. By the late 1770s, the city was hauling water from Brooklyn, but even those additional supplies didn't suffice to control fires, including one in 1776 that destroyed one-quarter of the city's buildings. By the 1820s, city leaders were already thirsting after the Croton River, forty miles upstate in what are now Westchester and Putnam Counties. The 1832 cholera epidemic made local votes for a Croton water supply project come easy, and in 1837, with the aid of 4,000 immigrants, work began on this major engineering feat.

The east and west branches of the Croton were dammed, and aqueducts were built to reservoirs in downtown Manhattan. In 1842, the river's water finally arrived in the city, celebrated with fountain displays and a parade of unprecedented proportion featuring thousands of volunteer firefighters and temperance society revelers. Supplies from free hydrants linked to the Croton system began to substitute for water from the polluted wells. Property values shot skyward. "Oh, who that has not been shut up in the great prison-cell of a city, and made to drink of its brackish springs, can estimate the blessings of the Croton Aqueduct? Clean, sweet, abundant water!" exclaimed the Massachusetts-born poet Lydia Maria Child. Yet within just a few decades, increasing population and demand meant the city once more had to search for ways to expand its water supply.

In 1905, the New York State legislature created the New York City Board of Water Supply, charged with identifying and delivering new water sources for the growing metropolis. Board officials soon looked to the Catskill Mountains, twice as far away as the Croton system, and within a few years workers were blasting bedrock for tunnels and damming tributaries of the Hudson River, at last completing the Catskill Reservoir System in 1928. The pattern of grow-and-reach continued throughout the Roaring Twenties, with the city also claiming tributaries of the Delaware River. New Jersey, just downstream of the new dams, challenged this move in court, fearing it might reduce the water's flow to the point of harming the state's fisheries, one of its most important commercial resources. But in 1931, the United States Supreme Court nonetheless upheld New York City's right to tap the Delaware, providing it released enough water to protect the fish. The construction of new reservoirs went on for decades more, and in the process, New Yorkers not only offended the Garden State but also earned the abiding resentment of thou-

sands of upstate New Yorkers whose lives they had severely dis-
rupted. Nine upstate villages had been flooded and nearly 3,000
people displaced as parts of the watershed were claimed and reservoirs established. Cemeteries were moved, property was condemned,
and farms and businesses were relocated, leaving bitter feelings that
would come back to cost the city decades later.

Still, the prize was irresistible. Completed at last in 1964, the
Catskill/Delaware Watershed today provides about 90 percent of
New York City's water. Together with the Croton Watershed, it
encompasses nineteen reservoirs and three controlled lakes, storing
580 billion gallons of water. Some 6,000 miles of conduits and
pipes—some big enough to drive a bus through—transport water to
five city boroughs and a few upstate communities en route. Yet however awe-inspiring it is in its scope, the process is surprisingly low-
tech for so huge and sophisticated a city. The water arrives powered
almost entirely by gravity and routinely untreated except for some
chlorine, used as a disinfectant, and fluoride, to prevent tooth decay.
The only filter it passes through is a big metal screen designed to
catch dead fish.

This system worked fine through most of the twentieth century,
when the Catskills area was a wilderness and what are now the city's
northern suburbs were only sparsely populated. Yet as the new millennium approached, tourism was taking off in the upstate mountains, with new ski resorts, golf courses, inns, and second homes
under construction, and growth in the suburbs was exploding. By the
late 1980s, fertilizers, pesticides, oil, and exhaust particles had con-
tributed to what one official called a "creeping cumulative impact"
on the water supply. Meanwhile, inadequately treated sewage was
occasionally being discharged directly into the reservoirs from a few
large treatment plants, including one at the Bedford Hills Correc-
tional Facility.

City officials were already growing concerned about water quality
by the time the United States Congress directed the EPA to promul-
gate rules specifying when public water supply systems supplied by

surface water sources would have to be filtered. In 1989, the EPA released the Surface Water Treatment Rule, which said that *any* system using water from reservoirs, streams, lakes, and rivers must build a filtration plant—unless its managers could show they could control human activities within the watershed "that may have an adverse impact on the microbiological quality of the source water."

New York readily agreed to build a plant for the small Croton system. Its water was indisputably sullied, and the cost of a filtration plant was not expected to exceed $300 million. But the city's officials balked at the much greater expense to filter the rest of the supply. They started to investigate their options.

The local officials were eager to take the EPA escape route, avoiding filtration by showing they could control watershed contaminants. But they faced an immediate problem, one shared in other cases explored in this book. Protecting a natural asset is always easier if you own it. And whereas other big cities with unfiltered surface water supplies, such as Seattle, San Francisco, and Boston, owned most of the land around their systems, this wasn't the case with New York. Before 1997, the city owned only 80,000 acres of the million-acre area, with nearly half of that land actually under the reservoirs. (New York State owned an additional 200,000 acres, protected as part of the Catskill Forest Preserve.)

What's more, New York's watersheds had a lot of people living in them: about 160,000 in Croton and 45,000 in the Catskill/Delaware system. Clearly, city officials needed some powerful tools to control watershed residents' behavior and fight the pollution. And luckily, they had some, thanks to state legislature decisions made almost a century earlier. Concerned, even back then, about the city's ability to preserve its water quality, New York State in 1905 had given city officials the power to condemn land in all its watershed areas, and six years later it added the power to regulate regional development. The delicate question was how the city might wield that power and maintain cooperation from the already embittered populations to its north.

In January 1991, the New York State Department of Health, acting as the EPA's designated agency to carry out the Safe Drinking
Water Act, ordered New York to build a filtration plant for the
Catskill/Delaware system. The city lobbied furiously to reverse the
decision, and after a year the EPA was persuaded to suspend the
order temporarily. But it was clear that time was running out. Pressures on the city to move rapidly were now coming from two sides.
On the one hand, the EPA's threatened filtration fiat had given financial value to the Catskills' natural water purification services, making
the conservation option attractive. On the other, environmental and
consumer activists had begun to agitate for the city to protect its
water at the source and move forward with alternatives to building a
filtration plant for the Catskill/Delaware system.

In the lead was Robert F. Kennedy Jr., son of the late senator.
Kennedy was also the chief prosecuting attorney for Riverkeeper, a
gadfly group that had formed in 1966 to protect the Hudson River,
whose dammed tributaries made up half of the Catskill water supply
and all of the Croton system. He was eager to provide what he said
would be a "stark symbol of the foolhardy choice the City was contemplating" in even considering whether to go ahead and build the
costly filtration plant. In 1989, beginning what would be his long,
high-profile role in city watershed policy, he solicited a study to
investigate the alternative of buying every acre in the
Catskill/Delaware Watershed. A real estate agent who volunteered
her time estimated it would cost just $1 billion, which of course
would be several billion dollars less than the potential cost of a filtration plant.

"The contrast between those economic choices was really obvious and really persuasive," Kennedy said in a conversation in the fall
of 2000, as he sat at a picnic table outside his office at Pace University School of Law's Environmental Litigation Clinic. He radiated
celebrity as he squinted into the sun, in shirtsleeves and a silk tie
printed with a red fish motif. A group of young assistants hovered by
respectfully. At forty-seven, Kennedy had been wrestling for more
than a decade with what he saw as official apathy about the water-

shed. He clearly was as keenly interested in preserving the Hudson River valley's beauty, wildlife habitat, and recreational opportunities as in maintaining its water purification service, but he spoke of both goals as inextricably linked. He was convinced that the EPA's filtration mandate should be used as a "gorilla in the closet," forcing the city to focus on watershed protection. But his image of what protection should look like made city officials understandably nervous. The real answer to ensuring water quality was to "stop development," Kennedy had previously told a reporter. "That's what you have to do, [but] nobody wants to say it."

To advance his view that the city wasn't doing even the minimum it should to protect water supplies, Kennedy waged a kind of guerrilla war, making the most of his access to the media. He led television crews to the Putnam Hospital Center's faulty treatment plant, where hospital waste and sewage was flowing into a reservoir, while his younger brother, Douglas, a reporter at the *New York Post,* kept up the fight with periodic exposés. In a typical scoop in 1994, the *Post* reported that the Croton reservoir had been shut down because of sewage pollution. A city spokesman subsequently contended that the closure was due not to sewage but to "organic material"—after which late-night television host David Letterman dryly joked that the whole story "scared the organic material out of me."

In *The Riverkeepers,* which Kennedy coauthored with fellow activist John Cronin in 1999, the two accuse city officials of belonging to an "institutional culture wed to chemical and engineering solutions and sympathetic to intensive real estate development." This stance, and Kennedy's tactic of frequently suing the DEP, not surprisingly has stirred some rancor among city employees who believe they're doing their best.

"His approach is fundamentally different from ours," said Hilary Meltzer, an attorney with the New York City Law Department who for years has been deeply involved in overseeing the watershed regulations. "I heard one of his cohorts recently saying it's not so much that the road to hell is paved with good intentions as that the road to hell is *paved.* They think paving is intrinsically bad for the environment. And that may be true, but our view is there has to be a balance. We don't think it's a realistic option to stop all development in the watershed. We have to live with the political realities, and we'd just never get, or want, regulations that prohibit all construction."

As much as he has vexed the watershed managers, Kennedy's confrontational tactics have helped raise the issue's profile from an obscure bureaucratic dilemma to front-page news, and his celebrity and family contacts have generated support in Washington, D.C. For his own part, he defended his legal suits as necessary to keep New York City's government honest. The politicians who claimed they were championing New York's watershed program were "all indentured servants to the real estate industry," he contended in the conversation at Pace University's law school. "They'd never come to the table if we didn't sue them; it's the only thing they respect."

In the early 1990s, Riverkeeper devoted itself to educating New York about the source of its tap water in order to pressure officials to get more serious about watershed protection. Kennedy helped draw together a coalition that included labor unions, HIV advocacy groups, local community boards, and Hispanic and African American activists who were upset that the worst water was going to the poorest neighborhoods. Part of Riverkeeper's effort involved the preparation of shocking posters, such as one depicting a water tap attached to a naked man's lower torso and spewing yellow liquid into a glass. The caption read, "Human Waste Is Discharged into 88 Percent of New York City's Water Supply."

Throughout this time, Mayor David Dinkins' staff and Riverkeeper members were negotiating with the federal government for another stay of the filtration order. In January 1993, those efforts paid off when EPA administrator William Reilly announced a compromise. He said that New York City should plan for filtration, but if it were able to show, within a year, that it could protect its reservoirs from contaminants, the order to filter the water would be reviewed. The city was also ordered to start an enormous new water-testing program.

City officials were well aware that their existing laws were woefully inadequate for the task of protecting the watershed. The regulations hadn't been seriously updated since 1953 and, as Kennedy wrote, were "better suited to Li'l Abner's Dogpatch or Andy Griffith's Mayberry" than to the modern regional development boom. Although the old rules governed the placement of outhouses and chicken manure piles, for instance, they were silent on toxic waste or the discharge of polluted storm water runoff from construction sites. The maximum fine for an infraction was $25, and no one had been prosecuted in forty years.

By the time of Reilly's order, Dinkins' administration had already been working for years on a comprehensive overhaul of the rules, a process that made it clear reform wouldn't be easy. Three years earlier, upstate residents had learned of the ambitious changes being contemplated when a draft of the proposals was circulated. They included severe restraints on development, a ban on new buildings in certain areas, limits on construction of new sewage treatment plants, and a directive obliging property owners to collect and treat their own storm water. There were also strict limits on the amount of paved surfaces allowable on any property and a crackdown on watershed farming activities. The draft generated a huge outcry—including upstate newspaper cartoons portraying city officials putting diapers on cows—and led to the formation of a protest group called the Coalition of Watershed Towns.

The upstate protests continued even after the regulations were modified—Kennedy's group said "watered down"—by a new city administration in the months after Rudolph Giuliani was elected mayor in November 1993. This new version dispensed altogether with the notion of limiting pavement or restricting farm practices, prohibiting only intentional, knowing, or reckless acts that significantly increase pollutants in the water supply. In a series of public hearings on the rules, environmentalists slammed them as too lax, and watershed residents complained that they were going to have to carry the cost of New York's drinking water, arguing that they would lose out on development and their future tax base. Major lawsuits were initiated. Upstate developers paid for a direct-mail campaign against New York's alleged usurpation of the land. As the crisis bloomed in the spring of 1995, Governor George Pataki, who had just taken office, stepped in and offered to mediate.

The negotiations that followed lasted two years, eventually including representatives of New York City, New York State, the EPA, upstate towns, and three leading environmental groups. They ground on through more than 150 public meetings, many lasting late into the night. "It was like a rolling Thanksgiving dinner with relatives you only want to see once a year," summed up Chris Meyer, who represented the New York Public Interest Research Group (NYPIRG). The long process ended in a compromise aimed at appeasing everyone, and, unwieldy as it was, it worked: the agreement released in 1997, known as the memorandum of agreement, or MOA, had support from sixty towns, ten villages, seven counties, and several major environmental organizations. The upstate communities agreed to drop almost a dozen lawsuits and cooperate with new limits on growth in watershed areas. In return, the city promised to spend what was then calculated to be $1.5 billion on, among other things, buying land, constructing new storm sewers and septic systems, and updating existing sewage plants. This was in addition to about $35 million already budgeted to help upstate farmers limit their pollution. The EPA rewarded the efforts with a five-year stay of its filtration order, with the possibility of an extension in 2002. "This agreement is a great victory for New Yorkers who believe, as I do, that environmental protection and economic growth go hand in hand," Pataki said. Yet the victory merely ensured that New Yorkers would have to keep working on their watershed program. To continue getting reprieves, perhaps indefinitely, the city would have to not only show that its water met EPA standards of purity, with low levels of sediment and fecal bacteria, but also never be the source of a waterborne disease outbreak. On top of that, officials would have to prove that they had a program that would help meet all these demands in the future.

The biggest single item in the budget for this determined venture was $260 million to buy property around the reservoirs, creating "buffers" of undeveloped land. In addition to preventing new sources of pollution, the buffers would let Nature do its water-purifying work: soil and plants, left unperturbed, would absorb and filter contaminants. The city would be responsible to the upstate local governments for property taxes on the purchased land—an expense that had climbed to $68 million per year by mid-2001.

Through all these payments, the city would be internalizing the costs of providing its workers and inhabitants with naturally clean water. An additional hefty expense, and the most novel one, was more than $140 million to be paid directly to local governments and businesses in the thirty-five watershed communities whose land would be supplying the natural water filtration. It was a considerable transfer of wealth from city water consumers to newly designated stewards, now committed to forgo environmentally harmful types of development to protect the watershed. The total included $68 million divided between Putnam and Westchester Counties for use in projects relating directly both to improving water quality and providing jobs. Another nearly $60 million was slated for the Catskill Fund for the Future, to be distributed among local businesses to encourage environmentally sound development, and an additional $13 million was earmarked as "good neighbor payments" for distribution among all the local governments that signed the MOA, to be spent on public works.

"All this money is to be used at the local officials' discretion," said city watershed scientist Kimberlee Kane, "and their discretion right now is to leave it in the bank to earn interest. I guess that's why a few unkind souls say we bought the regulations."

One of the most vocal of those souls has been Putnam County developer and far-right Republican Party activist Ed Heelan, who has a real estate office on the outskirts of the village of Brewster. In October 2000, his walls were adorned with posters supporting the presidential bid of Pat Buchanan, for whom Heelan was state campaign chairman that election season. From his distinct end of the political divide, Heelan has goaded the city with fervor equal to Robert Kennedy's. His concern, as he put it in a long conversation that month, was primarily with property rights and what he saw as the grave violation thereof.

Before New York City got into the conservation business, Heelan's county of 90,000 residents, less than an hour's commute from Wall Street, had been enjoying an extraordinary real estate boom, in which Heelan himself represented some 10,000 acres as principal, partner, consultant, or broker. But the boom was stifled by the crackdown on watershed growth, and the negotiated MOA had done nothing to make that any easier for him. Despite a recent heart attack that had made him resolve to scale down his commercial activities, the sixty-one-year-old mogul had been busy organizing at least half a dozen suits against the city. None had prevailed in the first three years of the MOA, but Heelan held out hope that the courts would eventually sympathize.

"It's been an absolute outrage, a thievery!" he exclaimed, banging his hand on the table as his face turned pink. "If you or I did what the city did, they'd put us in prison for bribery and extortion. That's pretty strong language, and I'm comfortable with it. What they did was illegal. They went around to the townships and said, 'Hey, towns, we'll give you hundreds of thousands of dollars, in most cases to do what you want. You can balance your books and look good, and not raise taxes.' The public officials had to waive the right to sue later on. And now they're reading the fine print. Now they're wondering how they're going to build their schools if they can't have development."

Heelan figured he'd personally lost several million dollars in "opportunity costs" due to development forgone, and he named several entrepreneurs whose property values, like his, had plummeted. (The properties were mostly in the area around the Croton system, which was to be filtered, yet where watershed protection rules were still being applied.) Consequently, Heelan predicted, thousands of residents' taxes would have to rise to make up for decreased commercial activities. He also forecast "a flood of demands for lower tax values" because Putnam properties were still being assessed at their pre-watershed agreement levels.

"People are waking up, starting to realize they can't carry this vacant land," Heelan said, gesturing toward his window, though the forested slopes of which he spoke were well beyond view. He insisted that New York officials had access to reliable filtration technology to deal with water pollutants and pathogens. To his mind, the decision to focus instead on watershed conservation simply switched the financial burden from the government to the taxpayers. "The city and Kennedy are radical and no-growth, and I think that's unrealistic and unreasonable and un-American," Heelan said.

Indeed, Kennedy's and Heelan's positions demonstrated two dramatically opposed ways of looking at Nature, with New York City caught somewhat awkwardly in between. Whereas Kennedy's view implied that property owners had an obligation to society to act as stewards of the environmental assets on their land—though they might also be compensated for their costs—Heelan's suggested that buying land entails the purchase of an incontestable right to pollute. This debate is at the crux of the conflict over New York's watershed, and much like several controversial federal environmental laws of the 1970s, including the Endangered Species Act of 1973, it's a sign that Americans are increasingly willing to rethink private property rights once viewed as inalienable for the sake of the common good.

ALTHOUGH BATTERED BY LAWSUITS from the right and the left, New York's watershed bureaucrats have ultimately been more concerned about microbes. The greatest risk to all the progress they'd made lay in the enormous uncertainties involved in understanding adverse human effects on life-support systems. They had seen, in the early 1990s, how farmers and towns could spew waste into their environment for years, with little perceptible change in drinking water quality, until an unseen threshold was crossed and, seemingly overnight, a disastrous outbreak of a new pathogen such as *Cryptosporidium* could develop. And they were well aware of the stakes involved if this were to occur in the watershed: under the agreement in effect with the EPA, any serious outbreak of a waterborne disease in New York City would be grounds to lift the stay and order immediate planning for a filtration plant.

Another looming scientific concern was the phosphorus accumulating in the reservoirs from continued runoff of sewage and fertilizer in the populated and farming areas. Too much phosphorus can lead to eutrophication—algal blooms and weed growth that deplete oxygen from water and in some cases actually suffocate fish. Water from sources overloaded with phosphorous looks, tastes, and smells bad. But the cure—more chlorine—can be worse than the disease because chlorine creates dangerous by-products such as carcinogenic trihalomethanes. These dangers from phosphorus overload were the reasons the watershed program's funds to build and update sewage treatment systems—another major expense on the list—were so crucial. According to New York City's plan, more than 100 wastewater treatment systems for schools, towns, and condominium complexes in the watershed area had to be brought up to modern standards, fast.

Down the line, yet another danger was lurking: that the forests so key to maintaining New York's clean drinking water could eventually be seriously impaired by acid rain from smokestack utilities and exhaust from cars and trucks traveling more than 100 miles away. For decades, the healthy forests had absorbed most of the sulfuric and nitric acids in the rain, keeping them out of the water supply. In late 2001, nitrate levels in the upper watershed streams were still below EPA limits. Yet the forests "aren't an infinite sponge," warned Kathleen Weathers, a forest ecologist for the Institute of Ecosystem Studies, based in Millbrook, New York. "The $64,000 question is: Where's the break point? When do you get to the point where it does affect water quality?"

Money troubles compounded the city's worries. Original estimates for the wastewater treatment plant upgrade program—one of the few watershed programs without a funding limit—were $75 million, yet by the summer of 2001 the cost of upgrading all the plants was projected to be more than three times that amount. The city was also far behind schedule in dealing with the facilities. "We're buried. We won't make it," Meltzer, the city attorney, acknowledged, though she said planners expected to be able to upgrade the most important plants by the EPA's May 2002 deadline.

WHEREAS NEW YORK'S challenge in heavily populated Putnam County is to limit further development and thereby minimize water pollution, its mission in the Catskills, which are still thickly forested, is to protect the forests and other foliage that help generate clean water in the first place. This means working closely with local residents, who own about 80 percent of the forested areas. The healthiest of those parcels, with the most intact ecosystems performing their environmental services most efficiently, are those owned by careful timber managers. Next in line come the farms, and far after that, the subdivisions and second homes. City employees thus see an important part of their mission as trying to keep foresters in forests and farmers on farms.

A century ago, a full 95 percent of the Catskills area was forested with native elderberry, silky dogwood, maple, black cherry, and red oak trees. Now there is no virgin forest left, but small private landowners—many of them amateur foresters, with average properties of about thirty acres—sell timber from secondary forests in what has become an $80 million industry. A city-funded program aims to help these businesses with everything from financial management to instruction in the techniques of sustainable forestry—cutting selectively and replanting judiciously—so that they can afford to stay on the land. "Property tax pressures are a major force causing people to sell or subdivide," said John Schwartz, a forester with the New York City–sponsored Watershed Agricultural Council. "So we end up doing some tax counseling as well as economic development work."

Upstate farmers are also getting lots of free advice, and even free infrastructure. At Holley Hill Farm, a tiny family-owned business in the speed-bump town of Walton, more than 100 miles from New York City's center, David Holley's calves take shelter in a $50,000 solar-heated tent, paid for by urban taxpayers. Moving the eight calves out of the cramped, dank barn to their state-of-the-art new quarters in a spacious bovine greenhouse has dramatically improved their health—and the success of Holley's dairy farm. "I haven't lost a calf in two years . . . and I'm doing a lot less doctoring," he says. And just as the greenhouse saves him money, so does the neat new fence along the creek running through his property, which keeps his cows from fouling the water or stumbling on rocks. With milk prices at historical lows, Holley never could have afforded these improvements on his own. But New York environmental officials deemed them worthwhile in order to minimize the chances of waterborne diseases such as crypto originating in polluted runoff at Holley Hill or hundreds of other small farms.

With such boons in mind, the city initially tried to make farmers conservationists by fiat. Among the controversial regulations proposed in 1990 was a mandatory 200-foot setback from streams to allow room for trees and wetlands to hold back water long enough to break down and remove its pollutants. But the farmers simply rebelled. "Our most productive land is beside streams," protested veteran upstate corn farmer Dave Fulton. "We insisted it be a voluntary program." New York City's emissaries subsequently returned with a sweeter offer of voluntary fifteen-year contracts, paying $100 per acre per year, to plant native species along the streams. This approach bought greater goodwill, but because so many farmers could earn more with crops such as corn, only about 400 acres were involved in the streamside rehabilitation program by the fall of 2000.

On the other hand, the great majority of watershed farmers have signed up for the free consultations and infrastructure aid, including fences and pumps, that have helped out on Holley Hill Farm. However, even though these improvements are helpful and welcome, local farmers say they aren't enough to eclipse the larger economic forces, such as the downward trend of milk prices, that would ultimately decide whether the land can stay in agriculture. "We're helping out the city, and we're benefiting, too, but we can't say how long it'll last," said Holley.

Many other Catskills residents seemed to share this idea of their duty as local water stewards and what was owed to them in return. "When we go home for Christmas, we always ask our relatives, 'Where do you think you get your water?'—and they simply have no idea," said Karen Rauter, an outreach worker for the Watershed Agricultural Council. Rauter had moved from Manhattan in the late 1990s to the tiny town of Halcott, a few miles from Dave Holley's farm. "I had no idea myself before we moved here," she said. "But now I live here and feel it's our responsibility to keep the land as it is. And it's the city's responsibility to pay."

Crucial as the Catskills may be, the heart of New York City's watershed protection efforts is the Kensico Reservoir, a thirteen-square-mile reservoir in Westchester County, about a half hour's drive north from Manhattan. Under normal circumstances, all the water from the Catskill/Delaware Watershed enters and leaves from Kensico. It's where all the care taken by city consultants, upstream farmers, and foresters could be outweighed by a single event, such as runoff from a breach of a nearby sewage line or a big construction project sending sediment into water. Maple and ash trees around the reservoir were bursting into fall reds and yellows on the sunny morning when Michael Principe, deputy commissioner for New York City's water supply program, explained how the system worked.

The water enters the 30-billion-gallon reservoir from two aqueducts, he said, and there it spends, on average, about twenty days as it is chlorinated and fluorinated before traveling for three more hours to the city. "You know who the biggest enemies are? Birds," Principe said, laughing. "We had a major problem with geese and ducks in the early 1990s." The flocks of waterfowl relieved themselves in the reservoirs, dramatically raising bacteria levels. "We zeroed in on these thousands of Canada geese who've migrated here as their habitats have been destroyed in the south," Principe said. "In 1993 we implemented our 'waterfowl control program,' which was basically chasing them with motorboats every morning and evening." City geesefighters even set off propane cannons to scare the birds, he said, until neighbors complained about the noise.

A limnologist, an expert in the science of lakes, Principe seemed much more at ease discussing the watershed's basic functioning than the fiery politics surrounding it. Watching his relaxed, open face as he spoke, one could easily imagine that New York's problems might be as simple as geese. "I'm fairly optimistic," he said. "The fact is, the water quality is excellent and only going to get better. The EPA feels we should be buying more land and speeding up our wastewater treatment program. But it's an incredibly ambitious deadline that they had, and I really don't see the reasoning for why we should build a filtration plant. When you look at the rest of the world and what's going on with freshwater supplies and then look at New York, well, we have problems—but by and large we're very lucky."

But was New York City's luck starting to run out? It certainly looked that way later that morning on a second tour of Kensico, this time with attorney Marc Yaggi, a young Kennedy lieutenant, and Cathleen Breen, an activist with NYPIRG. They pointed out all the construction taking place around the strategically important reservoir despite the city's efforts to control new growth. And to be sure, the city had been greatly challenged in its effort to buy buffer zones in that prime real estate area. Plots near the Kensico Reservoir, within an hour's drive of New York City, had cost as much as $350,000 per acre, and many landowners simply balked at officials' offers. (By 2001, the city had spent about one-third of its budget for land acquisition to buy 27,000 acres, mostly in the Catskill/Delaware system.)

Meanwhile, developers were moving ahead, buying land and building properties all around the Kensico Reservoir. One new subdivision was rising just 600 feet from the water's edge. Elsewhere, sprawling new "McMansions" took up enormous plots on land the activists said should instead be used for buffers. Outside one grand residence, a developer had actually filled in a stream to build a drive-way. (Riverkeeper sued in that case and won an order for a $1.3 million remediation.) In a more dramatic development, a major highway expansion was being planned along the reservoir's shore, near a complex of offices for large companies including IBM Corporation and Swiss Re. "We were dumbfounded when we heard about it," Yaggi said. "It's such a critical area, and paving the land is the worst thing you can do. You get this huge impervious surface, with the water rolling over, carrying the pollutants. . . ." He made a sudden U-turn on the empty road. "The rationale was the heavy traffic," he said. "Yeah, like I'm really scared to drive here." (Subsequent to that afternoon, Riverkeeper and twenty civic and environmental groups brokered a deal with the New York State Department of Transportation in which the agency would make traffic and safety improvements with no net increase in impervious surfaces.)

Convinced that the city lacked the political will to effectively control development, Riverkeeper and other environmental groups were continuing to monitor the Department of Environmental Protection as rigorously as the DEP was monitoring potential outbreaks of intestinal disease. Kennedy's group, which had made so much use of the "gorilla in the closet" threat of a budget-breaking filtration plant, was particularly concerned that the conservation fight would be lost altogether were the gorilla to be set free. They charged that the city had already lowered its vigilance around the Croton system, where a plant was planned for completion in 2007. In the Catskills, Yaggi predicted, "filtration would be a green light for developers. Once it started, the City just wouldn't have any other reason to care. . . . We'd have beachfront condos before you know it, with septic tanks spilling right into the watershed."

In the summer of 2001, however, city officials remained confident that they could avoid a filtration order for the larger Catskill/Delaware system, at least for another five years. "The EPA rhetoric has been such that we're working on the terms of a filtration-avoidance scheme rather than on the question of whether or not we'll get one," said Meltzer, the city attorney.

Even so, the strength of the economic argument against filtration had been reduced with time. The anticipated expense of a Catskill/Delaware filtration plant appeared to have come down dramatically since 1989—Principe, eleven years later, estimated that such a plant might cost as little as $4 billion, although other city officials were still citing higher estimates. On the other side of the equation, the conservation program's costs were approaching $2 billion, primarily because upgrading the wastewater systems had turned out to be so much more expensive than anticipated. "The higher the costs of these programs go, the less clear is the economic argument in favor of the watershed conservation program," said a worried Meltzer.

City employees and environmentalists nonetheless agreed, at least in interviews, that it would be wrong to assume they could rely on technological solutions alone, given that even the state-of-the-art technology wasn't completely dependable. The EPA claimed that combining filtration with chlorine as a disinfectant "removed 99.9 percent of *Giardia* cysts and 99.9 percent of enteric viruses." Yet this assumed that the filtration plant was running flawlessly. Milwaukee's water supply had been filtered, yet that hadn't sufficed to prevent its deadly outbreak of *Cryptosporidium* after one of the filtration plants was overwhelmed during heavy rains. In fact, one 1999 Massachusetts study, the results of which were presented at an EPA workshop, found that children living in towns with an unprotected, filtered surface water supply were nearly twice as likely to have been exposed to crypto than those in towns with a protected, unfiltered surface water supply. Nor were technological solutions addressing watershed problems such as nitrogen runoff from farms, or toxic or hormone-mimicking chemicals from household cleaners, paints, pesticides, gas, and fertilizers. Finally, neither filtration, chlorine, nor even cutting-edge treatment with ultraviolet light would help if the water tasted, smelled, or looked bad. It all amounted to a powerful argument in favor of preserving the purity of water at its source, which, with surface water systems, means maintaining a healthy watershed.

Certainly, the safest solution, economic costs aside, would be to have both the filtration plant and effective watershed protection. This, in fact, was the recommendation of a blue-ribbon panel appointed by the EPA to look at New York's dilemma in 1991. For at least the near future, however, the choice between a costly filtration plant and a less costly watershed protection plan remained, for many New Yorkers, obvious evidence of the economic value of Nature's services.

Robert Kennedy said he hoped the lesson would last. "Good economic policy is always good environmental policy," he maintained. "Whenever you see people trying to pit the economy against the environment, it's always in terms of short-term benefits. If you want to treat the planet as if it's a business in liquidation, you can generate cash flow and the illusion of prosperity, but our children are going to pay for our joy ride. It's just deficit spending, a way of making a few people rich by making everyone else poor."

In New York, it was the city government, responding to federal and local activist concerns, that led the effort to recognize the value of Nature's assets and slow down the "deficit spending." On the opposite coast of the United States, meanwhile, a grassroots group was seizing the initiative to make rules of its own about recognizing Nature's role in the economy.

Napa, California: How a Town Can Live with a River and Not Get Soaked

"The life of every river sings its own song, but in most the song is long marred by the discords of abuse."

—Aldo Leopold

IN A CATTLE PASTURE south of downtown Napa, California, a clarinet, flute, and bass guitar strike up a jazzy version of "Up a Lazy River." About sixty people, if you count the rubber-neckers wandering over from a nearby retirement house, gather in the midsummer sun. Two young women in flowing dresses open paper boxes to release orange clouds of monarch butterflies. A few dogs wander through the crowd. It's a markedly mellower scene than your average U.S. Army Corps of Engineers groundbreaking ceremony. Yet the mood of this morning, in late July 2000, is triumphant. This blue-collar, backwater city has fought Washington, D.C., and won. It has taken control of the shape of its future, declared its right to choose its battles—and now, with low-key pomp, it is celebrating a promising armistice.

For several decades, Napa, the depressed county seat of the glamorous grape-growing valley that bears its name, had lived at war with the river that runs through it. The fifty-five-mile-long waterway, meandering from the high country redwoods of Mount St. Helena through vineyards and marshes to the San Pablo Bay, near San Francisco, was pinched and squeezed by earthen levees and low concrete bridges that blocked its flow when the water ran high. It was corseted, in the words of one city mother, like the Victorian ladies who once strolled its docks. But the river was no lady, and periodically, after heavy rains, it would burst from its jackets and flood, costing increasing fortunes in property damage and disaster aid.

The Corps, the main federal agency in charge of flood control, proposed a remedy. The river would be forced into a deep concrete channel running in a straight line through the city. Concrete steps would line its banks; rocky riprap would constrain it. Yearly dredging would speed the water along, and chin-high walls would block its periodic fury. Riverside marshes would be stripped, with the damage "mitigated" by restoration of wetlands someplace else.

There was just one problem. Napa residents, by law, would have to foot as much as half of the bill, and they balked at the Corps' aggressive river-subduing plan. So instead, in a process that took several years and several million dollars' worth of studies, residents came up with their own design, a friendly truce that would preserve the river's integrity while containing its rage. They called it a "living river" approach, and it held the promise of bringing the city's submerged economy back to life.

Proponents said they'd work with Nature rather than trying to tame it; they'd let the Napa River *be* a river. The waterway and its adjoining land would be coaxed back into ancient patterns. Planners would relocate homes, businesses, and even railroad tracks built on the floodplain and would bar future development there. The Corps, in a stunning reversal of approach, would raze levees and either remove bridges or rebuild them at higher levels. More than 650 acres of wetlands would be created or restored—even right in the middle of downtown, where an oil-storage facility once stood—and the land would periodically sop up floodwaters as it had done in centuries past.

At its conception, in the mid-1990s, it was a pathbreaking idea, although it wasn't entirely original. A decade earlier, after a devastating 1984 flood, Tulsa, Oklahoma, had defied tradition by moving some 1,000 structures out of its floodplain. Napa's approach was much more comprehensive, however, and since its start, the idea of a river armistice has caught on in rain-soaked communities from Rapid City, South Dakota, and Louisville, Kentucky, to Argentina, Australia, and China. The scope for duplication in the future is great because the tactic is aimed at an age-old human problem. All over the world, people have crowded unwisely onto floodplains and filled-in wetlands, playing chicken with rivers that rise up every few years to teach them the same costly old lesson.

In contrast, Napa's project and those that followed represent vivid progress toward the establishment of a new economy of Nature, in which the labor of ecosystems is formally respected. It got off the drawing board in 1998 after county residents voted to raise their own taxes to help fund it. That was just one year after New York launched its watershed conservation experiment, and the two events had more than timing in common. In both cases, governments made major investments in Nature, treating local ecosystems as assets that, if managed wisely, would yield financial returns. But whereas New York's main goal was savings—conservation would be cheaper than a new filtration plant—Napa residents were counting on being enriched both financially and spiritually.

At the start, at least, Napa's plan would cost taxpayers and the federal government much more than the Corps' original scheme. But local environmentalists and city boosters alike hoped to profit from a host of extra benefits besides simple flood protection. In bringing back their river from the dead, they meant for it in turn to revive their beaten-down urban landscape, providing their city with lovely new natural settings that would encourage local commerce and tourism. Their hope was that, in the end, their plan's net benefits would outweigh those of the Corps' proposal. The cow-pasture groundbreaking ceremony marked the start of a grand experiment that would show whether the city's "green gold" prospectors had dreamed an impossible dream.

As a dozen local leaders took their places in front of a plot of pre-turned earth and a row of twelve gold-painted shovels, two women stood out in the crowd, much as their passionate efforts had stood out in the long campaign leading to that day. Moira Johnston Block, of course, would have stood out anywhere. Elegant in her white bobbed hair and lime-green silk jacket, she exchanged kisses and congratulations with a radiant smile. The author of eight books, Block had devoted her eloquence to convincing city residents and well-placed county, state, and federal politicians that their *personal* interests, as well as the interests of the larger public, would be served by preserving the river.

On the other side of the field, striding toward the portable podium, Karen Rippey was surrounded by her own gaggle of well-wishers. A former welder and truck driver who wore her hair pulled back in a bun emphasizing her strong Scandinavian jaw, Rippey had been a faithful warrior through four years of political battles that hammered out a consensus on the plan. She had written letters, made telephone calls, collared public officials, and organized nearly fifty community meetings. The lesson she took away from it all, as she later described it, was that "the public can decide its own future—as long as you have a really *loud* public."

At stake from the start in Napa's battle, as every local resident who'd ever dreaded the winter rains knew, were not only environmental ideals but also property, income, and lives. Throughout the world, floods are by far the most common natural disaster. In the United States alone, in an average year they cost dozens of lives and more than $4 billion in insurance claims and emergency relief. These costs have been rising as a result of more people taking out insurance, but also because of some extraordinarily heavy weather. An analysis, by the major reinsurance firm Munich Re, of the worldwide flood toll in 1999 and 2000 counted more than 37,700 deaths and nearly $29 billion in economic losses. That trend is expected to accelerate in the twenty-first century as climate change boosts the power and frequency of storms.

Despite the mounting costs and casualties, there was wide agreement for most of the past hundred years that flood prevention was possible and people could live safely in flood zones if only their levees were high enough. During this time, North America developed one of the world's most extensively engineered hydrological systems, thanks mostly to the U.S. Army Corps of Engineers, with its stalwart faith that Mother Nature could be conquered with technology. (Even Dan Quayle, as a U.S. senator, once remarked that the Corps had "kind of a beaver mentality.") In part, it was an institutional problem: in an agency long blessed with the power to distribute political pork and run by can-do engineers, Corps stalwarts were by nature disinclined to switch to gentler approaches.

Toward the century's end, however, and after repeated levee failures, the Corps' tactics had widely fallen out of favor. One of Rippey's favorite quotes, from *Bay Country*, by Tom Horton, reflected the skepticism. "We grew up hearing so often that a straight line is the shortest distance between two points that we end up thinking it is also the *best* way to get there," Horton wrote. "A river knows better—it has to do with how it dissipates the energy of its flow most efficiently; and how, in its bends, the sediment deposited soon turns into marshes and swampy islands, harboring all manner of interesting life, imparting charm and character to the whole waterway. I would defy you to find a river on this planet that prefers to run straight, unless it has been taught so by the U.S. Army Corps of Engineers."

Horton was writing about Chesapeake Bay, but he could just as easily have been discussing the Napa River, whose untamed stretches are alive with beauty, with striped bass protected by the shade of lush marshes and great blue herons and red-tailed hawks soaring above.

Before the industrial age, the river's usefulness had been as evident as its beauty. Wappo Indians fished on its banks until they were wiped out by smallpox; subsequently, Spanish settlers used the waterway for commerce, shipping hides and tallow to San Francisco. The river trade continued through the nineteenth century, with schooners loaded with goods from nearby vineyards and farms plying Napa's docks.

Throughout this time, the river ecosystem was working in ways less evident to human eyes but no less vital. Before much of the surrounding land was cleared to make way for farms and subdivisions, trees and grasses broke the impact of heavy rains, soaking up the moisture like a sponge and meting it out slowly, minimizing flooding. When the river did spill over, the rushing water was slowed and absorbed by natural wetlands and plains. Silt deposits fertilized the soil, and fish and waterfowl flourished, long accustomed to the coming and going of the floods.

With the passing years, however, the mutually beneficial relations between the river and the people living near it broke down. Napa's population grew to 70,000. Cars, trucks, and trains diminished the waterway's transportation value; factories dumped toxic chemicals into streams, and buildings rose on the riverbanks with windowless back walls facing the water. The river became a muddy, brown enemy to be feared every few years. From 1960 to 2000, floods took a toll of three lives and $542 million in property damage.

But just as a river sometimes insists on going where it pleases, so does a well-motivated city, and in the mid-1990s, the wills of the river and the city coincided. By then, Napa badly needed a shot in the arm. The millions of tourists flocking to the valley's vineyards, mud baths, chic inns, and gourmet restaurants found little to attract them in the city's few hundred Victorian homes, old-fashioned diners, and small shopping mall dominated by a Mervyn's department store. Nor did the evening-news shots every few years of waves coursing over city streets lure outsiders. Robert Mondavi, the local grape baron, compared the downtown to a morgue.

Moira Johnston Block, a Canadian who had moved to Napa after more than thirty years of living in New York and San Francisco, had a strikingly different vision for her adopted home. She imagined it as no longer a city at odds with its river, but a *river city.* She could close her eyes and see shoreline parks and promenades; she envisioned open-air restaurants packed with tourists watching herons fly over a lush marsh that once was a lumberyard.

Johnston had settled in the city in 1990, when she married a local doctor and added *Block* to her name. The couple bought a condominium with a dock on a tidal canal and cruised the river on their pontoon boat. The stretches of wild beauty they enjoyed made it all the more depressing when they passed banks littered with abandoned cars and old factory sites. Johnston Block became convinced that the river needed saving—and that it, in turn, could save the city. In 1993, she took out an advertisement in the local newspaper and invited a few dozen like-minded volunteers to her home. The group founded the Friends of the Napa River.

Karen Rippey attended that first meeting in Johnston Block's living room, as well as nearly all those that followed. A plainspoken Napa native, she still lived on the ranch where she had grown up in a family of six children. Rippey, like Johnston Block, had a powerful vision of better days for the city and its river. She also was fascinated by the challenge confronting the community and determined to stand up to what she saw as the insensitive dictates of the U.S. Army Corps of Engineers. After working for several years in blue-collar jobs, Rippey had returned to school, at the University of California, Berkeley, where she would later receive master's degrees in architecture and regional planning. In her planning thesis, titled "The Environment, the Corps, and the Napa River," she strongly criticized the Corps' flood control projects for having "dramatically changed our relationship to, our feeling of ownership, and our understanding of our local waterways." Even so, Rippey early on recognized the Corps as Napa's only hope, the only government agency around with the funds and the mandate to help the city free itself from floods.

Johnston Block's own river activism had grown from different roots. As a child, she had learned about the Nature ethic of indigenous Pacific Northwest coastal peoples from the several books her mother had written; later, in the 1960s, she practiced urban environmentalism in Greenwich Village and in New York's black ghettoes, where she helped plant community gardens. By 1993, her idea of a fun birthday celebration was to fly with a small band of local activists who'd become known as "river rats," along with several city and county officials who shared their interest, for a working weekend in San Antonio, Texas, a city that had turned itself around with help from its river. In a project dating from 1939, developers had diverted the waterway through town and built a two-and-a-half-mile cobblestone trail along it called the River Walk. The new district, which blossomed with shops and theaters, became a major tourist attraction and won urban planning awards. But Johnston Block, looking it over, was amazed. San Antonio had done these wonders with a mere trickle, whereas Napa had a real river to work with, and a surrounding valley with real charm. Moreover, San Antonio's project lacked the environmental attributes the Napa group was imagining. The Texans had simply steered the water into a cement channel; their project lacked the grace of a quest to restore Nature. The Napans returned home inspired and doubly determined to work with the Corps on a flood project that would be both useful and beautiful. This made for important progress: the Corps, which had long been at odds with Napa residents, had at last found a strong grassroots ally committed to finding a solution.

The Corps began devoting attention to Napa's flood problems in 1939, but it was not until 1965 that the United States Congress authorized it to come up with a flood control plan. The wheels of bureaucracy didn't speed appreciably with the ball in the Corps' court, and eleven more years passed before the agency had a plan ready to offer for voters' approval. During that time, the federal government had grown much more environmentally sensitive, and many officials, including the new president, Jimmy Carter, were pushing the Corps to abandon its dam-happy ways. These concerns were absent from the plan Napa first saw in 1976, however, which, in Johnston Block's words, was "a classic case of river-torture," featuring twelve-foot levees, frequent dredging, and the concrete channel through downtown. Voters roundly opposed paying higher taxes to support it, and when the plan was presented again the next year, they repeated their thumbs-down.

Napa's attitude changed, however, in 1986, after a particularly horrendous flood killed three residents, forced 5,000 people to evacuate, and cost $100 million in property damage. The Napa County Flood Control and Water Conservation District formally pleaded for the Corps to return, and the agency agreed to try harder to make its plan more aesthetically pleasing. This new effort was to take nine more years.

By then, the pressure on the Corps to consider Nature in its plans had grown much more acute. A slew of groundbreaking regulations had been passed, aimed at saving wetlands and endangered species. Environmental protection had been made a formal part of the agency's mandate. And by the 1980s, the Corps had shown some willingness to change. Instead of damming the Charles River around Boston, for instance, it had bought development rights to 8,500 acres of floodplain wetlands, which it then put aside, preventing the building of new homes and businesses. The engineers calculated that letting the floodplain "store" the water would be just as effective as the proposed dam and would cost about one-tenth of the price. But the real turnabout for the Corps came in 1993, when the agency's favored tall levees and deep dredging proved useless against catastrophic floods along the Mississippi River. In subsequent years, the federal government spent hundreds of millions of dollars to buy and demolish thousands of riverbank homes and businesses, restoring the natural floodplain and tacitly conceding that flood fighting was a losing proposition.

Throughout this time, Corps engineers were working on their new Napa plan and periodically seeking input from city leaders, including the Friends of the River. At last, the agency was ready to show off the product of all its work. In early 1995, engineers led Johnston Block, Rippey, and several others on a tour around town, where they had tied ribbons to demonstrate the height and location of flood walls. "They were little yellow ribbons, like crime-scene ribbons, and as we walked up to look at them, we saw the plan was just intolerable," recalled Johnston Block. "It was going to be just as Draconian and sterile and ugly and river-killing as any of the previous plans. They were going to create a concrete barrier between us and the river. It was going to kill our downtown for good." The plan nonetheless had support from county flood control officials. They were concerned that if Napa continued to oppose the Corps, it might alienate the agency once and for all, ending all hope of the city ever getting federal aid for flood control.

Rippey, Johnston Block, and the rest of the Friends shared that worry. But they were more alarmed by their preview, on the waterfront tour, of what the Corps had in mind for their river and their city. Rippey in particular felt betrayed. "We went into it very innocent," she said. "We believed the Corps was listening to us and would change its design. When it didn't, we were shocked. We said, 'We can't let them get away with it.'"

Rippey's marriage to a Napa County supervisor had schooled her in local politics, and she decided that what the Friends needed most at that point were out-of-town allies. She and other members tracked down Ann Riley, a Berkeley-based urban waterways expert who was writing a guide for communities wishing to restore their streams. "The government works for you—you don't work for the government," Riley later recalled telling the group. "If you don't like a plan being handed to your community, you are obligated to speak up and define what that plan should be."

Specifically, Riley suggested that the Friends seek support from state and federal agencies, which would have to sign off on the Corps plan. "Don't limit yourself," she told them. Rippey took the advice and phoned every agency she could think of, including the California Department of Fish and Game, the San Francisco Bay Regional Water Quality Control Board, and the United States Environmental Protection Agency. "Our question was, 'We want to change the plan—what can you do; can you help us?'" she recalled. The agency staff members she reached all promised to oppose any plan that lacked environmental protections.

Riley also counseled the Friends to ask their congressional representatives to back new legislation authorizing a more river-friendly plan. Small as their group was, the river activists might be able to take advantage of the new "green" sensitivities in Washington to sway local officials and the Corps. The group sent letters to every one of its federal and state legislators, receiving in the end only one reply, from U.S. Senator Barbara Boxer. Still, Boxer proved a valuable ally, beginning with the powerful effect of her letter of support. As Johnston Block recalls, the senator's letter "created terror" among the Napa County flood officials, who worried that controversy on Capitol Hill over the plan might cause Napa to lose its precious authorization for any flood protection from the Corps. Only then did local officials agree to work with the community to seek a compromise.

The county assigned a veteran employee, Dave Dickson, as a community liaison. He would eventually earn admiration for his skillful handling of a difficult job, but in the beginning, Rippey worried that he was too sympathetic to the Corps' plan. She lobbied him relentlessly, often calling him at home, as she later recalled. "I felt kind of sorry for him," she said, "but I just couldn't let him get away with it." While Rippey was scrapping away, Johnston Block was playing social emissary, wooing influential officials, including Corps and county bigwigs and various state legislators, with wine-and-cheese and deli-lunch cruises on her pontoon boat. Johnston Block didn't share Rippey's gusto for confrontation; instead, she held faith in the humanizing power of food and drink. She was convinced that a sunny afternoon on the river, with a civilized repast and the persuasive power of river experts on board, could win over the hardest hearts.

The county flood control officials were key targets of this new offensive because they would have to approve and organize payment for any new plan. The Friends wooed them on Johnston Block's pontoon boat but also played some hardball. At one point, in August 1995, for instance, the group scored a tactical victory when its leaders organized a public meeting with the county officials, representatives of the Corps, and staff officers of the agencies Rippey had consulted. The agency personnel roundly trashed the Corps plan. An official of the California State Lands Commission told the audience that flood *control* was an unrealistic and outdated approach. Then an emissary from the California Department of Fish and Game explained in detail how one feature of the Corps' plan would create a kind of bathtub downtown, in which warm, stagnant water might prove dangerously uncomfortable for steelhead trout, which were already dying out in the river. With Boxer in Washington lobbying for a better plan and the agencies exposing the problems with the Corps' approach, the local engineers were being forced to face the new reality: to survive, the flood project had to be made more environmentally sensitive.

The county officials were also owning up to what seemed like the inevitable, agreeing to sponsor a search for a compromise between the Corps and the river defenders. The Napa County Flood Control and Water Conservation District set up and paid for an umbrella group called the Community Coalition for a Napa River Flood Management Plan, which held its first meeting in January 1996. With the Friends, the local chambers of commerce, and the county's economic development corporation as cosponsors, the coalition had two dozen members, including conservationists, local vintners and farmers, businesspeople, Native Americans, mobile home owners, and fishermen. Other regular participants were representatives of the Corps and of the various federal and state resource agencies, a design review committee of architects and engineers, and the mayors of all five of the valley's cities. Establishing the group was a last-ditch effort for the flood control officials, who decided to spend the last $1 million of a budget that had gradually been depleted by statewide tax reforms. They knew they would either go out of business altogether or wind up with a plan they'd be paid to administer, which would extend the life of their agency.

Using the county funds, the coalition hired professional planners and hydrologists and came up with what its leaders touted as the first formal definition of a "living river." It specified optimum levels of water quality, temperature, and sinuosity, a measure of how much the river bends along its route. In doing so, they pressed the point that the river would be of value to the city only if its health and natural beauty were restored and maintained.

The coalition labored for six months in an unwieldy, two-track process; even as Corps officials joined in the work, they continued to refine their own project, just in case the community-based alternative were to prove unworkable. For this lack of faith, Rippey blamed Paul Bowers, the Corps' project manager, who she complained in her thesis was an obstructionist, "a barrier in the process, rigid in his belief of meeting policy objectives." Bowers, not surprisingly, didn't see it that way. He would later look back at those six months as a blossoming of mutual understanding, the birth of a true compromise. "Everything changed when we came to the community and started dealing with people one on one," he said. "People realized we weren't just a bunch of old engineers sitting in Sacramento. We had a lot of young, enthusiastic people working for us, and we were all interested in coming up with the best possible solution."

By that time, Bowers acknowledged, he had a lot invested personally in coming up with some sort of solution. The Corps had been paying for studies for several years; the bill was close to $10 million, and Bowers, who'd been manager for seven years, didn't want to be known as the guy who spent $10 million for a pile of paper. In his memory of those months, he worked hard to see the other coalition members' side. And indeed, the two tracks gradually began to merge, even as Bowers regretfully lost some features of the Corps' original plan, such as the concrete steps, which he called beautiful. "You see them all over Europe," he said.

"That just shows how he *still* just doesn't get it," Rippey later remarked, contending that most Napans regarded the steps as "miserably ugly." But Johnston Block judged Bowers less severely, choosing to describe him as "a metaphor for the massive change being forced on the Corps, an engineer who began with the party line but who transformed to enlightenment through the two-year process."

In any case, the plan that finally emerged had little in common with the Corps' design. Under its auspices, Napa and its immediate surroundings would be the target of a remarkable investment in ecosystem capital. After a century of degradation and loss, the natural assets of the river and its floodplain would be restored, supporting ecosystem services such as flood protection; habitat for fish, birds, and other wildlife; and scenic beauty for outdoor recreation and tourism. All these services held the promise of new sources of income that would at least help justify the required financial investment—a sum that had started out high and was quickly mounting.

As then estimated, the coalition plan would cost $194 million— some $44 million more than the original Corps scheme, mostly because of the anticipated expense of buying land in what was then an extraordinarily hot real estate market. The Corps would also have to move a million cubic yards of dirt in order to widen the river with multilevel terraces that would become marshes and floodplains. A river bypass, a wide swath of open space cut through the heart of downtown, would serve as recreational parkland during dry weather and a conduit for floodwaters in the wet months.

Dozens of homes and businesses would be uprooted, and residents would be paid relocation assistance. Nine bridges would be removed, with five replaced at higher levels. But the good news was that it looked as if Napa residents would pay much less than half of the total bill. Among other donors, Senator Boxer had come to their aid with nearly $9 million in transportation funds to help replace one of the bridges, and the state government would reimburse local taxpayers for several million dollars more, in part because of Dave Dickson's hard lobbying for grants from environmental bodies such as the California Coastal Conservancy.

Years later, government officials would pour praise on Napa's design, calling it innovative, pioneering, a model for the country. "We've had pollution prevention, and now we have restoration," said Bill Leary, associate director for natural resources of the White House's Council on Environmental Quality, at the groundbreaking ceremony. "Restoration is fundamentally about optimism, saying, 'We can do it!' You can create trails for families to stroll, green places for your children to play. . . . You're doing more than inspiring others. You are, by your actions, illuminating the landscape."

Still, Napa's river backers never forgot just how much work it cost them. When it was Karen Rippey's turn to speak at the ceremony, after half a dozen dignitaries from Washington and the state capital, she pointedly read a page of names, determined to acknowledge at least the major players among the dozens of local residents who had helped their plan triumph. And at the ceremony's end, when it came time to pick up the gold-painted shovels and heave some dirt for the cameras, she couldn't help but notice that she was the only one bending to the task. "Come on, you guys!" she growled.

Producing the flood plan, which was ready in June 1996, was a formidable job, yet no more work than the subsequent task of getting all of Napa County to understand it, and to vote to pay for it. The local share would require a half-cent increase in the sales tax, to last for twenty years. It would be the largest tax increase in county history, and voters would have to approve it by a two-thirds majority.

The campaign to convince county residents to part with those funds "became my life," Rippey recalled. "I was going to school, but sometimes I worked on the campaign as much as forty hours a week." As head of the campaign's outreach committee, she assembled a group of local volunteers, who helped arrange scores of community meetings. In a particularly remarkable feat, she made sure that every single Napa County resident received a letter written by someone in the same ten-block area urging support of the flood plan. To pay for these efforts and elaborate propaganda, including large color brochures, a separate fund-raising committee raised $400,000 from vintners and other wealthy local residents.

"The issue of 'What's in it for me?'—that became the hue and cry of our coalition," recalled Johnston Block. "We wanted to identify for everybody in the county, regardless of who they were or whether they ever saw the river, that there was a reason they should vote for this and put money behind it. We had to identify often intangible benefits, and give them value for every voter. We realized that enlightened self-interest is a very healthy thing. It's all very well to expect people to rise to a righteous cause, but they don't always do that. So we weren't just selling the glory of the living river. It was, 'This will keep my business from closing, my job intact, my child's school open; my winery won't lose tourism; and they won't see us looking bad on the evening news.'"

In its brochures, the coalition laid out the financial benefits for Napa and the neighboring small city of St. Helena and town of Yountville, which were slated for flood plans of their own after a few years. County residents, the coalition said, would get a seven-to-one return on their sales tax contributions, which amounted to just $3.9 million per year. Some $22 million would be saved annually by eliminating flood damage to property, with an additional $4 million of estimated benefits from reduced costs of flood insurance, cleanup, and emergency aid as well as from "environmental improvements." The brochure's authors calculated those environmental benefits by judging how much it might have cost to establish habitat somewhere else similar to the new wetlands created by the flood plan, and included some $300,000 per year as the value of new river trails for hikers and bird-watchers. The additional promise of an increase in property values, accruing not only from flood protection but also from the charm of river views, wasn't specified in the brochures, but it was on many Napa residents' minds as they went to the polls.

On March 3, 1998, during a spate of El Niño–fueled storms, the

Napa River Restoration Project, Measure A on the county ballot, squeaked by with 68 percent support. "The naysayers pooh-poohed the idea that a community our size could afford such an extravagant project," said Dickson. "No one ever thought we'd get a two-thirds majority on this one. But we powered through the doubt."

Paul Bowers, the Corps' project manager, got in his car early on the evening of the vote and drove to Napa from Sacramento, about an hour-long journey. Pulling into downtown, he turned on his radio and heard that the measure had passed. Soon afterward, he spotted a group of the Friends, including Johnston Block and Rippey, headed toward a pub. Bowers got a hug from Johnston Block, and they all walked off to share a celebratory drink.

The approved plan made national news, and Corps officials embraced it with fanfare. "What we will be doing in Napa is radically different from anything we have ever done before," Corps spokesman Jason Fanselau told reporters. "It's going to totally change the way we do business."

To be sure, some of the enthusiasm waned with time. Costs continued to rise, along with skyrocketing land prices. Within a year after the groundbreaking ceremony, the estimated project price tag was running at more than $238 million and counting. "There are a lot of unscrupulous condemnation attorneys out there," said Dave Dickson in an interview in the summer of 2001. The overruns hadn't caused a problem until then, he said, because the county had greatly underestimated sales tax revenues, which were making up for them. But, he conceded, he was losing sleep over whether the costs would keep mounting, forcing planners to extend the duration of the sales tax or even stall work on the project.

Added to this was the pain of all the individual sacrifice by the more than 300 people who'd have to move their homes or businesses. Some residents were upset that historic structures, such as a stone bridge downtown built in 1862 and the Roughrider Building, a clothing plant built in the 1930s, would have to be demolished. Families were also displaced, including one whose members had just obtained a low-interest loan to raise their home six feet to protect it from floods. At the time, the proud owners had flown a banner depicting Noah's ark. But they had to sell their property and move elsewhere; the house would be destroyed.

The pastureland site of the groundbreaking ceremony was another property claimed by the flood project, and destined to be turned into a marsh. It was owned by the Ghisletta family, who had been farming in the Napa Valley for nearly a century, and they weren't giving it up cheerfully. "It was either that or have them take it with eminent domain," said Joe Ghisletta III, adjusting the visor of his cap over his deeply tanned face. "Perhaps it's for the best, but maybe not. We've talked to flood experts who've told us it's risky. We'll just have to hope it works."

Jeffrey Mount, a prominent flood control expert who is chair of the Department of Geology at the University of California, Davis, said he shared some of Ghisletta's concern. Napa planners, he warned, hadn't been sufficiently cautious with their flood protection design, a fault he predicted would catch up with them in time. The trouble was that they sought the standard 100-year flood protection, a calculation based on a flood with a 1-in-100 chance of occurring. Mount pointed out that in the years since that statistic was calculated, it had been outdated by the reality of climate change. "It's just a whole new climate now from that of the 1950s," he said. "In fifty years, there's going to be some finger-pointing." On the other hand, underestimating the effects of climate change isn't a flaw unique to Napa—most flood plans around the world are operating under old assumptions. And Mount stressed that in every other sense, he believed Napa was making the right choices. "It's far better than in most of the rest of the world," he said, "with cities crowded on top of floodplains with barely adequate engineering solutions, doing just enough to keep the water out of their living rooms for a while."

Mount is, in fact, a leading champion of flood promotion over flood prevention. "*Never* buy into a development called Riverbend

Estates," he says. Although he acknowledges that Napa's plan is costly, he says it's still a clear win-win for the city and the federal government, largely because of values derived from Nature but not reflected on the balance sheets. Leading that list is the project's sustainability. "There are two kinds of levees—those that have failed and those that will fail," Mount says. "It's just too expensive to design a bullet-proof levee, and even if you could, it would put pressure on the river somewhere else down the line. The weirdness of the Corps' projects is they give 70–90 percent of the funding and then move away. My argument is that they'd have to come back when the project failed. Another problem is the levees are growth-inducing. They give the illusion of safety, so more people move to the floodplain, and when the levees fail, the damages are extraordinary."

Mount went on to enumerate the other values of Napa's "softer" approach: the creation and protection of habitat, made more financially valuable in recent years by laws protecting endangered species, along with the improvement of water quality by the filtering action of wetlands, as seen in New York's watershed effort. "We're constantly surprised as we look at the ecosystem services enhanced by these kinds of strategies," Mount said. "There's some evidence they even help improve air quality."

Not that Napa residents lacked evidence of their plan's gifts in its first year. In the months that followed the July 2000 groundbreaking, the economic benefits surpassed even Moira Johnston Block's expectations. With a measure of flood safety finally guaranteed, commercial real estate prices rose by nearly 20 percent. By early 2001, flood insurance rates for the city had been reduced by 20 percent. Major businesses were vying to relocate downtown to take advantage of the promised new waterfront. The Napa Valley Opera House was undergoing elaborate remodeling; several new hotels were being planned; and, in the grandest show of faith in the city's new safety, an enormous new museum and education center was being built on the oxbow bend of the river near downtown. The $70 million Copia: The American Center for Wine, Food & the Arts, a fitting monument to the valley's hedonistic style, was sponsored by Robert Mondavi, who'd bought the land in 1996 and gambled on approval of Measure A. It would occupy twelve acres and have organic vegetable gardens, a 500-seat outdoor amphitheater, and parking lots lined with grapevines. It was scheduled to open in the fall of 2001, with plans to draw as many as 300,000 visitors per year.

Napa's experiment was getting such positive press throughout the world that county officials and the Friends' office were being deluged by visitors, including delegations from China, Argentina, and Australia, all interested in finding out how communities could save their rivers while saving themselves from floods. Within the United States, too, several other cities were trying Napa's ground-up approach to flood management. King County, Washington, for instance, now bans development on floodplains its engineers have determined are hazardous.

Federal funding remained indispensable for flood protection projects, "green" or not, because they're normally so expensive. Yet there were promising signs of new sources of support for cities eager to adopt "living river" projects of their own. The Nature Conservancy was beginning to work with the Corps, providing funds to buy land in flood-prone areas of California and Nevada in a people-friendly approach to conservation. And, as mentioned earlier, insurance firms were studying the possibility of lowering flood insurance premiums in communities that avoided outright confrontations with Mother Nature.

As flood promotion became ever more popular, two of the Napa River's staunchest defenders went on to make their careers in that field. David Dickson, the county liaison, became a full-time consultant for Napa copycats, helping communities in Reno, Nevada, and Monterey, California, devise similar grassroots flood plans. And Karen Rippey, who'd been so adamant in fighting Corps engineers, turned around and got hired by them, her long experience with the agency proving an advantage. For her part, she said she realized the Corps was turning more environmentally sensitive, and besides, it was the only game in town if what interested you was moving tons of dirt to restore Nature. Her new colleagues joked that they didn't know who had changed more—Rippey or the Corps. "She's still very strong environmentally, but I guess we've both moved a little more to the middle," said one engineer.

Rippey's new job forced her to resign from the Friends of the River to avoid a conflict of interest, a development Johnston Block watched with remorse. Rippey's combative energy was missed. The group was just then expanding to work elsewhere in the watershed while remaining vigilant to protect Napa's riverfront from overdevelopment; the promise of flood protection had lured developers eager to fill the riverfront with big hotels. Even so, Johnston Block said, one of the great successes of the river project was that developers routinely called the Friends before even applying for a permit, knowing how important it was to educate themselves about the guidelines stemming from the city's vision for the "living river," with its balance of commerce and open space. "They're learning that the real gold lies in sustainable revitalization around the river, not in quick hits," she said.

With that said, following several years of strong federal support for "living river" strategies, there were some signs in the summer of 2001 that the Corps was starting to retreat. In southern Missouri, the agency was going ahead with a controversial $60 million levee project that would close off one of the last remaining natural floodways on the lower Mississippi River. Meanwhile, the administration of President George W. Bush was planning to cut by 25 percent the federal share of the congressionally mandated program that buys property in prone areas and converts it to open space.

Nonetheless, Rippey and many of her Corps coworkers found it easy to agree that Napa's success pointed the way to what might be accomplished elsewhere in the world. Even considering Napa's budget problems, as well as the worries that its level of protection wasn't up to the realities of climate change, the immediate results were striking enough to encourage others on the path to a new economy of Nature. In Napa's crowded planning meetings, as in the Katoomba Group's more abstract discussions, the goal was the same: to turn from trying to conquer Nature to coexisting with it, while realizing the concrete benefits of peace.

Vancouver Island: Project Snark

"We have sailed many months, we have sailed many weeks,

(Four weeks to the month you may mark),

But never as yet ('tis your Captain who speaks)

Have we caught the least glimpse of a Snark!"

—Lewis Carroll

JUST AFTER 8:00 A.M. on October 5, 2000, Linda Coady sat watching Adam Davis stand up to address the first reunion of the Katoomba Group. A blunt-spoken, blue-eyed woman with short red hair, she was new to the group and struggling to ignore the frustration she'd been feeling since the conference began the day before. Coady, who held the unusual title of vice president, environmental enterprise, had convinced her firm, the timber giant Weyerhaeuser Company, to cosponsor two days of workshops at Tigh-Na-Mara Resort Hotel and Conference Centre, a cluster of log cabins on Vancouver Island in British Columbia. To put it frankly, she wanted something in return—something more than shrimp hors d'oeuvres and high-flying yuppie policy-wonk talk. Coady needed her colleagues' help.

She was actually just the sort of person the group had been formed *to* help—a lonely advocate for environmentally sustainable forestry in a company that still got most of its revenues from clear-cutting. With $12 billion in annual sales, Weyerhaeuser, based in Tacoma, Washington, was one of the world's top three timber companies; as such, it was under a harsh spotlight from environmentalists. But now its managers were trying to prove they had a conscience—especially when it came to their controversial dealings in the old-growth forests of Clayoquot Sound, on the western coast of Vancouver Island, a couple hundred miles from Tigh-Na-Mara.

Weyerhaeuser had strong reason to embrace "green" ideals on Clayoquot Sound, whose ancient fir, hemlock, and cedar forests had been declared a biosphere reserve by the United Nations Educational, Scientific and Cultural Organization (UNESCO). Environmentalists the world over, including some 3,000 indigenous residents of Clayoquot Sound, members of the Assembly of First Nations, treasured the area as one of the most stunningly beautiful places on Earth—and also one of the most threatened. Much of British Columbia's coastal temperate forests had already been clear-cut, leaving behind naked mountains and clogged rivers. So when the provincial government announced plans to open two-thirds of the sound to logging in 1993, it prompted the largest protest demonstration in Canadian history, in which 800 people were arrested.

MacMillan Bloedel (MB)—British Columbia's largest forest firm before it was purchased by Weyerhaueser in 1999—was the protesters' main target. Its directors were eventually forced to shut down local operations and lay off about 150 workers. The enormous backlash on Clayoquot Sound made it clear to MB that the social and political cost of treating Nature as a limitless commodity had grown too high. The company moved forward with a dramatically new approach, one that looked at forest ecosystems as long-term capital assets. Over the next few years, MB began actually to internalize the externalities—the costs its activities imposed on society—associated with the way the company had been logging. It began restructuring its operations in order to become more environmentally sustainable and, in the process, win certification to sell timber under an "eco-friendly" label. Among other reforms, it started to phase out clear-cutting, conserve old-growth forests, log selectively so as to maintain other forest habitats and streams, and invite scientists to assess its operations.

This approach, developed by a team that included Linda Coady, became known as the Forest Project. Among themselves, though, team members referred to the plan as Project Snark, expressing their worry that all their work might well lead nowhere. The name came from the Lewis Carroll poem "The Hunting of the Snark," about a seafaring expedition whose goal was to hunt for a creature that no crew member had ever seen or even heard described. The great danger, which the crew learned only well after embarking, was that snarks sometimes were also "boojums," in which case anyone who saw one would "softly and suddenly vanish away, and never be met with again."

The same brave spirit that produced the Forest Project was the guiding force behind a remarkable joint venture, announced in 1997, between MB and First Nations. Its goal was to resume logging, in a scrupulously "green" fashion, on Clayoquot Sound. This plan, which Weyerhaeuser inherited along with the Forest Project, was called Iisaak Forest Resources—*iisaak* meaning "respect" in the language of the island's indigenous Nuu-chah-nulth Tribe—and Linda Coady, who was also inherited from MB, was partly in charge. Iisaak took the Forest Project one step further, seeking to develop nontimber revenue sources, including tourism, forest products, and environmental services such as carbon sequestration and biodiversity preservation, to help compensate for the lost revenue and extra expense involved in the switch to more sustainable timber harvest practices. That expense would turn out to be enormous.

Logging had resumed on Clayoquot Sound just a few months before the Katoomba Group meeting. The only approach on which First Nations, Weyerhaueser, and several environmental groups had

been able to agree was an agonizingly delicate one. To avoid building new roads into the old-growth areas, Iisaak had turned to
extracting one tree at a time by helicopter, with 250-foot grapples.
As a result, the timber harvest had dropped to a tiny fraction of what
MB had collected before 1993, and costs had skyrocketed. Iisaak was
paying U.S.$95 per cubic meter to produce logs to sell for approxi-
mately U.S.$77. The sale price would certainly increase if Iisaak man-
aged to get certification from the Forest Stewardship Council, allowing the company to market timber under a "green" label. Yet Coady
suspected the price would not rise high enough for any profits to be
made. Consumers simply weren't paying enough of a premium for
certified wood—not yet, at least. And she had yet to find anyone
interested in paying for the services of carbon sequestration or biodiversity preservation. Nor did she have much longer to try. If Iisaak
failed to develop any successful nontimber products, its low-impact
harvesting scheme would last a year or two at best, she feared, before
Weyerhaeuser pulled the plug on its experiment in eco-friendly
business.

A lot was hanging on the outcome. If Weyerhaeuser couldn't
make a successful go at sustainable timber management in temperate
woodlands in a wealthy country such as Canada, what did that bode
for the world's forests? Endangered tropical forests face much more
daunting prospects, given that most are in countries far less stable,
with less trustworthy land titles and more threats from illegal activities such as invasions by squatters.

In that broad context, Coady knew her plan had a lot going for
it. She had come to Vancouver Island with a Nuu-chah-nulth chief
named Larry Baird, with a beautiful twenty-five-page business plan
full of graphs and charts, and with endorsements from Greenpeace,
the Sierra Club, and the Natural Resources Defense Council. But
what she painfully lacked was a working model of a similar program,
anyone to give her concrete advice based on experience, or any
assurance at all that at the end of the day, her project would be able
to make money.

Around the conference table were many faces from Katoomba as well as some new ones, including the director of a research center at the Chinese Academy of Social Sciences, a Swedish representative of the trendy furniture shop IKEA, and a contingent of Brazilian economists and entrepreneurs. The gourmet jelly beans were back, together with another luxury: windows looking out on a road lined with maple trees turning red and gold. To Coady, whose mind was wandering, everyone else seemed intently focused as they listened to Adam Davis get to the gist of his short speech. "Imagine you've all just inherited a piece of land in Australia," he was saying, "and now you have to decide what to do with it for the next twenty years."

Coady rested her chin in her hand. Having been closely involved in the conference preparations, she knew what was coming next, and she wasn't keenly interested. Six months after the group's first meeting, Davis' dream of a Conservation Exchange, in which ecosystem services would be traded in a new market, had morphed into a complicated role-playing exercise. By agreement with Michael Jenkins, director of Forest Trends and founder of the Katoomba Group, he'd been working on it during the few hours each day he could spare from running his company and spending time with his wife and two young daughters. He'd had help from a few other members of the group, including David Brand, but they had never had enough time, and even as the meeting opened they were huddling around their laptop computers, still trying to work out the rules.

The idea of the role-playing exercise was to demonstrate how the conservation incentives the group was discussing might play out in real life. It was a tactic used widely by management experts to educate groups about unforeseen consequences of their decisions. The aim at Tigh-Na-Mara was to see, first of all, whether carbon and biodiversity credits and the like would make any difference to people's decision making and thus to environmental quality. If so, the next question was whether blind pursuit of profit by the players would lead the world into unintended disasters, with some crucial assets of Nature being liquidated in favor of preserving others, or into greater well-being, as hoped. What sorts of rules were needed to achieve socially beneficial outcomes? Davis' game was meant to find out, in a laboratory test of the grand visions of a new economy properly valuing Nature.

The participants would imagine themselves as farmers trying to figure out how to reap profits from land in Australia's breadbasket, the Murray-Darling river basin; at the previous conference they had learned about these farmers' troubles with salinity. They were divided into five landholder teams, and each team was awarded 12,000 acres divided into three zones: irrigated, dry, and pasture. The teams received detailed information on revenues per acre and what investment would be necessary to convert land from one use to another. The game was to be played in four rounds, each requiring the farmers to make five-year commitments. With each new round, Davis and the other game-masters would roll dice to decide on changes in global commodity prices, reflecting fluctuations in the markets.

The economists, entrepreneurs, and think-tank members on each team squinted at their handouts, trying to agree on what to do. Most ended up keeping their zones as they were in the first round while they waited for more information. That came in the early afternoon, when the game-masters brought in a large cardboard box filled with dime-store hats. The hats heralded the creation of three teams of buyers of forest services, including big utility firms (in black hats) interested in carbon credits, local governments (red hats) in search of water purification rights, and wildlife conservationists (white hats, naturally) looking for biodiversity credits.

The farmers' groups spread themselves out, taking over tables in the resort's rustic dining hall and haggling over their new choices. Should they continue raising sheep or plant forests? And if they planted forests, would it be more profitable to grow a single species of tree in a plantation or diverse native species, which might reap biodiversity credits? Meanwhile, the new buyer groups circulated to try to make deals. Jenkins passed Coady in a hallway and warned,

"Don't get caught between the conservationists and the corporate guys; you'll get polarized!"

"It's the story of my life," she retorted.

Any comic relief was welcome. The tone of the conference was generally much more sober than that in Katoomba, when everyone was still excited by the novelty of the ideas. Coady wasn't alone in her frustration with the emphasis on theory, the feeling that progress was more virtual than real. "What's it going to take for us to learn how significant such incentive schemes really are for conservation, to ramp this up?" Nels Johnson, a World Resources Institute analyst, asked the group at one point.

Events taking place far from the cozy conference room increased the sense of urgency. In the United States, presidential elections were just one month away; earlier that week, several in the group had watched George W. Bush unexpectedly hold his own in his first televised debate with Al Gore. Were Bush to win, it could be terrible news for the environment in general and the Kyoto Protocol in particular, given that he adamantly opposed the draft treaty.

Even worse was the feeling that no real progress had been made since the Katoomba conference. In fact, there had been a reversal: the Sydney Futures Exchange had abandoned its long-advertised plan to launch the world's first carbon exchange. Stuart Beil, the nervy young Australian broker who had announced the details six months earlier with such bravado, had quit his job after a falling-out with the new director. Still, he hadn't lost faith in the carbon market. He had since formed his own firm, the Universal Carbon Exchange, to trade carbon credits, and in conversations at the Canadian reunion he strove to keep up his bluster. He called the retreat by the Sydney Futures Exchange a "speed bump," saying that the more important issue was what would happen in The Hague, The Netherlands, where the parties to the Kyoto Protocol were to convene that November to nail down rules for reducing carbon dioxide emissions. In a move that brought hope to the heart of every Katoomba Group member, the administration of President Bill Clinton was to attend the meeting and had plans to lobby hard for a scheme of credits for forestry and soil "sinks" that would sequester carbon. These flexibility measures, allowing businesses to offset their fossil fuel emissions, were designed to soften the effect of any future carbon caps. If the tactics won support from other countries, leading to clear rules for designating and managing carbon sinks, Beil said, billions of dollars could be unlocked for new forests.

It was clear by then that the Katoomba Group had already become a kind of lifeline for Beil and many of his colleagues. Having left their studies and fieldwork to meet first in Australia, then in Canada, they reveled in the shared belief that their convictions were more than fantasies, that, indeed, their work might eventually make them part of history. "You'll know you're in the New Forest Economy when you see forest companies and Aboriginals joining together as Biodiversity.com," Coady boldly told the group at one point.

To be sure, there were reasons to take heart. The first day of the reunion—a public meeting in Vancouver, before the core group retreated to its workshops on Vancouver Island—featured a stirring speech by David Berge, head of the Social Investment Forum in Washington, D.C., who told them of the huge demand he saw in the United States for "green" investments. As of 1999, Berge said, U.S. citizens had invested some $2.16 trillion in "socially responsible" funds. Investments in these funds had increased by a phenomenal 82 percent since 1997 and were growing much faster than investments in any other kind of fund. Nor were all these riches flowing from sheer benevolence: the socially responsible funds were racking up a performance record generally twice as good as their counterparts.

Socially responsible investing had taken off in the 1970s as part of grassroots campaigns to boycott firms in South Africa as well as the nuclear weapons and tobacco industries. The way it usually worked was that investors had their portfolios "screened" to eliminate support for objectionable policies. Berge told the group that nearly 80 percent of the $2.16 trillion invested had been screened to rule out companies perceived, on the basis of lawsuits or government sanctions, as harmful to the environment. Even better news, however, was that investors were starting to take the next step, demanding that fund managers seek out firms that were actually doing something good for the environment. "I really don't know of any active investor who wouldn't be interested in the work you're doing here," Berge told the group.

Linda Coady joined in the loud applause that followed Berge's speech. At last, the discussion had turned to concrete, practical ideas that were proving their promise in the world. Maybe it didn't matter quite so much that neither government nor industry was coming forth in a significant way to finance change. Maybe there really was a Third Way.

Over the three days of the conference, other speakers pressed home the point that demand for environmental services was in fact greater than the group might realize—that there were actually several groups of potential buyers for the products they hoped to provide. These included not only socially responsible investment firms but also government agencies and, increasingly, wealthy conservation philanthropies seeking new ways to preserve water quality and reduce threats from environmental disaster. All could be powerful players in helping transform the economy to incorporate the value of ecosystem assets.

The presenters, mostly biologists and economists, spoke in particulars, using handout charts and PowerPoint slide presentations generated from their laptop computers. One analyzed a group of World Bank projects testing market instruments for forest conservation; another explained the workings of an experimental ecological value-added tax in Brazil. Then Ron Sims, the political chief of King County, Washington, which encompasses Seattle and its surroundings, got up to speak, without notes.

The title of his speech was "Innovative Policies and Incentives for Biodiversity Conservation." Yet after just a few words about his county's growth management tactics, the tall, beefy politician abruptly launched into a series of stories about his late father, who had been a preacher in Spokane. "He took me down to the beach one day," Sims told them, "and he said, 'Bud, you know what? There are three kinds of waves. There's the kind of wave that makes no impression on the shore. And there's the wave that just gently caresses the shore. Then there's the kind of wave that rearranges the shore. Which kind of wave do you want to be?'"

Between these reminiscences, Sims conveyed a few points about King County's projects to buy development rights on forestland, recycle treated sewage as fertilizer, and organize volunteers to plant tens of thousands of trees. But then he abruptly switched gears again to tell about his girlfriend in high school. He spoke of her in an intimate, confiding tone, and as if he had all the time in the world. "Your first love is stupid. It's *sssucculent,*" he said. He detailed the courtship: the Smokey Robinson tapes; the pound cake she baked for him, forgetting to add sugar ("You're all the sugar I need," he'd said). A few scientists shifted in their chairs. Sims just kept going, well over his time limit. He told of how she'd gone on to be a teacher, until she'd gotten sick. He told about crying at her bedside and how she'd said to him, "Silly man, my time is over, but you have the rest of your life to make a difference."

He looked out at his audience, now hushed and rapt, and paused portentously to nod toward the windows and the forests outside them. "One more day. We have this precious gift," he said. "I hope you find the commitment to save this place. Save this place. You have one more day to rearrange the shore."

The scientists and executives gave Sims a standing ovation and mobbed him on his way out, handing him business cards. He'd spoken to their hearts, to their best intentions, the reason most of them had come to the meeting in the first place. With the drive of a coach leading his team to the field, he'd reminded them that there were limits to analysis; it was now time to act.

In fact, at least one Katoomba Group member had already left the locker room. Even as Sims was giving his talk, David Brand was pacing in the hallway, spreading the word about something called the New Forests Fund. As he revealed the details, the project seemed almost like something invented as part of Adam Davis' trading game, but this was real life, with potential fortunes involved.

A few months earlier, Brand had been hired away from his job at State Forests of New South Wales, Australia, by the Hancock Natural Resource Group. The Boston-based group, a division of the behemoth John Hancock Financial Services, was the world's leading manager of forest investments for institutional investors. With its multibillion-dollar resources, it gave Brand the opportunity to test a scheme he'd been developing for some time. He soon convinced John Hancock executives to launch an unprecedented fund based on two types of income from newly planted forests in Australia and the United States. Investors would receive shares based on future harvests of sustainably managed timber, with carbon credits paid as a dividend. The value of the credits was uncertain but probably not zero: it would depend on what transpired in the development of a global agreement on climate change and an associated carbon market. Calling on his earlier experiments in Australia, Brand hoped eventually also to sell the forest's biodiversity rights to large conservation organizations. The promise of that extra income could provide an incentive to plant diverse native forests rather than plantations of a single species of tree, chosen solely on the basis of its carbon-storage capacity.

"I know this can work because I've done the market research," he told his colleagues on Vancouver Island. "I've interviewed more than fifty companies. There's a lot more interest than you'd think." His mind was already racing ahead to imagine the forests he'd sow, replacing failed soybean crops along the Mississippi River with native oak and hickory trees, regenerating aspen forests in the Great Lakes area, and replanting native hardwoods in fields of sugarcane in Hawaii.

Brand's goals for the week after the conference were particularly heady for a guy who used to work on logging trucks. Three days after leaving Vancouver Island, he would fly to Boston to present his business plan to John Hancock's board (which would approve it unanimously). The next day, he'd meet with environmental entrepreneur Richard Sandor, who was flying in from Chicago to discuss a possible partnership. On the next, he'd see representatives from The Nature Conservancy and other large environmental organizations to sound them out on buying biodiversity credits. And one month later, Brand would launch the New Forests Fund at a glitzy cocktail reception during climate treaty negotiations in The Hague.

Brand and John Hancock were taking a calculated risk in the hope that jumping so early into the carbon market would pay off. It was a huge risk, all the same. No one could predict what would happen in The Netherlands, even though at that point it seemed likely that the strong U.S. support for carbon sinks would prevail. After all, the other political leaders negotiating the terms of the treaty realized it might well prove ineffective without U.S. participation and therefore, it seemed, would make extra concessions to keep the U.S. government on board. "I feel pretty bullish," Brand said. In the worst-case scenario, were Bush to be elected and the protocol declared dead, Brand said, he could still market the New Forests Fund in Australia, where power firms were already under government orders to cap their greenhouse gas emissions. But Brand had faith that it was only a matter of time—regardless of who ended up in the White House—before the U.S. government would have to develop similar regulations. Eventually, he figured, a weather calamity, or a series of them, due to global warming would force the United States out of its complacence.

As word of Brand's plan circulated at Tigh-Na-Mara, the group's mood was lifted. Unlaunched and untested, the New Forests Fund already seemed, to them, a success, if only in the sense that a major corporation such as John Hancock was taking it seriously. The presentations and role-playing exercises wore on, but the scientists and investors poured new energy into their conversations during the breaks, talking excitedly, in the dining hall and along the paths to the log cabins, about such issues as the fair market value of water purification. They also embraced their roles in Adam Davis' game. The "conservationists" argued among themselves and got little accomplished. One farmers' association announced a decision to become buyers of carbon. Others declared mergers.

In the end, the team that won had converted 80 percent of its high-yielding irrigated cropland to forest while strategically selling ecosystem services. This seemed a wonderful vindication. Yet there was also a distressing surprise: each of the five teams clear-cut its forest and cashed in during the final round. It was completely logical behavior under the rules, showing how the best of intentions can easily go awry. But it ended the game on a jarring note for many in the group, with the emphatic exception of Adam Davis.

Upbeat as ever, Davis pronounced himself "incredibly gratified" by the results of the game. "The specific question we had was whether cash from these new sources could influence demand, and it clearly has," he contended. "This took the game from an academic vision to the world of self-interest." The players had obviously learned a lot, he said, even though it was clear that the game-masters would have to get back to the drawing board before the next round. The problems with the first-draft rules were numerous and, in some cases, reflective of the real world, with high uncertainty over how to plan sales of ecosystem services, poor access to information about markets for them, and high transaction costs between potential sellers and buyers. Still, Davis maintained, "I could see people walking away with the feeling that they got it, that they understood how to shift the role of forests from suppliers of commodities—that's the dinosaur view—to suppliers of services." He said he felt energized, as he had after the Katoomba conference, and more convinced than ever that his Conservation Exchange would someday become a global trading force. In fact, he'd already bought the Internet domain name.

In the meantime, Davis was getting more interested in marketing the trading exercise as an educational computer game. He counted 8 million potential buyers just by calculating the members of major environmental groups, adding there might be "a bazillion versions" adapted for players in different regions of the world. "It's like Beanie Babies!" Davis exulted, anxious to get cracking. The idea was so good, he couldn't imagine that someone else wouldn't also try to market it.

Linda Coady was much less positive about what had been accomplished on Vancouver Island. She would leave feeling just as torn as when she'd arrived, too enmeshed in the gritty realities of trying to squeeze profits from sustainable forestry to get excited about new ways to educate consumers. Back when she'd worked for MacMillan Bloedel, she'd been personally involved in Clayoquot Sound's "eco-wars," even to the point of having been burned in effigy—an event broadcast on the television news—by irate loggers and their families in one hard-hit town where she was blamed for caving in to environmentalists. Although she certainly cared about the ancient timberlands, she also understood the bitterness of all the families whose breadwinners had been left unemployed since the logging had stopped. It was as clear to her as to anyone that Iisaak Forest Resources and the Forest Project had been born as a corporate escape route to defuse unbearable tensions. Yet she insisted she wouldn't be satisfied with a simple propaganda scheme that wouldn't last and an operation that wouldn't generate real income. Coady had long ago stopped thinking in terms of Project Snark. She could *picture* the notion of a market for ecosystem services as a road to the future, an international model, and as a particularly dramatic change in orientation for Canadians used to thinking of forests as either timber or parks. Whether the hopeful vision she had for Iisaak would materialize in time to save it, however, was another question altogether. Iisaak, she told her colleagues, "is a child of the mother of environmental conflicts in Canada, but no one knows if that child will ever get to be a teenager."

The four dozen Katoomba Group members rode the ferry back to the city of Vancouver, planning to catch planes that night and the next morning to their homes in China, Brazil, Australia, Sweden, the

United States, and elsewhere. They'd resolved to meet again in Brazil the following March.

About a month later, just a few days before the opening at The Hague of the sixth conference of the parties to the United Nations Framework Convention on Climate Change (called COP 6), David Brand sent out an e-mail message lacking any vestige of his habitual Canadian reserve. "Living in this global carbon market over the last couple of weeks is a really weird feeling," he wrote. "There's this sort of pre-COP 6 frenzy building. It's like a friend of mine who used to work in the stock market [once told me]. He said the old-timers in the pits could just sense when something was going to happen. . . . I have so many deals, partnerships, joint venture opportunities, web e-trading ventures thrown at me. Everybody wants to do a deal and our reception at the Hague is looking to blow out the venue size, plus we have all these lawyers and tax accountants working and rumors of competing funds being cooked up! I got up this morning and there were like 40 e-mails in overnight. What did those cowboys say—'Let's light this candle!'?"

As it turned out, however, the excitement before the COP 6 meeting only made the disappointment that followed more cruel. European nations roundly rejected the Clinton administration's plan to soften the effect of the greenhouse gas reductions with flexibility tools such as carbon trading and sinks. There were a few more-than-impolite suggestions that carbon credits and sinks were a scam. "We have strong interest groups in German society," said Jürgen Tritten, the German environment minister, in one of the more scathing comments. "What shall I tell them if the United States makes a fire road in a forest and flies airplanes over it and says that is an emissions project? They'd say you're ridiculous." The meeting broke apart without a deal.

A few weeks after the COP 6 deadlock, Brand sent around another memo, this time substantially more sober, though still optimistic. He blamed the failure on "human frailty and the lack of a strong central negotiating capability out of Europe" but said he still hoped COP 6 could resume and reach agreement by June—a scenario he thought likely if Al Gore became the next U.S. president. "At the end of the day, we still have the best product available with the best environmental and social credentials," he concluded, "and while it may be a bit harder to sell than if COP 6 had succeeded in The Hague, I am sure enough companies and investors will judge that the writing is on the wall."

One month later, following the most closely contested election in U.S. history and weeks of suspense over ballot recounts in Florida, George W. Bush was granted the presidency by means of a controversial ruling of the United States Supreme Court. Bush's future national security adviser, Condoleezza Rice, had already publicly warned that his presidency would oppose the "multilateral approach" of the Kyoto Protocol. The Katoomba Group's heady dream that the climate negotiations would lead to multibillion-dollar markets for Nature's services had never seemed more like a Snark.

C h a p t e r   S i x

King County, Washington: The Art of the Deal

"Without wilderness, the world is a cage."
—*David Brower*

Ron Sims ambles into the bar of the TPC Snoqualmie Ridge golf course, his big, handsome face stretching into a grin. The political chief of King County, Washington, population 1.7 million, he's got the Clintonesque charm of a pol who loves his job, and who expects to be loved back. He's not disappointed this evening.

R. "Fuzzy" Fletcher, Snoqualmie's mayor, has been watching the door. Sims is nearly an hour late, having left his Seattle headquarters behind schedule for the thirty-mile drive east, and Fletcher is halfway through the dinner they'd planned to share. But he shows no signs of annoyance, rising from his chair as Sims stoops toward him for a backslapping bear hug, drawling: "Hey, Mayor! Peace and prosperity to you!"

Fletcher and Sims are a study in contrasts: the mayor (a machinist by day) with his ponytail, four-inch beard, and wrist tattooed with the Harley-Davidson insignia; the county executive with his smooth shave, blue suit, and silk tie. Yet while Fletcher's attire says rebel, his attitude plainly shows his awe of Sims' powerful position, which makes him a kind of super-mayor, responsible for countywide services such as mass transit and wastewater treatment and land use in the unincorporated areas. In his congenial way, Sims, too, is clearly conscious of his power, looking pleased but not surprised as Fletcher says how proud he is to have him there.

Both men have reason for cheer this late-spring evening, some seven months after Sims got his standing ovation at the Katoomba Group meeting in Vancouver. Sims has come to Snoqualmie to clinch a landmark pact that promises to boost the two politicians' careers as much as it helps the local environment. Its chief accomplishment will be the preservation of nearly 150 acres of forested landscape above the 270-foot Snoqualmie Falls, a major tourist attraction as well as a sacred site for local Native Americans. The area, Washington State's most visited place after Mount Rainier, had been about to be developed by Puget Western, which owned the land and planned to build homes and shops on it. "You would have looked above the falls and seen Chuck E. Cheese," bemoaned one local environmentalist. Instead, the falls' pristine backdrop was rescued by a complicated compromise.

The deal that saved the forest was worked out over three anxious months through elaborate negotiations Sims helped orchestrate between environmentalists, local politicians, and the powerful Weyerhaeuser Company. Its approval this evening by the Snoqualmie city council is assured. Afterward, Sims will celebrate, back at the golf course bar, with a few staff members and a friendly Weyerhaeuser executive. Once again, Sims and his enterprising aides have pulled off a win-win-win conclusion.

As urban sprawl threatens the quality of life throughout the world, the art of the deal—always a key skill for politicians—has become even more pivotal. Faced with increasing constituent complaints about polluted air and water and diminishing open space, they know that the problems' sources, and often their solutions, lie outside their jurisdictions, where they have no formal power. What they

must enlist instead is a gift for swaps and arm-twisting—and sufficient public relations savvy to show rural and city folk how their
interests are linked.

Sims isn't alone in capitalizing on such talents. In Boise, Idaho,
Republican mayor Brent Coles in 2001 spearheaded a successful
campaign for a two-year, $10 million property tax to buy land and
development rights to preserve open space in the foothills in and
outside the city. The effort was based on an extraordinary management plan for the foothills area that brought together city, state,
county, and federal officials. In that same year, in De Kalb County,
Georgia, newly elected county executive Vernon Jones proposed a
$125 million bond referendum to preserve and protect green space
and rehabilitate parks, which voters approved by a two-to-one ratio.
In both of these cases, as in an increasing number of others around
the country, local officials drew a direct connection between a
healthy environment and economic gain by praising the value of
green views and clean air—and in Boise, at least, also less obvious
gifts of Nature such as wildlife habitat and water purification by
streamside foliage—in attracting lucrative new business. Like Sims,
many have achieved these environmental goals by forging innovative
agreements between normally uncooperative groups.

Compromise wasn't Sims' forte back in 1970, when he wore an
Afro and dashiki, marched against the Vietnam War, and threatened
to close down Central Washington University over its admissions
policies. Nor did environmental issues grab him in his first years of
politics, as he rose from fighting for health clinics and parks as a
neighborhood activist in Seattle's South Side to become a member
of the county council. "He hated land-use issues at first," says Sims'
deputy chief of staff, Ethan Raup. "His eyes would glaze over."

But today Sims is fifty-two, the father of three boys, and head of
a generously forested county, whose seat, Seattle, has been dubbed
the Emerald City for its urban greenery. And he has helped refine a
model of a new kind of political activism in an age of environmental distress. He simultaneously tunes in to the needs of wealthy local

corporations, green activists, and local and national politicians, mobi-
lizing all of them to value, and *pay* for, the concrete benefits of
Nature's labor. "You've got to make the market move on your
behalf," he says, "because the government just doesn't have the
resources to buy what needs to be bought."

Unlike the Katoomba Group thinkers, Sims spends little time
debating theory, and he's not expecting global policy, such as the
Kyoto Protocol, to enlarge his options. Instead, he's dealing with the
pressures of population growth and land degradation in real time,
always balancing his heartfelt environmental commitment with his
politician's caution, and inventing solutions as he goes. He makes the
market work with sixteen-hour days full of jawboning and wheeling
and dealing, boosted by a charisma that his fans say borders on
genius. "I've watched county executives for twenty years, and no one
holds a candle to him," says Gene Duvernoy, head of the Cascade
Land Conservancy, a nonprofit conservation group, referring to
Sims' environmental commitment and effectiveness.

Sims is the son of a minister, with an eloquence all his own. His
trademark, on the stump for the Pacific Northwest environment, is
his penchant for telling homey, sometimes hilarious, and always
poignant stories about his family. Most of the tales leave audiences
rapt, run over his allotted time, and end with some urgent call to
public service, in particular the service of preserving sylvan places.
After a long, rambling reminiscence about cutting the umbilical cord
of his youngest son, Aaron, for instance (Aaron, now thirteen, "was a
surprise," he relates, "a loving surprise. There'll be no more surprises
after Aaron . . ."), he'll pause to draw in his breath and then declare,
"I love my kids immensely. And I made a promise to them I'd leave
the world a better place. I don't want people 100 years from now to
ask, 'Where did the forests go?' They won't know Ron Sims from
'boo,' but they'll know someone was *thinking*."

If it's true, as some say, that environmental values are a luxury, pursued almost exclusively by societies that have achieved a certain level
of comfort, King County has all the makings of a green voting bloc.

Encompassing thirty-nine cities within 2,100 square miles, it became a new-economy showcase in the 1990s, ranking eighth among U.S. counties in generating new jobs. Local firms such as Microsoft Corporation, Amazon.com, and RealNetworks expanded dramatically in those years, with average wages rising by 58 percent.

All that wealth and all those new jobs naturally attracted newcomers. From 1980 to 1998, King County's population increased by more than half a million people, a 44 percent increase—nearly the size of a new Seattle. The price of housing shot up with real wages, and so did demand to expand development into rural areas.

The growth engendered a backlash, however, especially in Seattle, which is so green that its city council in 2001 pledged to cut local carbon emissions even beyond the U.S. target set in Kyoto. "By the end of the 1980s, people freaked out that King County was becoming Los Angeles," says Sims' deputy, Ethan Raup. An alliance of environmental and citizen groups in Seattle came up with a radical anti-growth initiative, successfully countered—Raup says co-opted—by Washington State, which passed a more conservative law modeled after legislation passed in Oregon. (The Seattle initiative subsequently failed to win voters' approval.)

The new Washington State law set up an urban growth boundary aimed at keeping newcomers out of areas designated as rural or forested. That limit restricts urban development to the westernmost 20 percent of King County and allows only low-density rural residential development, such as farms and woodlots, in the next 20 percent tier to the east. The rest of the county, about 800,000 acres, is known as the Forest Production District and designated as permanent forestland. One-third of it is devoted to wilderness, parks, and municipal watersheds; another third is state or federal forest in active timber production; and most of the rest is privately owned timberland. It's the last third that is the most at risk, and which Sims is fighting to protect from private development by wealthy immigrants threatening to love Nature to death by buying huge wooded plots for their estates. "They drive up and say, 'Wouldn't it be beautiful to build my half-million-dollar mansion here with this view,'" Sims says. "Our concern is that there are lots of people in that position."

Sims and his staff know that once forest lots are subdivided, for homes or farms or anything else, something irreplaceable is lost. Paved roads, sewage systems, and all the other infrastructure of human settlement destroy the coherence of an ecosystem, compromising its ability to provide habitat for wildlife and perform a range of other services useful to humans, from purifying water to reducing air pollution, all labors that would be tremendously costly to try to replace.

State policy, enforced with zoning limits, calls for no growth in the permanent forestland areas, but many landowners still hold unrealized development rights granted prior to the change in state legislation. That gives Sims and his crew the hard task of trying to persuade people not to exercise their legal rights to build a dream home in this particularly property rights–conscious state. Similarly, he's trying to restrict the options of corporations with a powerful voice in state and local politics.

Not surprisingly, he has sometimes failed. Just outside the growth boundary bloom bunches of signs advertising new luxury subdivisions. There are plugs for Renaissance Ridge "view homes" ("Rise above it all!") and the tony Estates of Treemont. Raup drives a county four-by-four past one giant-sized new home set amid forests of cedar and fir about a fifteen-minute commute from Microsoft's headquarters in Redmond. It has a mammoth stone fireplace and a twenty-foot-tall statue out in front of a cowboy on a horse. "There are no sewers here and no water—people dig wells," Raup says, shaking his head. "Meanwhile, they drive up the land prices so high that the few other homeowners would rather subdivide and sell than keep their houses."

As county chief, Sims has a lot of issues on his plate, from bus routes to drug-abuse programs. But avoiding more Treemonts has become his signature, and he conveys his concern in terms calculated to win the hearts of his constituency. "Our goal is simple," he says.

"Two-thirds of King County is now in forest, and 200 years from now, two-thirds of King County will be in forest."

At the same time, Sims is so keenly green that he occasionally suspects he's getting ahead of his constituents. He'll wax eloquent, for instance, about frogs. "Amphibians are dying at a rate that requires our attention," he says. "They're a great barometer of the health of a system. They tell us how our air and water systems are working. We monitor them religiously. But I can't go around and say I want to save frogs. Can't do it. I'd get clobbered. So instead I talk about clean air and clean water." He'll often go further than that, however, testing audiences' sophistication as he describes the Pacific Northwest landscape in terms of all the vital services it provides for urban dwellers. He'll go into detail about how forests buffer cities from storms, help stabilize the climate, and even provide a measure of protection from floods. "I call them 'working forests,' because they're working on our behalf," he says. "And I want King County to be a model of how urban areas and forestry areas have something in common."

Sims has held this worldview for several years—he blames his wife, business consultant Cayan Topacio, for converting him when he was still serving on King County's council and she was catching on to environmental issues while working as a community liaison for the Bonneville Power Administration (an agency of the U.S. Department of Energy that sells electrical power, wholesale, from federal dams). But in March 1999, he was given a major new incentive to think in terms of the financial value of Nature's work when the federal government listed the once bountiful Puget Sound chinook salmon under the Endangered Species Act of 1973 (ESA).

"Here's where forests really work," Sims says. "Salmon die if the water is too warm, but the forest canopy keeps the water cool. We could not have engineered a system to do that. We couldn't have put refrigerator coils in the streams. But forests do the job. That's why investing in forests for wildlife habitat is one of the smartest things we can do."

The ESA listing created financial value for healthy salmon habitat in two ways. One is that local governments with jurisdictions that have salmon streams now risk federal sanctions or suits by environmental groups if they fail to protect the fishes' homes. Another is that, thanks in part to Sims' wheeling and dealing (including setting up a tri-county response team and flying east to meet with Bill Clinton during his presidency), King County now gets about $16 million annually in federal funds for habitat protection, including tree planting and outright acquisition of land. "We didn't fight the listing: we embraced it," he recalls. Key to this approach is managing growth, and Sims is proud of his record, which shows that since 1995, just 5 percent of all growth throughout the county has occurred in rural areas.

Much of that success owes to a series of innovative plans offering financial benefits for environmental conservation, most of which were prepared under previous administrations but which Sims has energetically pursued. Mark Sollitto, who says he has worked for "sleepy bureaucrats" since 1985, enthuses that under Sims' management, "I come to work every day and it's like coming to work at NASA in the 1960s. There's a mood here like, 'Hey, let's do something we've never done before!'"

One such moonwalk, called the Public Benefit Rating System, involves property tax cuts of as much as 90 percent for landowners who agree to maintain healthy habitat for wildlife. Some 4,700 acres are currently enrolled in this program. Another project involves the sanitary recycling of treated human waste, politely called biosolids, for use as fertilizer on wheat crops and forests owned by Weyerhaeuser and by Washington State. Revenues from the program are used to buy more forestland to make sure it stays in forest.

Sims and his staff have particularly high expectations for yet another program, which creates a market in transferable development rights (TDRs), trading population pressure much as other programs have involved the buying and selling of pollution permits. In this instance, King County plays matchmaker, connecting property owners wanting to sell their rights to develop rural land with developers seeking to add density to urban projects. The goal is to preserve fish habitat and forests by lowering density in rural areas and increasing it in cities. Similar transfers have been brokered in Montgomery County, Maryland, and Boulder County, Colorado.

It's probably easiest to understand King County's TDR program by reviewing the most celebrated deal Sims has made with it, one he frequently cites in his speeches. Back in the year 2000, Port Blakely Communities, a residential development firm, was building a large planned community in Issaquah, a city of about 13,000, eighteen miles from Seattle. The firm had permits to build a 3-million-square-foot complex but wanted to add half a million feet more to accommodate a planned expansion by Microsoft. Sims offered to help Port Blakely—on the condition that Port Blakely help him save a forest.

The woodland covered 313 acres in an area known as Mitchell Hill. Its private owners had recently put it up for sale, and a developer already had plans to cut through it to build sixty-two new mansions. The hill has views of downtown Seattle and thick stands of second-growth western red cedar, Douglas fir, and bigleaf maple. More important, it holds the headwaters for two bodies of water important to salmon: Sammamish Lake on the west and the Snoqualmie River on the east. With several hundred acres of open space on each side, it was a strategic parcel that environmental groups were clamoring to save.

King County and Issaquah had previously capped the growth they'd accept in the new Port Blakely development, known as Issaquah Highlands. But they agreed to stretch that limit after Sims and his staff did some dealing. In the agreement that emerged, Port Blakely bought the development rights to Mitchell Hill for $2.75 million, thereby reducing its property value so much that King County could subsequently buy the land itself for a mere $250,000. Issaquah, in return for accepting more urban density, wound up with several advantages, including additional open space for its residents to enjoy and credit with state officials for helping to create jobs, reduce sprawl, and save salmon habitat. City officials also received $1 million for road improvements from Port Blakely.

Sims has other TDR deals in the works and has even put together a "bank" of $1.5 million worth of development rights already purchased by King County. The biggest obstacle, quite similar to the problems that have cropped up with markets in pollution permits, is finding buyers. City councils have been reluctant to accept more density, despite Sims' argument that density makes cities more vibrant, and even despite the new federal requirements that local governments on Puget Sound help preserve salmon habitat. Still, Sims scored an important victory with the city of Seattle when it designated the depressed downtown Denny Triangle neighborhood as a "receiving site" for development rights from rural areas, thereby signaling that it would accept more density there.

Although Sims has had to work hard to peddle his density-swapping concept in some King County cities, he had no such problem with his effort to save the forested property above Snoqualmie Falls, known as Falls Crossing. There, the incentives were clear; the situation was ripe for Sims' intervention, and everyone, from Mayor Fuzzy Fletcher to the newly recognized Snoqualmie Tribe, was grateful when it came.

As Fletcher waited for Sims at the gleaming new Snoqualmie Ridge golf course, he gazed out the full-length windows at the Cascade Range foothills. Downtown Snoqualmie lay in the floodplain a few miles below the ridge. An old mill town with a population of barely 1,500 in 1990, it served as the setting for the television show *Twin Peaks.* (Special Agent Cooper rents a room in the real-life Salish Lodge overlooking Snoqualmie Falls.) The Weyerhaeuser Company has been a powerful force in these parts, where it still owns a lot of land; in years past, Snoqualmie was such a company town that Fuzzy Fletcher's predecessor as mayor was a career Weyerhaeuser employee.

The downtown still looks a bit ragged around the edges, with

abandoned railroad tracks and a few rusty wrecked cars on its bor-
der. But Snoqualmie has been caught up in the growth that has taken
off all over Washington State, making towns that, like it, are near the
interstate highway more desirable. Aspiring to accommodate new
residents on the ridge above the floodplain, Snoqualmie's city council had recently annexed about 1,300 acres of undeveloped King
County land and agreed that Weyerhaeuser could build a grand
"planned community" there, which would ultimately include 2,000
upscale assembly-line homes and the golf course where Sims and
Fletcher planned their dinner.

But Weyerhaeuser could no longer dictate terms as in the past.
Original plans for the development were scaled down considerably
following one of the most acrimonious debates in county history.
Weyerhaeuser finally had to settle for a "community" about half the
size of what it had hoped for, with an agreement that Snoqualmie,
King County, and the firm would meet again in 2010 to reconsider
expanding it.

That potential expansion became known as the Joint Planning
Area (JPA), and it seemed destined to remain widely unpopular. Sims
had said publicly that King County had enough urban land to handle growth for years to come. Fletcher voiced his resistance in
stronger terms. "I probably did say, 'Over my dead body,'" he said. "I
know I said, 'No way with the JPA.' I just didn't want any more
sprawl in Snoqualmie."

But then Puget Western, a division of Puget Sound Energy, began
to move ahead with plans to develop its Falls Crossing property, and
the mayor had a much tougher problem on his hands.

The Falls Crossing backdrop was precious to Snoqualmie in several ways. It was serenely lovely, with its fir, hemlock, and cedar
forests. It was historic, an ancient site of the Snoqualmie Tribe. And
it was also lucrative, in the sense that it provided the scenic setting
for the town's star tourist attraction. Sensitive to these considerations,
Puget Western, which first proposed its development in 1992, had

already scaled back its plans several times, but the one on the drawing board in early 2000 called for 370 homes, which would still represent dramatic change.

Mayor Fletcher, in particular, was in a bind. He was up for reelection and knew that allowing the development to proceed might cost his political future. But he had no legal way to halt it at that point, and buying the land was out of the question for the city council. Its market price, about $13 million, was four times Snoqualmie's budget.

"It was worth just about anything, short of burning down the town, to save the Falls," Fletcher said. He told his staff members to "be creative," and they started talks with the Cascade Land Conservancy. These discussions soon grew to include Weyerhaeuser's real estate division, which saw in them the chance to make some kind of arrangement that would let the company push forward with the JPA, the expansion of Snoqualmie Ridge. Weyerhaeuser's directors had invested huge amounts on that project and now needed to sell more homes to make a profit. That's when Sims and his aide Lori Grant also got involved, because a Weyerhaeuser expansion of Snoqualmie Ridge development would need some county-approved zoning changes.

Over the next three months, Sims and Grant worked with the Cascade Land Conservancy, Weyerhaeuser, and Snoqualmie to crank out a deal by which Snoqualmie and King County, bankrolled by Weyerhaeuser, would buy the forest above the falls. The deal's complications and compromises were typical of those Sims forges, as were its payoffs for the public. Over time, Weyerhaeuser would reimburse almost all the money spent and also give up the development rights to two coveted parcels: one that encompassed 2,800 acres of working forestland in the Raging River basin, on King County land just a few miles away, and on another 600 acres traversed by King County's regional trail system. The firm additionally promised to pay $1 million for a bridge connecting trails north of Snoqualmie Falls.

Weyerhaeuser would be well compensated for this largess. It

would get immediate permission to build 268 additional homes on Snoqualmie Ridge and, more significantly, a promise by Snoqualmie and King County to speed up consideration of the Snoqualmie Ridge expansion. Weyerhaeuser would time its reimbursements for Falls Crossing to its receipt of permits for Snoqualmie Ridge, which of course gave the public officials an incentive to move quickly to approve the permits.

As generous as this deal may have seemed, however, Sims and Grant believed that Weyerhaeuser negotiators were dragging their heels throughout most of the talks. To be sure, the firm entered the talks with some hard feelings: as acknowledged by Lynn Claudon, the executive who shared drinks with Sims after the Snoqualmie council vote, past relations with the county chief had been "spotty at best." Sims is a staunch Democrat who brands Weyerhaeuser a Republican firm. For their part, Claudon and her colleagues thought Sims, in other dealings, had been trying to usurp state authority to regulate timber, overstepping his bounds and landing on their toes. "Our institutional memory of King County is not positive," Claudon said. "We had to get through all that to make this deal."

A breakthrough eluded them until Sims came up with one more inducement for Weyerhaeuser. The company's timber division had been lobbying him to soften a new county ordinance he'd proposed, the purpose of which was to ban the construction of homes on newly created lots in the Forest Production District. The intent was to deter the big timber firms—in particular Weyerhaeuser, which owned a lot of land there—from selling their large holdings to developers who would subdivide them. Weyerhaeuser's timber division had already indicated it wanted to get rid of some of its large Pacific Northwest timber holdings, on the grounds that tough state environmental laws made it too hard to make money selling logs. If the ordinance went through, it would greatly reduce property values in the eyes of any potential buyer, a prospect that had Weyerhaeuser officials extremely upset.

Sims' solution was to replace the proposed ban with a resolution to study the issue for another eighteen months. During that time, Weyerhaeuser would still be barred from building homes on the new lots. Yet if it chose, it could pursue negotiations to sell the land at market price. Sims let Weyerhaeuser know he expected more flexibility on Falls Crossing in return. Suddenly, the negotiations in Snoqualmie started showing real progress.

Claudon later conceded that the backdown on the ban on new homes in the designated forestry area "could have made us more willing" to deal on Falls Crossing. "It affected Weyerhaeuser senior management's perception of King County's ability to work together, to have a trusting relationship. That had not existed before," she said.

To be sure, a devoted environmentalist hearing of King County's strategic retreat and then bumping into Sims and Claudon sharing drinks at the Snoqualmie Ridge golf course bar, with Claudon, a contributor to Sims' reelection campaign, humorously calling Sims "boss," might reasonably worry that relations between the county exec and the timber firm had become a bit too comfy. But in fact, environmental activists throughout King County are resounding in their approval of Sims' technique. "The majority of those who really know about his deals think that if he weren't doing them, we'd probably end up with nothing," says Ed Zuckerman, executive director of Washington Conservation Voters. "Ron balances what he needs to balance just about better than anyone. His heart is in the right place, and he thinks outside the box."

Compromise is a daily reality of Sims' job and a key to his political future, as he'll readily admit. But even old college friends maintain he hasn't sold out. "He set a foundation of values in the '60s and '70s, and he has stayed there," says John Drinkwater, who now works at Central Washington University in student affairs. "He's obviously become much more savvy, but often you see politicians who give way to everything, and Ron hasn't done that. He butts a lot of heads and has never backed down from a fight."

Back in Snoqualmie, the vote on Falls Crossing is coming up. Sims makes his way through the city council's packed meeting room, hugging and shaking hands with all five council members during a break in the evening session. He then takes a seat near the front as proceedings resume. The vote is read out; approval is instantaneous, and Sims is invited to make a brief comment. He stands, clearly savoring the opportunity.

"This is one of those projects that makes my heart sing," he says, and launches into a story about a relay race involving the eighth-grade track team of one of his sons. The audience chuckles as he draws out the bit about how, between the third and fourth runners, the team missed the handoff. "But in this case, no one missed the handoff," he says. "This is clearly one of those projects where people will look back and ask, 'How'd they do it?' It was a win-win-win-win-win-win!"

A couple of hours later, while driving back through the night to his Seattle home, where he'll arrive near midnight, he's still buoyed by the Falls Crossing purchase. "It's like we're getting all these crown jewels," he says. He's excited about the deals he has made and those yet to come, and he muses dreamily about how he'll get more power to broker deals of even greater scope if he attains higher office, as is his oft-declared plan. Sims ran for the United States Senate and lost in 1994—"a bad year to try," he says—and since then has set his sights on the governorship, even though the current occupant of that office, Gary Locke, has not declared he plans to leave it anytime soon.

Sims understands that his county's pro-environment leanings are all too often tempered by concerns over money, but he's confident that he can work with that tension. The formula is to show big corporations that they can gain from conservation and conservationists that they can't afford not to work with big corporations. By following that rule, Sims has stored up enough goodwill on both sides to stand him very well in any future race for higher office.

"I've always said that King County is great preparation," he says. "But of course the state can do a lot more. It's got the ability to establish a really aggressive environmental tone, and there's this big menu of issues just waiting. Salmon. Conflicts with agriculture.

Arsenic. Columbia River basin irrigation. Spokane's sprawl. I love desserts—just look at my waistline—and this is like walking into a banquet room and just being able to choose whatever you want, because there are so many of them. One has to salivate at the challenges. They're so *do*able."

On the road to a new economy of Nature, Sims' artful deal making points out how much a single motivated person can do, even within the confines of a local government bureaucracy. Business entrepreneurs often have a freer power, depending on the reach of their bank accounts and imagination. John Wamsley, the subject of the next chapter and one of the most imaginative environmental entrepreneurs around, does his business in South Australia, where he combines a zeal for making money for his investors with a passion for saving native wildlife.

C h a p t e r   S e v e n

Down Under: How to Make a Numbat Turn a Profit

> "Death is one thing—an end to birth is something else."
>
> —*Michael Soulé and Bruce Wilcox*

THE EVENT WAS BLACK-TIE, so John Wamsley donned a dark suit before leaving home to accept yet another regional tourism award—he'd already won a dozen—for his management of Warrawong Earth Sanctuary outside the South Australian city of Adelaide. A six-foot-two bear of a man who spends most of his time in wading boots and jeans, he frowned into the mirror at the jacket's tight fit. His wife, Proo, smoothed the lapels beneath his long, scraggly beard. Then Wamsley reached for the crowning touch: a Davy Crockett–style hat made from the carcass of a large feral cat. Its toothy death-grimace would adorn his forehead, its tail swing down behind him, and Wamsley would be talked about for days—which was precisely the point. Most who would see him that night already knew the message he had in mind. He had long ago won notoriety as a man sworn to kill as many feral cats as possible, and to do so in the most remorseless manner. Among other things, this meant urging his countrymen to cook "pussy-tail stew" and selling bumper stickers reading "The Only Good Cat Is a Flat Cat."

"You have to shock people a bit to get them to think," he told the television crew following him around the Adelaide Convention Centre that night. The camera caught faces watching him pass: shock and thoughtfulness were among the milder reactions to his choice of attire. Over the next few days, photographs of Wamsley in his cat-hat landed on front pages throughout Australia. The 1991 event inspired several days of death threats. One caller to a radio show compared him to Hitler. But it may be fairer to say that Wamsley takes militant measures to address an urgent problem. He seeks to halt the 200-year slaughter of Australia's native wildlife, and his fierce hatred of cats stems from their leading role in the ongoing bloodbath.

Before Europeans began arriving in 1788, the world's smallest continent maintained an abundance of strange and wondrous creatures found nowhere else: dainty, jewel-colored fairy-wrens; raucous cockatoos; furry duck-billed platypus; tiny, anteater-like numbats; cuddly koalas; and more than two dozen species of tiny kangaroos.

Yet barely two centuries after cats came on the scene—brought over in the 1700s to kill rodents on ships from Europe—the felines' expanding numbers rivaled Australia's current 19 million human population. Feral cats grew to enormous proportions—males weighing as much as 13.5 pounds, the size of a small bobcat—and made mincemeat out of the smaller native species. Scientists estimate they currently kill more than 400 million native mammals, birds, and reptiles each year. Increasing the toll are European red foxes and rabbits, imported by hunting devotees. The foxes have joined in the slaughter, and the rabbits have competed for food. And as if four-footed threats weren't enough, logging, farming, and shortsighted government support of land clearing by bipeds have steadily destroyed the animals' homes, fouling rivers and toppling billions of trees—about half of the country's forests. The net result is that at the century's turn, Australia had one of the world's highest rates of species loss, having hosted a full quarter of the world's mammal extinctions over the previous 200 years.

To be sure, the Land Down Under isn't the only place where biodiversity is under siege. Throughout the world, with every passing hour an estimated two to three species are committed to extinction, mostly as victims of habitat destruction and the spread of non-native species, which kill or compete with natives. Both forces might in theory seem simple to control, yet the reality is complex, sobering, and often bizarre, as a glimpse of related developments in Florida shows. In recent times, out-of-town guests on the loose in that state have included piranhas, walking catfish, green African savanna monkeys, and giant Madagascan hissing cockroaches—all deliberately released and many, including the roach, popular as pets. Hundreds to thousands more exotic species are accidentally released in the state each year.

Wamsley has made it his life's work to do battle with these trends—and, in the process, as founder and director of Earth Sanctuaries Ltd. (ESL), make money for several thousand investors, including himself. Like Ron Sims in Washington State, he has shown genius in zeroing in on people's self-interest as a reason why they should care about Nature. Yet his plunge into the predatory world of high finance, beginning in May 2000, when he listed ESL on the Australian Stock Exchange, has been nearly as controversial as his one-man war on felines. At a time when many conservationists still oppose the notion of imposing bottom-line accounting on Nature, Wamsley embraces the trend. He scorns the more traditional technique of waging fund-raising campaigns for animals about to go extinct, saying this has succeeded only in creating large, inefficient private bureaucracies. Instead, he has found some remarkable ways to make a numbat turn a profit. He calls ESL the world's first publicly traded company with a "core value of conservation."

The sixty-one-year-old former mathematics professor lives at Warrawong, the smallest and busiest of three private wildlife parks managed by ESL and open to the public. (Six others were under development in mid-2001.) Wamsley has applied the same formula to all: buy up pristine wilderness or degraded farmland, fence it off, remove harmful non-native species, and restock the land with native flora and fauna. As he describes it, he has been "setting up a bit of Australia as we think platypus would like it, rather than as people would like it."

Not so surprisingly, people have actually liked it quite a bit. By 2001, some 50,000 Australians and foreigners were visiting Warra-wong each year to tour the sanctuary, lunch at its outdoor café, and shop at its boutique for such novelties as jigsaw-puzzle pictures of endangered frogs and platypus-shaped chocolates. The visitors included families on outings, wildlife photographers, local school-children, and small businesses hosting conferences.

Wamsley's experiment is intriguing because it seems so concrete an example of the Holy Grail of getting revenues from conserving biodiversity. Perhaps you really don't have to choose between saving a species and saving for your child's education—perhaps you can do both at once. Perhaps the profit motive could even expand the ranks of conservationists. Wamsley was proving the case, albeit on a small scale—ESL's market capitalization (the number of outstanding shares multiplied by the share price) was just $24 million on its list-ing. His way of mining "green gold" from ecosystem services was to capture the financial value of habitats for interesting animals. Tourists, he'd found, would pay quite a bit to see the wombats and wallabies nurtured by the wilderness he protected. With all the talk at Katoomba Group conferences of using markets to protect Nature, an ESL share seemed to come closest to making it real. It was based on the belief, so energetically espoused by Adam Davis, that the value of the natural capital—in this case, Australia's native plants and animals—would increase as people realized its worldwide supplies were growing more rare.

Wamsley had good reason to assume that. In fact, already people were rapidly coming to this realization. As the world's trove of pris-tine wilderness declined, tourists were traveling farther and paying more to see it, and there was no sign the trend would slow down. The more pavement, grit, and noise filled neighborhoods, the more people craved clean, green antidotes. In a 1998 study, the Alliance Internationale de Tourisme found travel experts from every continent predicting that "nature and a clean environment, and increasing environmental awareness" would become top determinants of consumer demand over the subsequent fifteen years. Inexorably, Nature's works of art were gaining the prestige of those housed at the Louvre.

To be sure, people had been traveling to enjoy Nature—to hike, raft, ski, bird-watch, and go on safari—for generations. But as consciousness deepened of the wear and tear on the planet, beginning in the 1970s, it led to a particular kind of travel that usually implied as light a footprint as possible. That travel became known as ecotourism, and over the next couple of decades it turned into a thriving niche of the tourism industry, the world's largest profit-making enterprise. In 1997, people traveling internationally for pleasure spent $425 billion on everything from hotels to meals to taxis to museum tickets, according to the World Tourism Organization. The International Ecotourism Society has estimated that Nature-based tourism may make up as much as 60 percent of those expenditures. What's more, it says that while tourism overall has grown annually by about 4 percent, ecotourism has increased by 10–30 percent.

A main attraction of journeys to wild places is the chance for a glimpse of wild animals—an experience with a strong, primitive pull for human beings. As competition sharpens for the dollars of wildlife-loving tourists, several countries hold natural advantages. Ecuador has the exotic iguanas and booby birds of the Galápagos Islands, drawing tens of thousands of foreign visitors each year. South Africa, where visits to Nature reserves grew, on average, by an amazing 108 percent per year in the 1990s, has its lions and giraffes as well as good airports and roads and a relatively stable government. Australia has many blessings that draw tourists, but its class act is its uniquely charismatic fauna. Visitors know they'll be asked, on return, whether they saw a koala or kangaroo—preferably in the wild. Still, as human development marches on throughout the world, such sightings have become ever harder to achieve without a lot of help.

Wamsley hasn't been alone among entrepreneurs in understanding these growing market forces. As the new millennium began, thousands of businesses around the world were hanging out ecotourism shingles, hawking anything from a simple Nature walk to an air-conditioned stay in a 200-room hotel. Many stressed their conservationist virtues, some more deservedly than others. Some Brazilian businesses, for instance, have offered "ecotourist" outings on boats that chase dolphins while blasting pop music on their radios. But a more respectable and innovative approach was represented by the South Africa–based Conservation Corporation, which beginning in 1990 maintained animal sanctuaries across Africa, offering luxury suites with such backdrops as Victoria Falls and the Serengeti Plain. The firm owned only a few small land parcels but contracted with surrounding landowners for conservation "services" and access to game viewing and hunting. Contracts were made for access only to land that retained high biodiversity values, where Nature-oriented visitors wouldn't be disappointed. The firm's success owed to its ability to show surrounding landowners that they could earn twice as much from conservation contracts as they could from cattle ranching.

Wamsley's vision was even more ambitious. His plan was to own in perpetuity, through his corporation, as much land as possible. By the time he listed his company, he and 6,700 private shareholders controlled 225,000 acres, or 351 square miles. ESL's goal was eventually to manage native Australian biodiversity in a full 1 percent of the country, about 30,000 square miles, roughly the size of Maine.

THE HALF-HOUR DRIVE from Adelaide's airport to Warrawong Earth Sanctuary leads up a gentle slope into the mostly barren Mylor Hills. Along the way, the distance between homes steadily grows. Welcoming guests to the spartan hotel, with its simple cots and $110 per weekend "luxury" tents, is Mark Edwards, a twenty-seven-year-old

Warrawong staff member with a bachelor's degree in ecotourism from nearby Flinders University. An unabashed Wamsley loyalist, Edwards regales visitors with stories of his boss' accomplishments and of the hopes they share for ESL's international success. "We're trying to position ourselves as the world's best provider of the Australian experience, the marsupial experience," Edwards says. He speaks of "John" in hushed tones, underscoring how Wamsley's fans lionize him. ESL's World Wide Web site has actually featured an adoring Wamsley biography titled "The Lion Next Door."

Wamsley has won more than his share of critics with his in-your-face style, yet Australian government wildlife officials enthusiastically praise his record as a caretaker of rare wild animals. His successful breeding of platypus is by many accounts unrivaled, and ESL promotional materials tout his efforts to restore several other threatened species. At the 12,000-acre Yookamurra Earth Sanctuary, a ninety-minute drive from Adelaide, ESL says it hosts almost 20 percent of the world's population of numbats, which can't survive in zoos because they must eat several thousand termites every day. At Scotia Earth Sanctuary, a 160,000-acre reserve in New South Wales that is Wamsley's largest property, ESL officials say that endangered stick-nest rats and critically endangered bridled nailtail wallabies are thriving. Warrawong managers say they care for more than 100 brush-tailed bettongs, one of the most common kinds of kangaroo in the 1700s but numbering fewer than 200 worldwide as recently as the early 1990s. Although these claims couldn't be independently verified, Australia's government has shown its faith in Wamsley by leasing him public land assigned to wildlife conservation. "ESL is doing the best job of anyone in Australia in terms of preserving native animals," says government economist Carl Binning.

Wamsley's other main point of pride is to have lobbied aggressively for what turned out to be a momentous change in Australian accounting standards, the creation in 1999 by the Australian Accounting Standards Board of "self-generating and regenerating assets." This new and unprecedented accounting category obliges businesses, including fish farmers, foresters, and vintners, to count on their balance sheets and profit and loss statements the value of non-human living organisms held for commercial purposes. This has allowed Wamsley to include his stick-nest rats and yellow-footed rock wallabies, among other threatened animals, using prices that government breeding programs charge when selling them. On ESL's listing, the financial value of his entire menagerie was approximately $2.3 million, which could rise or fall from year to year, depending on the success of his breeding programs. In 2000, the first year after the accounting standard change, the new technique had the effect of increasing ESL's net worth by $1.9 million—a kangaroo-sized leap forward in valuing biodiversity.

Warrawong means "water on the side of the hill" in Aboriginal dialect and refers to the many natural springs that once flourished in the area. But by the time Wamsley bought the land for his first sanctuary, much of the region had been tamed to farmland and degraded by deforestation. In 1969, Warrawong was a dilapidated dairy farm; thirty years later, Wamsley had replanted it with tens of thousands of native trees and shrubs. In the process, he'd made it a small (thirty-five-acre) but lush model of what Australia might have looked like millions of years ago, before it dried out as the landmass drifted north. This was the type of land in which kangaroos evolved, a lost paradise brought back to life for Wamsley's proselytizing purposes. Warrawong guests tour his wonderland before dawn, when the air is full of hoots and hisses and most of the large nocturnal animals are still awake, looking for food.

Wamsley himself is not usually a guide, but his staff includes many trained naturalists, among them the amiable John Gitsham. Gitsham leads tourists along boardwalks and narrow trails through small forests of mountain ash trees. The boardwalks are part of Warrawong's rigorous strategy of minimizing visitors' adverse effects on Nature, from their consumption of energy to their accidental trampling of plants in the fragile reconstruction of a long-gone landscape. Eventually, the group arrives at a gully that has had water pumped in to turn it into a swamp. Wamsley planted some trees to provide an upper canopy in the early 1970s and filled in the understory with shade-loving ferns from Victoria and Tasmania. An irrigation system installed by volunteers keeps the woods fogged; the artificial rain-forest habitat is not yet sufficiently mature or extensive to maintain a cool, moist microclimate on its own. Frogs have been lured to the area from less habitable surrounding farms, and flocks of birds have settled in to enjoy nectar-rich native shrubs. As the morning light breaks, coots and moorhens begin paddling about. With a little luck, a quickly swimming dark shape may come into view—one of about two dozen platypus living in the area.

The shyness of platypus (the word is commonly used for one or more alike) makes sightings of them all the more thrilling. This strange amalgam of duck and beaver is among the oldest species of mammal around: its ancestors flourished with the dinosaurs 160 million years ago. But from about 1970, platypus have been classified as extinct in South Australia, hunted for their waterproof fur, drowned accidentally in fisherman's nets, and devastated by river pollution. Beginning in 1988, Wamsley received government permission to bring five platypus from Kangaroo Island to Warrawong; three years later, the first two babies, known in Australia as puggles, had appeared. The secret, say Warrawong guides, is simply providing them with suitable habitat—in this case, the human-made swamp, which Gitsham proudly calls "the Taj Mahal of platypus living." Falling eucalyptus leaves and bark from the trees Wamsley planted blacken the water, adding tannin and acidity to make it just the way a platypus would like it. Muddy banks let the animals excavate burrows and feed on plentiful invertebrates, which they dig out with their bills. For viewing, Wamsley has built a "platypussery"—a submerged concrete structure with a window looking into the murky pond, through which patient visitors might see a "platy" swim past. "They can't survive in zoos, where they're put in tanks with clear water," Gitsham explains on his tours. "It makes them so stressed they go mad. Because conservation is our number one priority, we'll never put a platypus on display."

Well, perhaps not. Yet Gitsham doesn't hesitate to scatter oats from a large bag at several stops along the trail to summon long-nosed potoroos—small kangaroos—and wallabies, which gobble frantically at what he calls a "snack," while tourists' cameras snap. When people point out that such feedings seem to blur the line between sanctuary and zoo, and that the snacks perhaps are making the animals incapable of living on their own, Gitsham responds that ESL is "always fighting between the demands of conservation and tourism." An honest answer, but the practices leave Wamsley vulnerable to some ridicule. "He makes little Jurassic Parks for the Chardonnay set," scoffs an investment banker in Sydney.

By and large, the firm's shareholders have not been put off by such compromises. Barbara Harkness, a local Web designer married to a postal clerk, bought ESL stock at $0.36 per share in 1994, thinking of it as charity, and watched it nearly quintuple in value in six years. "It's amazing to see how it's grown, and how this place has grown," she says, gesturing at the new boardwalk skirting the swamp, during the morning tour with Gitsham. "We come here every few years. If we ever make any money, we'll invest more. It's our legacy." Harkness, who is forty-six years old, confides that she wouldn't have been so taken with ESL's approach when she was younger. Experience has moderated her views. "A lot of people try to save the world, but it's too big a task," she says. "You can only do a little bit, and you have to do that with rules, do it within the system. It takes an enormous amount of money to save wildlife, and where is it? In the market. A lot of people don't like that; it kind of sticks a bit, making money off wildlife. But bake sales aren't going to do it."

After the tour, visitors routinely end up on a sunny terrace at Warrawong's café, with views of rainbow lorikeets screeching and chattering to one another on nearby perches. Included on the lunch menu is grilled kangaroo, initially jarring after one has just spent a couple of hours watching the marsupials at close range. Yet whereas thirty-eight species of kangaroo are on the edge of extinction, eleven occur in plague proportions, like deer in some parts of the United

States, and Wamsley is as unperturbed about eating kangaroo filets as he is about dispatching cats and foxes.

At last, as noon approaches, the mastermind appears, looking like Tolstoy in a bush hat, with squinty blue eyes and a tiny gold platypus pin adorning the suspenders on his faded jeans. He is accompanied by Proo, who is carrying their pet southern hairy-nosed wombat, Danthonia Ruby Thing. As Proo strokes Thing, Wamsley begins with his beginnings.

"My dad was a farmer, citrus and poultry. He bought 166 acres of bushland in the central forest of New South Wales, and we went to live there when I was ten," he explains. "I had six sisters; the home was unbearable to be in. So I spent most of my time outside, and it was a paradise for an impressionable boy, an incredible place in the middle of millions of acres of bush. The creeks were full of fish and platypus."

Wamsley remembered seeing lyre birds, bandicoots, and gliders. But by the time he turned 12, foxes and cats had entered the area, and just two years later, native animals seemed to have disappeared. Two years after that, he watched brush fires consume much of the wilderness—the fire danger increased, he charged, by the absence of foragers to clear the forest floor of easily ignitable debris. "The whole thing was gone," Wamsley said. "It was like an empty church—no wildlife at all."

Wamsley left home for good that same year. His plan was to make his fortune and do something, though he wasn't sure what, for the wildlife. He worked as a door-to-door encyclopedia salesman, a nurse in a mental asylum, and a buyer of derelict homes that he fixed up and sold for a profit. "Money was never a problem for me," he said. By 1969, he had made his first million, and he used some of the money to buy land—in some parts for as little as $0.40 per acre—which he replanted with native trees and shrubs to welcome back native animals.

Even this first step was controversial, at least locally. Back in those years, some town councils in Australia actually made it a policy to plant only imported species. The Australian forestry department told farmers that Monterey pines grew better and faster than eucalyptus, Wamsley recalls, adding dryly, "It's called conventional wisdom." As he carried on with his reforestation plans, one local paper, the *Mount Barker Courier,* ran a front-page story showing a neighbor standing amid Wamsley's seedlings. The caption was "A Picture of Despair— After Years of Clearing His Roadside of Scrub, It Has Been Replanted." In 1976, Wamsley even spent a night in jail, charged with illegally cutting down an imported pine tree. Photographs of Wamsley with a paper bag over his head ("The reporters told me it would sell more papers that way") and bearing his ax made front pages throughout Australia; it marked his entry onto the national stage. "I faced five years in jail, but the authorities didn't pursue it," he says.

As the afternoon wears on, Wamsley takes a stroll on the trails. Most of the small animals are nowhere to be seen, but he finds two large, gray kangaroos sleeping on a grassy slope. They're reclining on their backs like dogs, legs twitching as they dream. Wamsley sits in the sun beside them and continues his story.

Soon after the pine tree incident, the ever unrepentant Wamsley began to fence off his property and use dogs to destroy the cats, foxes, and rabbits therein. He calls these three non-native species the "terrible triad": the rabbits were easy prey for the cats and foxes, which meant the predators multiplied even faster, as did their harm to native animals. Shooting cats, even on private land, was illegal until the early 1990s, but that didn't faze Wamsley. "You do what you have to do," he says grimly.

In fact, many Australians sympathized with Wamsley's combative stance toward non-native animals, particularly rabbits. What farmers would come to call the "gray blanket" originated in 1859 with the arrival of a shipment of a dozen rabbits meant for shooting-party game on the Victoria State property of a gentleman farmer named Thomas Austin. By 1865, some 20,000 rabbits had been killed on Austin's estate, but many more were running free, and the population expanded to the north and west with a speed unparalleled in the history of animal invasions. By 1996, estimates of Australia's rabbit population ranged from 120 million to 600 million. They nibbled pastures bare, eating even the bark off trees, costing hundreds of millions of dollars in damage and in efforts to control them.

The government resorted to increasingly drastic counterattacks. Beginning in 1902, workers toiled on a 1,100-mile-long netted fence running from south to north in Western Australia in a pathetic attempt to preserve at least part of the country as rabbit-free. The effort took five years but was in vain. Half a century later, authorities went to the extreme of releasing a rabbit-killing virus from Brazil. The disease it caused, myxomatosis, brought slow, painful death to the rabbits and made the first real progress in cutting down their numbers—until survivors built up their immunity.

By 1995, with rabbits more rampant than ever, it was time to try again. The new and purportedly more humane technique in bunny bio-warfare was calici virus, which guaranteed rapid death by organ failure within thirty-six hours and had been shown to be harmless to other species. After two years of tests for safety in high-security laboratories on the continent, government scientists retreated to a bunker on a southern island to start tests in the wild. But the virus was accidentally released on the mainland sooner than planned. Bush flies on the island picked it up and were blown across the water by a rare Antarctic gale. The disease spread rapidly throughout the states of South Australia and New South Wales, where reports came in of twenty-two dead rabbits per acre in some of the national parks. In some areas, it knocked back rabbit populations by a stunning 90 percent. "Dramatic regrowth of grasslands and shrublands, on a scale unseen in living memory" was taking place, nurturing the return of both wildlife and ranchers' livelihoods, according to Brian Walker, a scientist leading the government's research on biodiversity and sustainability. Only time will tell how long this solution remains effective.

In Western Australia, meanwhile, attention has been focused on foxes and feral cats. There, the biggest wildlife conservation program ever undertaken in Australia aims to bring at least thirteen native species back from the brink of extinction on about 12 million acres of land. Called Western Shield, the program, launched in 1996, was reporting success as late as 2001: populations of threatened native animals including numbats, ring-tailed possums, and noisy scrub-birds were climbing. More dramatically, three forest-dwelling mammals— the woylie, quenda, and tammar wallaby—have been removed from the state's threatened fauna list as a result of the program. The main weapon in Western Shield's fight against the fox and feral cat is the naturally occurring poison "1080," found in native plants called poison peas. The native animals, having evolved with these plants, are tolerant of the poison, but introduced animals can be killed using the poison in bait.

Wamsley has fought his own rabbit, fox, and cat wars with cool efficiency. The first thing he'd do after buying a property was put up a 10,000-volt electric fence. Although they don't kill the fauna, he contends, "no animal would want to touch them voluntarily." The fence would usually be electrified on both sides, which Wamsley said was necessary in case a wombat, for instance, tore a hole in it to get out, leaving space for a fox to come in. Once the fence was up, ESL employees would track the non-native animals, one by one, with dogs and guns. "One rabbit can take a week to catch, but if you don't get the last two, you may as well have not gotten any," Wamsley says. ESL workers once tracked a single fox for seven months at Yooka-mura.

Such strategies have made Wamsley public enemy number one for Australian animal liberation groups. Some opponents, who he dismisses as "nutters," threw cats and foxes over the fence at Yookamura. It only egged Wamsley on. He continued to wear his cat-hat at public events, and he once told a television interviewer, "I suppose the message is, do your bit for the environment: go home and 'hat' your cat tonight."

In private, he says, "I'd sell my soul to the devil if I had to, to save an animal from extinction. That's what my life's about." That, and the drawing of clear lines as to who is with or against him. It's a rare conversation that doesn't include a dig at Australia's government or the "greenies" who he charges have "stuffed up the world." ("If you say, 'I'm going to save the gorillas,' and we all accept that and give you a couple hundred million dollars, then it's your fault they're gone," he says. "If you take on these responsibilities and don't do your job, you should be sued.")

In 1978, Wamsley's first marriage, of twenty years, broke up over Warrawong, as he tells it. "I didn't know there was a problem until she announced it," he says. "She couldn't handle me 'wasting the inheritance.' When I built the swamp at Warrawong, my mother-in-law wrote a letter to my mother saying, 'I can prove he's mad now; he's building a swamp. . . .'" His three children by that first union didn't talk to him for twenty years, he says. Only in the year 2001 did he meet two of his grandchildren for the first time.

As a result of the divorce, Warrawong was put on the market, and Wamsley almost lost his dream. But that same year, he married Proo Geddes, then a Warrawong neighbor and a science advisor for South Australia public schools. Together, they borrowed money to buy back the sanctuary. By that time, Wamsley had gotten his Ph.D. degree and was teaching mathematics at Flinders University. But he was spending more time on the sanctuaries than in classes, and he lost his job shortly after he brought his pet wombat to an algebra lecture in order to, as he said, illustrate a theorem. "I wasn't fired over the wombat, but it didn't help," he says.

Wamsley's history wouldn't seem to make him a natural advocate for working within the system, yet he appears to have become an ardent member of the establishment. By 2001, ESL's board of directors included a veteran investment banker and a mining firm executive. Wendy Craik, who took over from Wamsley as chief executive officer that year—after all agreed, as one board member described it, that the firm finally needed a diplomat at its helm—is a former executive director of a national farmers' group. Wamsley contends conservation is one of the few world concerns still working under "socialist" rules and that ultimately you can't save anything on which you can't put a price. "I've always found the concept of charity bizarre," he says. "To be effective, you have to be realistic. There are really only two motives that drive people: greed and fear. And the fear is the fear of missing out. Once you realize that's happening, there's no problem with these kinds of investments. Idealism would argue against it, but idealism hasn't worked. And I don't mind if you stand in front of a bulldozer in the name of idealism, but don't put the native animals there."

To be sure, many other environmentalists aren't swayed by such arguments, and some worry about Wamsley's turn to markets. Once a company such as ESL is publicly owned, contends the World Wildlife Fund's conservation-finance director, Barry Spergel, "there will always be a tension between conservation and maximizing profits. If the shareholders pressure Wamsley to make higher returns, will he compromise his values by building mega-lodges or overstocking his reserves? Is he really conserving natural ecosystems, or just creating large zoos?"

An equally potent critique is that Wamsley, in his battle for biodiversity, is chasing the simplest aspect of a highly complex global problem. He's a charismatic guy fighting for charismatic animals. In Australia, tourist dollars for photo opportunities of tame kangaroos are truly low-hanging fruit, and Wamsley can whip up investors' enthusiasm simply by featuring photographs on his Web site of baby platypus and numbats. (There was even reason to fear, given the accounting standards ESL was bound by—and its fiduciary duty to its shareholders—that its interest was to keep those cute rare animals rare. Once they became less rare, they'd become less valuable, and so also might ESL shares.)

But what about the rest of biodiversity? The world at large is losing species at a faster rate than ever before, with the peril to numbats the tiniest part of the problem. Humanity, which came into being at a time of unprecedented biodiversity, is threatening to bring on a mass extinction comparable to that which wiped dinosaurs off the face of Earth. Extinction rates in the year 2000 were an estimated 1,000 times higher than typical prehuman levels and were projected to rise sharply. As Harvard University's Edward O. Wilson has said, this mass extinction is the folly our descendants will be least likely to forgive.

This loss of biodiversity has been taking place even as new species—bees, beetles, fungi, microbes, and also occasionally birds and mammals—are being discovered, meaning we are clearly losing creatures we don't yet know we have. While people mourn the possible end of our ability to see koalas, the sad truth is that we have little idea how many species share the planet with us nor how their lives entwine with our own. In ignorance, we've been defying naturalist Aldo Leopold's famous warning that "to save every cog in the wheel is the first precaution of intelligent tinkering."

Anecdotal evidence abounds as to the ways we're dependent on the vast variety of other life-forms around us, how they help us survive and prosper. The world's biodiversity is a huge bank of treasures, most still hidden but some the basis of medical, agricultural, and industrial advancements. Two of the most touted of these discoveries are Pacific Northwest yew trees, which yield taxol, a cancer-fighting substance, and the rosy periwinkle flower, derivatives of which have helped cure some forms of childhood leukemia. Animals also play important roles: the venom of some snakes reduces blood pressure, and some insects produce anticoagulants.

Often we haven't understood the importance of a species until it has nearly disappeared. In the United States, people have only recently learned to appreciate the role of beavers in making dams that create rich wetlands and the fertile soil surrounding them. And only after the sea otters off the California coast disappeared, overhunted for their pelts, did we notice their importance in local ecosystems. The otters, it turned out, had eaten sea urchins that grazed on kelp plants. As the number of otters declined, the urchins began to destroy the kelp forests, which serve as nurseries sheltering young fish and thereby support a variety of creatures higher in the food chain, such as harbor seals and bald eagles.

Yet despite the evidence of the great value of biodiversity, our attempts to preserve it, as the century turned, were still limited in scope and basically primitive in style. One of the most popular conservation techniques, for instance, has been the purchase of land by philanthropists. This has included the growing "land trust" movement, particularly strong in California, and the single-handed efforts of individual entrepreneurs. Ted Turner, for example, has bought hundreds of thousands of acres in Montana and New Mexico to save them from development and to raise native bison; Doug Tompkins, founder of the Esprit clothing line, in the early 1990s purchased nearly 700,000 acres of some of the planet's most gorgeous land, in southern Chile, to keep it pristine. (Tompkins' tracts included clear blue-green lakes, dense rain forests, towering mountains, and an estimated 35 percent of the remaining rare alerce trees in Chile, some of them as much as 4,000 years old. After long negotiations with Chile's government, he agreed in 1997 to turn the land over to a foundation, which would run it as a park.)

Private philanthropy for Nature has flourished as a consensus has grown that public tactics have not reached their goals. The U.S. Endangered Species Act of 1973, for instance, was hailed in its early years as one of the world's toughest wildlife preservation laws. Yet it failed to turn the tide of extinctions even as the federal government spent billions to protect birds and mammals teetering on their last legs. Critics blamed everything from budget constraints to "biological brinkmanship"—attending to the most critical cases rather than spending more efficiently to prevent species from getting to the critical point. But economist Geoffrey Heal deems the main problem a "Stalinistic" focus on prohibitions instead of incentives. In the early years of the law, especially, landowners were essentially penalized for finding endangered species on their property because what they could do with their land from then on was severely limited. "The way it works is that if you find such a species, your motivation is to destroy it before anyone knows it's there," Heal says. "Shoot, shovel, and shut up," as the saying goes.

In his book *Nature and the Marketplace,* Heal describes an alternative approach that incorporates flexibility and economic incentives into the operation of the ESA. This approach is being tested in efforts to save a remnant population of the red-cockaded woodpecker, an endangered bird that nests in forests owned by International Paper (IP) in Florida. The U.S. Fish and Wildlife Service set a target number of breeding woodpecker pairs on IP land and then stated that the paper company could use its land as it wished—as long as it maintained at least that target number of breeding pairs. Any surplus pairs could be "banked," or used by the company to offset ESA requirements with respect to red-cockaded woodpeckers someplace else. This scheme even allowed IP to sell its "woodpecker credits" to other landowners needing them, much like the cap-and-trade system with sulfur dioxide permits. Woodpecker habitat, in effect, had—*presto!*— become a salable commodity, so much so that IP soon calculated it could sell credits for each breeding pair at about $100,000. Eventually, Heal notes, this could cause the value of land for woodpecker breeding to greatly exceed its value as a source of timber.

This experiment, to be sure, represented a compromise distasteful to many environmentalists. The underlying logic was cynical, after all: preserve woodpeckers here and you may massacre them there. In an ideal world, woodpecker banks wouldn't fly. Yet in the real world of economic pressures and trade-offs, they represent progress. Regulators drew that critical line in the sand, delineating what minimum number of breeding woodpecker pairs was acceptable. Then they introduced flexibility into the conservation game so that IP could do as it wished as long as the number of woodpecker pairs didn't drop below the limit. Finally, the strategy financially rewarded extra-good activities—those resulting in extra breeding pairs. In ways like these, flexibility and incentives may be part of the necessary revolution. Whatever the mechanics of their birth— whether they're inspired by regulations or by business opportunities, as in Wamsley's case—they may significantly expand the places protected for wildlife and wilderness.

Still, there's a deeper, more troubling issue here in the question of which species and places get to enjoy the special status of the red-cockaded woodpecker and the animals at Warrawong. How do we decide which ones we'll fight for? So far, many of the choices have been aesthetically motivated. In the 1980s, economists conducted surveys asking people how much they'd be willing to pay to keep certain natural resources in existence. Whooping cranes cadged $10 per household nationwide, seemingly justifying all the federal money spent on trying to save that threatened bird.

But what about all the uncharismatic invertebrates on which our lives depend? As Edward O. Wilson has put it, "The truth is that we need invertebrates but they don't need us. . . . If invertebrates were to disappear, I doubt that the human species could last more than a few months." So, what about the bees and other insects—known to be in serious decline in some places—that pollinate crops, gardens, and wild places? What about microbes and earthworms, which work their tiny guts out in improving soil fertility, yet whose "services" can't be sold as easily as a photograph of a whooping crane?

Some interesting answers to these questions have come from another Australian innovation, a small firm called BioTrack with the big ambition of "using biodiversity to monitor the environment." In 1997, BioTrack was conceived by conservation biologist Andy Beattie, a professor at Macquarie University, north of Sydney, who claims: "We can tell you if the way you're using land is increasing or decreasing biodiversity. We do that by examining large samples of hundreds of thousands of species—aquatic, terrestrial, marine, plants, animals and some microbes."

Beattie's firm uses sophisticated computer software to calculate the ebb and flow of huge populations of invertebrates in the soil. "I can bar-code an ant," he boasts. Among those who have hired him so far are Australian government agencies seeking to monitor the effects on biodiversity of logging and mining, and managers of habitat restoration efforts like Wamsley (though not including him) who want a scientifically sound way to measure their results. Beattie said BioTrack one day might also help educate ecotourists by providing digital images of invertebrates, lichens, fungi, and seeds, which resort guests could view on desktops in lounges or Web tablets in the field.

For the future, however, Beattie sees his most lucrative opportunities in contracting with big mining companies, farms using pesticides, road builders, and other firms that, he says, are "scared stiff about biodiversity" and the policies emerging on its behalf, and eager to gauge their effects on it. In a broader sense, BioTrack seems to offer a glimmer of salvation for the little-known and unsung creatures overlooked by big, glossy conservation campaigns, the Endangered Species Act, and the ESL sanctuaries.

In fact, however, some scientists suggest that the special attention given to "charismatic" species helps ugly ducklings, too. "Huge numbers of small, obscure, unlovely species shelter under the umbrella of the charismatic," says conservation biologist Stuart Pimm at Columbia University. "About 300 or so in the case of the northern spotted owl. The more aesthetic the species, the more species it likely protects." In this respect, Wamsley's sanctuaries are probably doing a lot more good than one might think.

Still, there's a problem of scale. "In how much of Australia—in how many representative ecosystems—will it be possible to attract investment?" asks the Australian government scientist Brian Walker. "Wamsley's operations are making a contribution; the question is how much, and how significant, in terms of what is needed." To be sure, one could ask the same question of parks and other conservation efforts worldwide: how close have traditional approaches come to stopping the hemorrhage of biodiversity? If the ongoing slew of extinctions is any guide, the answer must be "not very."

Beattie, meanwhile, worries about Wamsley's strategy for a very different reason. He says governments, not entrepreneurs, should be responsible for long-term conservation, contending there's no substitute for national park laws aimed at saving land and species forever. Although laws can be changed, he notes, they still offer better guarantees than private enterprises, which are subject to the vagaries of the market. "While the winds of change in politics are severe, they're nothing to the gales that rock economics," Beattie says. "We now have national parks over a hundred years old, which have survived all kinds of governments. Few companies survive that long, especially with their original goals and principles unchanged."

As it happened, Earth Sanctuaries felt some gales shortly after its stock market debut. Wamsley failed to get underwriting for the stock issue and came up about $1 million short of the modest goal he had previously announced, of raising approximately $7 million. Then, within six months after going public, ESL lost nearly 40 percent of its value. (In the same period, the Australian Stock Exchange average gained 4.4 percent.) "The market has said we're not an acceptable business," Wamsley said, his voice flat, in a telephone interview in January 2001. "The disappointing thing is that the investment community hasn't even tried to figure out what we're doing; we haven't had one broker come here. But it's not their job to change. The marketplace is the marketplace. It's our job to change, and we simply have to do that by making a bigger profit than other companies in Australia."

Wamsley may have been putting the worst face on things, according to David Fleming, portfolio manager for Rothschild Australia Asset Management, which held 1.25 million ESL shares in 2000 but sold off 20 percent of that amount after ESL's listing. Fleming said the decision to sell amounted to profit taking, which he blamed for the bulk of the firm's fall in stock price. "It's no reflection on the company," he said. "ESL is a good investment, and now they're going into a stage where they're getting more commercialized."

ESL profits in 2000 came to $1.26 million, which Wamsley hoped to double in 2001. His main scheme for doing so was to boost revenues through a major company expansion, developing three new Nature reserves on Australia's eastern seaboard, its richest tourist area. The first to open, in 2001, would be the Little River Earth Sanctuary, near Melbourne—larger than Warrawong, at about 2,600 acres, but following the same practices, with "model" habitats and snacks for the wildlife. The model format was a compromise, Wamsley acknowledged. So, of course, was the location of the sanctuary—determined by the potential number of visitors rather than the potential to save local species. "You make compromises every time you get out of bed," Wamsley says. "National parks are a compromise. We'll make all the compromises we need to protect the native animals."

Included in this category, presumably, was also ESL's push for government approval to sell platypus to zoos in Japan and other countries—despite Warrawong tour leaders' disparaging comments on the ways zoos have managed platypus in the past. Fleming, at Rothschild, said such a move could be "very profitable." Wamsley said he expected to receive about $600,000 per platypus. He added that koalas are "far better cared for in Japanese zoos than they are in Australian zoos. I believe the same would hold for platypus," adding that interested Japanese buyers had vowed to spend "enormous amounts" on research into platypus care.

In the meantime, Wamsley was expanding a foundation to research diseases affecting native species and techniques of restoring habitat. But he was proudest of all of ESL's stock market listing, which he called a breakthrough that would be recognized as visionary, just as soon as the investment community took notice. "We've shown that conservation can be a viable concern," he says. "Anyone who has money can do conservation, but our work has been setting an example of a new way to do business. The majority of businesses will do it this way in twenty-five years. They'll simply have to start looking after the earth, or they'll fail as businesses."

In short, he was saying, businesspeople have to start acting more like conservationists to succeed in the long run. Yet Wamsley's more insistent message has been that conservationists have to start acting more like businesspeople if *they* want to survive. His life's story underscores his fierce determination to do the right thing by Australia's native animals. Yet sitting among his kangaroos at Warrawong, Wamsley had boiled down his philosophy like this: "Look," he'd said, "You can say let's change the world, or you can say we've evolved the way we are, and we're a lot of bastards, and let's work with that."

C h a p t e r  *E i g h t*

Costa Rica: Paying
Mother Nature to Multitask

"Partly by default, partly by design, all of nature is now in the process of being domesticated—of coming, or finding itself, under the (somewhat leaky) roof of civilization. Indeed, even the wild now depends on civilization for its survival. Nature's success stories from now on are probably going to look a lot more like the apple's than the panda's or white leopard's. If those last two species have a future, it will be because of human desire; strangely enough, their survival now depends on what amounts to a form of artificial selection. This is the world in which we, along with Earth's other creatures, now must make our uncharted way."

—*Michael Pollan*

DANIEL JANZEN, a University of Pennsylvania biologist who has made it his business to know everything about everything going on in Costa Rica's northwestern Guanacaste Province, was talking to Norman Warren, a local citrus firm manager, back in late 1995, when Warren happened to mention pulp. Warren's company,

Grupo del Oro, had just opened its first juicing plant, with vast, imposing machinery that, as Janzen would later describe it, "eats oranges, pees juice, and shits pulp." *Pulp* is the trade term for peels, seeds, and fiber, and Warren had to figure out some way to get rid of more than 300 tons of it each day. Standard procedure was to invest in a plant to turn the waste into cattle feed, but Del Oro hoped to avoid that. The small company had rigorously cultivated its environmental credentials, niche-marketing organic juice in the United States and Europe. A big, fossil fuel–fired feed producer didn't fit with that image, aside from the fact that it was sure to cost several million dollars.

As Janzen mulled it over, his thoughts turned, as usual, to the Area de Conservación Guanacaste (ACG), the enormous biodiversity reserve that had been his home and major project for the past fifteen years. Abruptly, a smile broke through his wild white beard and his hazel eyes lit up behind slightly crooked wire-rims. "I've got 235,000 species in the ACG," he told Warren. "Some of them are going to like to eat pulp."

That insight was the starting point for one of the strangest, most innovative, and ultimately most controversial business deals ever struck between a corporation and a wilderness. It yielded a contract, signed in August 1998, specifying several "services" to be rendered over a twenty-year period by the conservation area's biodiversity. They included water from the ACG's high, wet "cloud forests," natural pest control by local bugs, and the biodegradation of orange pulp. In return, Del Oro would hand over 3,445 acres of lightly logged forest lying between the ACG and the orchards, valued at $480,000.

The juice firm agreed to pay for these benefits, most of which it had already been getting for free, for the sake of the most original and, for Del Oro, most valuable part of the contract: the disposal of pulp. As agreed, 1,000 truckloads per year of the orange waste would be trucked to the reserve and spread on strategically chosen pastures. There, they would be plowed through by stratiomyid and syrphid fly larvae and then gradually devoured by thousands of species of fungi and bacteria, providing a benefit for which Del Oro would pay with its land, the equivalent of $12 per truckload of pulp. This arrangement promised both to solve Warren's problem and to help Janzen's ACG.

An award-winning tropical scientist who combines Adam Davis' energy with David Brand's imagination and Ron Sims' deal-making savvy, Janzen had long been on the lookout for opportunities to raise money from Nature's labor to funnel back into conservation. His chief laboratory, to which he has devoted most of his career, is the ACG, yet he insists that the methods he has tested there could be models for much of the world. Janzen calls himself a tropical real estate developer; his specialty is coming up with different ways by which an ecosystem can make money to pay for its own preservation and maintenance.

He had come to Costa Rica thirty years earlier to study that country's wealth of biodiversity, specifically the animal–plant interactions that were his specialty. Yet he soon found his raw material vanishing before his eyes. Until the late 1980s, the small country, the size of West Virginia, had one of the world's highest deforestation rates. Oak forests were being demolished for charcoal, and fires were sweeping out of control across their razed remnants. Species were going locally extinct by the week, and the immensely complex webs of relations that make up healthy ecosystems were collapsing. Along the Pacific coast, only a few miserable patches were left of the magnificent dry tropical forest that five centuries earlier had reached from Mexico all the way to the Panama Canal.

That dry deciduous forest was nearly as rich in biodiversity as tropical rain forest, which has more successfully captured the public's imagination, but was even more endangered. The besieged forest's trees include the majestic, wide-canopied *guanacaste,* the province's namesake, and are home to such rare and charismatic creatures as jaguars, howler monkeys, scarlet macaws, toucans, and tapirs. When the Spaniards arrived, tropical dry forest occupied as much or more of the lowlands as did rain forest, yet by the 1980s less than 2 percent of it was still relatively intact. Even so, by Janzen's calculations, about 120,000 species of insects, 60,000 species of fungi, and 9,000 species of plants were still clinging to the decimated wilderness within the ACG.

Janzen's scientific devotion is deep. He loves mice and moths and can talk for hours about caterpillars. In 1978, after two failed marriages—"nice, intelligent women, but they didn't like the Tropics"—he found a soul mate in biologist Winnie Hallwachs, seventeen years his junior, who shares, among other things, his fascination with warble flies (*Dermatobia hominis*), which lay their eggs on the undersides of mosquitoes. While the mosquitoes suck their victim's blood, the warble fly larvae hatch and burrow into the skin of their prey, seeking a comfortable way to spend their infancy. Hallwachs, who like Janzen has spent many years in the Tropics, estimates she has "reared" half a dozen of the flies in her ankles, wrists, and scalp. She once let a Cornell University camera team film a larva emerging from her arm, which, of course, for most people would be a rather upsetting process. But, as she explained, "For both Dan and me, there are certain kinds of curiosity that are really part of the wonder of life, and can way override the kind of reactions most people would have."

All the same, what Janzen witnessed in Costa Rica made it intolerable for him to remain in the role of someone who, as he said, "would study the flames while Rome burns." He felt as if he were watching people burn the Library of Congress during a fuel oil shortage. Ornery by nature, he became more so. He did what few scientists do: he paused from his studies to, quite literally, fight the fires. Together with Hallwachs and a team of Costa Rican collaborators, he lobbied the government and raised the money to expand Guanacaste Province's tiny Santa Rosa National Park, then a barely surviving island amid the phantoms of the dry forests, into a 580-square-mile land and sea refuge from the pressures of the twenty-first century. The effort, eventually involving a full 2 percent of Costa Rica's land area, would in time become the world's largest tropical restoration project and an inspiration for others seeking innovative ways to finance environmental rescue missions.

The initial pieces of the project included lowland dry forests, upland rain forests and cloud forests, and reefs, rivers, and beaches, all with some protection status. The remarkably ambitious plan was to combine them into one vast area by buying all the barren tracts of degraded pastureland that lay between them. Then the newly protected areas would be revived to their former richness as the forests gradually regenerated. In the lowland dry forests, the largest part of the ACG, that meant, first of all, controlling the fires. In this task, Janzen faced a stubborn enemy common to conservation efforts the world over: non-native pasture grasses, known in Costa Rica as *jaragua* and imported from Africa by ranchers in 1943. In more than half of the reserve, the *jaragua* fueled the fires, traditionally set by farmers and ranchers, that annually burned through the area. Janzen needed a way to kill the grasses and nourish the earth underneath. That's where the orange pulp came in. He realized it might just accomplish both tasks.

In 1996, he set up an experiment. He asked Del Oro to deposit 100 truckloads of pulp on a one-hectare plot of pasture a couple of miles downwind from a patch of forest. Within eighteen months, just as Janzen had hoped, the *jaragua* had been smothered, leaving behind dark, moist earth. Broad-leaved herbs and trees whose seeds had been blown in from the forest were already sprouting in abundance. Janzen was sure the pulp had degraded much more quickly than it might have in other landscapes because of the great variety of species in the ACG available to tackle the work.

Both he and Del Oro's managers were elated by the results. Janzen had obtained a new tool against the *jaragua* and the promise of a valuable new forest parcel, without having to draw on the ACG's beleaguered budget. For Del Oro, the arrangement meant not only avoiding a major new expense but also building up its environmental credentials, which were key to its financial survival. The small firm, with sales of just $25 million per year, was competing with giants from Florida and Brazil by using the minimum of agricultural chemicals and pitching its juice to the most environmentally conscious consumers. Its efforts had already won it the Rainforest Alliance's ECO-O.K. label, and Del Oro was the world's only citrus company certified as being in compliance with the environmental management criteria of the International Organization for Standardization (ISO), a prestigious voluntary association.

As Del Oro expected, the unique biodegradation scheme won applause from environmentalists. But soon afterward, a competing citrus company, TicoFrut, struck a fatal political blow. In noisy appeals to the government, press, and congress, TicoFrut said Del Oro's pulp disposal arrangement was sullying a national park. The complaints led to an uproar that ended with the government canceling the project.

Janzen contended that TicoFrut's claim was groundless, arising from envy of Del Oro's novel competitive edge. "It just proves the worth of the services," he said with undiminished zeal in February 2001 during a bone-crunching two-day tour of the ACG in his Toyota four-by-four.

The comment typified the way Janzen looks at wilderness. His Costa Rica years have made him a fierce champion of the idea of wild places in effect paying for their own survival in societies that tend to think of them as costly luxuries. Use it or lose it, he argues. Use it, moreover, in as many ways as possible, as long as they aren't destructive. Most of the time, no one service of Nature pays enough to protect an entire ecosystem.

This notion of making wilderness work for a living repels other equally devout conservationists. "I would describe it as use it *and* lose it," says John Terborgh, codirector of the Center for Tropical Conservation at Duke University. Terborgh worries that, with the exception of ecotourism, many "sustainable" activities, such as selective timber harvests and cultivation of nontimber forest products, in fact do great damage. Among other risks, he says, they tend to attract more people to the new sources of income until the resource ends up being overused and often completely destroyed. In his book *Requiem for Nature,* Terborgh describes a series of efforts to combine conservation and development in Southeast Asia, West Africa, and elsewhere that ended up only accelerating forest destruction. Condemning the "mirage of sustainable development," he argues instead for enforced protection of parks as the last bastion of biodiversity. He even suggests a full "internationalization of nature protection" under the auspices of the United Nations. "If peacekeeping has been widely accepted as an international function, why not nature keeping?" he asks.

But Janzen contends that Terborgh's complaints don't apply to his specific experiments in the ACG. And he holds fast to his utilitarian perspective. Humans are hard-wired to cultivate Nature, something we've done since the Pleistocene epoch, Janzen says, adding that in the future, "tropical wildlands and their biodiversity will survive in perpetuity only through their integration into human society." Not all of wilderness can be saved, he insists, only those parts that have specific value to people. He hates the word *park* because he thinks it restricts options. Instead, he has coined the word *gardenification,* implying, as he explains, "you invest in Nature, use it, think of it as having an owner and a future, as producing goods and services for the country, rather than as a frontier to exploit or destroy."

"Attempts to conserve biodiversity for its own sake just make local society mad," Janzen barked as the Toyota bumped furiously down a dirt road, in the brook-no-argument tones of his pre–Vietnam War U.S. Army Military Police years. Far ahead to the east, the 1,500-meter peaks of the Orosi and Cacao Volcanoes could be seen, wreathed in clouds and capped by dense forest. Janzen's hands flew around the steering wheel for emphasis. "We've got to get rid of the Smokey-the-Bear, guard-the-gold idea of a park," he said.

Janzen demonstrated his various proposed alternatives on that two-day guided exploration of the ACG, with stops along the way to tour Del Oro's factory and eat beans and rice at a new thatched-roof restaurant aimed at visiting ecotourists. By the year 2000, the conservation area had long been producing revenues, primarily through tourism. Some 50,000 travelers, most of them foreigners, were visiting each year, paying $6 gate fees collected by the government. Besides that, Janzen estimated that visiting scientists, himself included, had recently been adding about $600,000 per year to the local economy, some of it paid directly to the ACG in return for lodging and research facilities and some as salaries to resident research assistants.

These, of course, were obvious winners: gardenification's low-hanging fruit. Janzen had been involved in many more innovative plans, most prominently a 1991 "bioprospecting" contract, which he helped write, between the giant drug firm Merck & Company and the Instituto Nacional de Biodiversidad (INBio), which inventories Costa Rica's biological wealth. In the groundbreaking contract, Merck agreed to pay more than $1 million over a two-year period for samples of chemical extracts from plants, animals, and microbes as well as royalties to INBio and the government if any new drug based on the samples were to prove commercially successful. The first materials came from the ACG, and the agreement with Merck has since been extended twice.

The commercial potential of Costa Rica's wealth of flora and fauna was becoming increasingly obvious in the years before the first Merck contract. Worldwide, at least forty-seven major drugs had come from rain-forest plant species, with an accumulated net worth of $147 billion. "We don't have gold. We don't have petroleum. But we do have biodiversity—green gold," Roger Blanco, an early ACG official, told author William Allen, as recounted in *Green Phoenix,* his book about the early years of the ACG's development.

Following its contract with Merck, INBio made deals with several other foreign firms seeking new antibiotics, fragrances, and natural pesticides derived from tropical plants. The first glowing headlines about these contracts, in Costa Rica and elsewhere, raised expectations of instant wealth from developing countries' rain forests—expectations that still hadn't been met by the millennium's end. But sobered enthusiasm for the concept persisted. In 1996, for instance, officials from Yellowstone National Park visited INBio and the ACG to learn from their experience. One year later, they announced that a San Diego corporation had agreed to pay for drugs or chemicals derived from the national park's resources, with revenues to help pay for conservation.

Pleased as he was by these developments, Janzen eventually grew frustrated by how few revenues from bioprospecting were directly funding conservation. "There is no big mystery in the technology," he has written of the art of bioprospecting. "The mystery lies in how to construct the income stream so that some portion of the prospecting profits are paid back to the wildland garden itself." Pointing at a cup of coffee one morning, he said, "I'll tell you what this is. It's the world's most popular rain-forest drug." Coffee, in fact, is the world's second-ranking commodity in monetary terms, right after petroleum. With trillions of cups of coffee brewed each year, Janzen claimed, "A one-cent tax on each cup worldwide would fund all of tropical conservation forever. Now, no one is going to succeed in imposing that tax . . . but if the bioprospecting contracts are written right, it'll be there for the next cup of coffee to come along."

Shortly after his experiments with bioprospecting, Janzen turned to another technique for marketing Nature's labor: the sale of carbon credits. The concept caught his imagination about the same time David Brand, in Australia, was working on the first carbon-rights legislation. In the early 1990s, he developed a plan to sell credits from Guanacaste's fledgling forests and aggressively courted General Public Utilities (GPU), an energy firm based in New Jersey that was among the first big U.S. companies to start acquiring carbon sequestration projects.

Dennis O'Regan, in charge of GPU's environmental auditing, said he met with Janzen in the fall of 1995 to review his proposal, which to his surprise turned out to be a multimillion-dollar project. "His price for a ton of carbon was very, very high," O'Regan said. "We were looking for a dollar a ton, while his estimates were on the

order of four. . . . Basically, he was appealing to our altruism to protect Costa Rican rain forest at a price four or five times what we
were willing to pay." O'Regan praised Janzen's "creativity" but said,
"I had a hard time getting $100,000 out of my company. We basically
told him no thanks."

Janzen countered that market prices for carbon by 2000 were
between $2.50 and $6.50 per ton and that companies that bought in
early gained valuable experience. But by 2001, he'd abandoned plans
to try to sell Guanacaste's carbon credits. He'd decided that its water
was a much more promising commodity and was working with officials from the Ministry of Environment and Energy on a plan to have
the ACG start charging tens of thousands of local farmers for the
water generation services provided by the cloud forests on its three
volcanoes.

Cloud forests are full of interesting sounds—from buzzes, shrieks,
and howls to soft peeps and melodious songs—but most of all the
sound of constant dripping. Dark green leaves crowd the spaces
between mossy trunks and stems in a confusion of shapes and sizes,
but with one design feature in common: the drip tip. The leaves'
enormous surface area condenses moisture out of the air and feeds
it, via the drip tips, to the soft and spongy forest floor. In the ACG,
cloud forests capture moisture as it blows inland from the ocean, storing and gradually releasing the water into the river system. The
ACG's cloud forests make rivers flow abundantly through the hot,
dry season and feed crop production far away in a vast, arid lowland
region in the rain shadow of the volcanoes.

Much of the prosperity of the lowland farming region owes to
the unpaid services of the cloud forests. Janzen's plan would recycle
part of the revenue stream flowing from agriculture back to its
source. His plan was proceeding, even though it was sure to be
unpopular locally. Water was still extremely cheap throughout Costa
Rica at the turn of the millennium. Nonetheless, officials recognized
that the ACG's water resources were bound to increase in value, particularly if global warming heated and dried the region. Janzen pre-

dicted that as the upland forest expanded, watersheds would be restored for eleven major rivers, creating a "water factory." He wanted to nail down a source of revenue for future factory maintenance. "The basic philosophy is no free goods, and protect the source," he said.

The more unconventional the strategy, the more Janzen liked it. At one point during the tour of the ACG, he braked his Toyota on a hilltop overlooking a small, green stand of new trees in a pasture. "These are gmelina," he announced. "They're fast-growing Southeast Asian plantation trees, and they provide most of the world's cardboard. They're anathema to most tropical conservationists because so often primary forests have been cleared to make way for them. Remember Ludwig?" He meant Daniel Ludwig, the U.S. shipping tycoon who'd bought a plot of Brazilian Amazon jungle larger than the state of Connecticut and deforested nearly 300,000 acres to plant gmelina and pine. Ludwig went bankrupt and sold out in 1982, but Janzen dreamed of success with a much smaller project. "The Nature Conservancy had a massive heart attack when I brought this up," he said, laughing, as he jumped down from the truck. "But then they saw the sense in it."

Janzen believed that gmelina could be a powerful tool in his effort to regenerate upland rain forest in the ACG. The tricks to restoring dry forest were comparatively simple: stop the fires and suppress the *jaragua* fueling them, and the natural process of succession to forest would immediately get under way, with wind and animals transporting seeds into the open pasture. Recovering the moist upland forest, on the other hand, posed more daunting obstacles. The seeds of most rain-forest trees are not dispersed by wind, and the ACG's moist uplands had few pasture-loving animals—like the lowland's magpie jays, coatis, and coyotes—to carry in seeds from the forest. Moreover, most young rain-forest trees can't survive in open pasture; they typically require shade to thrive. Topping it off, in order to survive, all the trees needed certain types of soil fungi to bind to their roots and supply them with nutrients. Although fun-

gal spores were blowing all over in the flat lowlands, the cloud-
enshrouded mountainous uplands had lighter winds, making the
chance fairly remote that both the seed of a rain-forest tree and a
spore of its special fungal partner would arrive at the same spot at
the same time.

The gmelina, as Janzen saw it, might kick-start the natural process
of succession to rain forest, potentially helping to solve a major problem not just in the ACG but also potentially elsewhere in the Tropics. The trees were easy to establish in open pasture and would fairly
quickly offer a canopy whose shade would kill the *jaragua* in as little
as two years and let native rain-forest plants and their hidden partners gradually establish themselves and flourish. "I happened to walk
by some plantation trees a few years ago and saw all this stuff growing underneath, and a lightbulb went off," he recalled. Subsequently,
he flew to The Nature Conservancy's headquarters in Virginia to try
to calm his conservationist colleagues with a briefing on the subject.
Helped by a $100,000 grant from the Michigan-based Wege Foun-
dation, Janzen began in late 1999 planting gmelina on about 125 acres
of pasture in the ACG. After as little as eight years, he said, he'd be
able to sell the logs, depending on market prices, and kill the stumps
with herbicides, leaving behind the start of a young rain forest. His
results thus far were encouraging.

Although Janzen contends that his forest restoration and revenue
models might easily be adapted to other places, his innovations in
Costa Rica arise from a unique serendipity of politics, biology, and
psychology. In few, if any, other parts of the world does the same
combination exist: a country so eager to prove its environmental credentials, such a vast store of biodiversity to draw on, and so audacious, persistent, and well-connected a guest. Over time, Janzen's
unorthodox approaches, aggressive ambition, and general lack of tact
have alienated various government officials. Nonetheless, he has
managed to wield extraordinarily enduring influence, especially considering his outsider status. "He's the hardest worker I know, and he's
Costa Rica's biggest salesman," said former minister of environment

and energy Alvaro Umaña, a founding father of the nation's environmental policies.

As the century turned, Costa Rica was a global showcase of environmental leadership. It had started out with the advantage of holding 5 percent of the world's biodiversity on less than 0.04 percent of the world's land. The reason it had managed to maintain such lushness was the same reason many Costa Ricans see irony in their country's name—"rich coast." "Costa Rica's secret is that it has exceedingly crummy real estate," Janzen told us. "Tall slopes; not great soil; only about 9 percent of the land is arable. And above all, very little gold, and very few Indians to enslave. Nothing to interest the Spanish, so they moved on."

Heavy European immigration didn't begin until the late 1800s, and the newcomers then were less rapacious than their sixteenth-century predecessors. The country has since been so blessed by peace and prosperity, compared with its war-ravaged neighbors, that it has become known as Latin America's Switzerland. No small part of this reputation is due to a tradition of relatively enlightened government policies, which included abolition of the military in the 1940s, provision of free and compulsory education to both boys and girls, and, in later decades, the establishment of environmental protection as a national priority. An announced national goal at the new millennium was to conserve a full 25 percent of the country as wildlands (compared with about 10 percent in the United States) within eleven declared "conservation areas."

In perhaps its greatest environmental success, Costa Rica has enacted an unusual environmental tax on fossil fuels, intended, among other things, to fund payments to landowners in selected areas who agree not to cut down their trees and to restore forest on land that has been cleared. The groundbreaking 1996 law allowing for those payments, Ley Forestal No. 7575, was set up to compensate thousands of property owners for "environmental services" provided each year by forests they maintain or reestablish on their land. The services include carbon sequestration, watershed protection, and biodiversity resources. Considering the depressed state of Costa Rica's cattle industry, the payments, of as much as $20 per acre per year, have been high enough to be attractive. (The program nonetheless suffered some problems in its early years, including poor monitoring of participants and suspected spotty compliance. But by 2001, there was new hope of improvement as Costa Rica's government received a $32 million loan from the World Bank and an $8 million grant from the Global Environment Facility to increase the number of participants and ensure their legitimacy.)

With such efforts in mind, Costa Rica's officials have bragged that their nation is a world model for conservation. Umaña conceded that the country is still losing biodiversity, but he added, "We're clearly the closest in the world to turning the tide on that." That reputation has brought definite payoffs, particularly in the tourism industry, which in 1993 surpassed bananas as the country's leading revenue source. Thanks in large part to Costa Rica's popularity among Nature buffs, tourism by the year 2000 was the country's second largest source of income (after Intel's silicon-chip manufacturing), drawing 1 million tourists and approximately $1 billion each year. At the same time, as "green development" became more fashionable among international banks and donors, Costa Rica's credentials attracted a healthy share of funding for development projects. Indeed, Janzen's colleagues have criticized him for having it too easy, saying his experiments couldn't have gotten past the blueprint stage anywhere else. Janzen counters that it was important to start where the innovations had the best chance of success, noting, "The Wright brothers didn't pick a blizzard in Minnesota in January to fly their first airplane."

Janzen grew up in Minneapolis, the son of a director of the U.S. Fish and Wildlife Service. At fourteen, his fascination with a butterfly exhibition at the public library decided the course of his future career; later, he went on a butterfly-gathering vacation through Mexico with his family in their Buick and grew addicted to Spanish and spicy food. He first came to Costa Rica in 1963 as a student in a traveling biology class financed by the National Science Foundation. He was taken by the country's sheer amount of wilderness—at the time, half of it was still forested—its rich stores of species, and the warmth of its people.

The previous year, a chance encounter in Mexico had turned Janzen into an ecologist, eventually also launching his reputation as a world-class scientist. "I was walking down a trail in Veracruz and saw a beetle land on an acacia bush," he recalled. "An ant approached, and the beetle flew away. I looked closer and saw that there were ants all over the bush." He studied the situation further and eventually confirmed that the stinging ants were protecting the acacia, which provided their nectar and home, in a striking cooperation. It was one of a continuing set of insights that in 1984 won him a Crafoord Prize, the Nobel Prize of ecology and evolutionary biology. Janzen continued his scientific research in Costa Rica, eventually settling in Santa Rosa National Park. Spending half of each year teaching a double load at the University of Pennsylvania, he has also managed to produce hundreds of scholarly papers and immerse himself in a project, funded by the National Science Foundation, to identify all of the ACG's approximately 9,000 caterpillars of butterflies and large moths, as well as their food sources and parasites. (In 2001, after ten years of this labor, his collection, as posted by him on the Internet, numbered 2,500 species.)

Janzen kept up his prolific output even as he found himself increasingly caught up in more immediate issues of local sociology and politics. In early 1985, Alvaro Ugalde, a longtime acquaintance who had become director of Costa Rica's park services, asked him to report on the environmental effects of 1,500 gold miners who had invaded the rain forests of Corcovado National Park, in the southern part of the country. The government, in desperation, was at that time preparing a paramilitary operation to remove the prospectors. After one day in the park, Janzen found it easy to answer Ugalde's environmental impact question. Intensive placer mining and unrestrained squatting were trashing the rivers and forests. But he then took several days to study the miners themselves and discovered they were

not the impoverished career criminals he'd been told they were—
many were middle-class; at least one was a corporate accountant.
Furthermore, they fully believed they were legitimately making use
of a "land with no owner" or, more precisely, no visible social presence. In the wake of Janzen's report, the government suspended its
plans for force and instead set an unambiguous deadline for the miners to leave. This proved to be the solution: one year later, only 298
of them remained to be arrested and peacefully removed. And Janzen
had more confirmation of his theory that wilderness had to have an
owner and be useful in some way to people in order to ensure its
own survival.

Another formative experience for Janzen came just a few months
later, when he and Hallwachs were invited by Australia's government
to spend several weeks in its sparsely populated but richly forested
northwest region and give advice on how the country should make
use of the area. They ended up recommending a combination of
long-term, low-yield forestry, ecotourism, research, and conservation, realizing, as they did, that the same kind of package might prove
to be the solution for the beleaguered Santa Rosa National Park.
"We had never thought before about how to make Santa Rosa be
'used,' and 'have an owner,'" Janzen recalled. They returned to Pennsylvania, preoccupied by events in their adopted home. Costa Rica's
economy was in the dumps, partly as a result of a global drop in coffee prices, and in the Guanacaste region the cattle trade, once a major
source of income, was suffering. As the cattle were removed from
pastures in and adjacent to the park, the *jaragua* was growing higher
and fire danger was increasing. Making matters worse, the park's
administrative costs were rising, with no corresponding increase in its
government budget.

In September 1985, Janzen and Hallwachs drew up an unsolicited
plan for what they then called Guanacaste National Park. The basic
idea was to create an area large enough for the long-term survival of
local plant and animal species still clinging to life in Santa Rosa
National Park and, as Janzen put it, "to absorb human activities."

Janzen hoped to do this by connecting the park with two others in a way that would allow animals to migrate during the dry season from the lowland dry forest to the upland rain forests and cloud forests to the east. This, he said, would be the only preserved intersection between the two major land-based habitat types in Mesoamerica, if not in all the Neotropics. Early the next year, Oscar Arias Sánchez, whose fame as a peacemaker came to overshadow his extraordinary environmental achievements, took office as Costa Rica's president and rapidly approved the conservation plan—providing it wouldn't require any government funds. Janzen and Hallwachs became unpaid foster parents for the future ACG, which would ultimately extend over more than 279,000 acres of land and 101,000 acres of sea.

Working with Nature Conservancy employees and a team of Costa Rican collaborators, they raised more than $17 million for the project. Besides buying land, the funds made the ACG the world's first fully endowed park. Rather than rely on annual appropriations, as had been usual practice, the conservation area's administrators could pay expenses out of $1.4 million in annual interest from funds housed at a Costa Rican nongovernmental organization called the National Park Foundation. Together with as much as $300,000 per year in income from Janzen's various schemes, that took care of most of the major bills from forest restoration, maintenance of ecotourism facilities, and salaries for 107 people, including caretakers, firefighters, teachers, guides, administrators, restoration staff members, and field researchers.

Creating the endowment was an adventure in itself. Most of the money came from a landmark debt-for-Nature swap in which Janzen, Umaña, and other Costa Rican leaders, aided by Salomon Brothers debt traders, leveraged a $3.5 million donation from Sweden to buy $24.5 million worth of Costa Rican commercial debt from around the world at huge discounts. Costa Rica's central bank then ended up paying 70 percent of the debt value, or nearly $17 million, into the ACG account at the National Park Foundation, with the understanding that the revenues generated would help pay for the conservation area. In a gesture of gratitude to the traders, who had worked without commission, Janzen later persuaded a friend, Ian Gauld, a taxonomist at The Natural History Museum in London (formerly The British Museum), to name several wasp species found in the park after them. *Eruga gutfreundi,* for instance, was named for John H. Gutfreund, then Salomon's chief executive officer. (One detail mitigated that honor: the wasp in question is a parasite that lays its eggs on the back of a "money spider," a species that some people believe brings good fortune.)

Purchasing land to expand the new conservation area took about five years. After protracted negotiations with more than 100 owners, Janzen, who had no formal title or authority for this task, arranged for the National Park Foundation to buy approximately 24,000 acres of low-grade ranchland. Fortuitously for the ACG, the decline in the cattle trade had decimated property values, and many owners were anxious to sell. Janzen negotiated prices as low as $31 per acre for some plots.

(One parcel with a particularly complicated history cost rather more. South of the Santa Elena Mountains, surrounded by ACG land, was a 39,000-acre property formerly owned by Nicaraguan dictator Anastasio Somoza and then sold to a group of Americans in the 1970s. With the permission of Oscar Arias Sánchez' predecessor, President Luis Alberto Monge, Lieutenant Colonel Oliver North's operatives in 1986 had leased part of this property to build an airstrip to supply the U.S.-backed Contra rebels who were fighting Nicaragua's Sandinista government. But Arias Sánchez had other ideas, and soon after coming to power he closed the airstrip. Several years later, the government ended up having to negotiate with one of the property owners, a wealthy North Carolina textile manufacturer, to integrate it into the park. The case was finally settled in the year 2000, with Costa Rica paying the businessman $410 per acre.)

In the midst of these deals, Janzen and his collaborators had started trying to restore the ACG's degraded lowland to dry forest, using seeds from the existing forest fragments. It was a startlingly new idea in 1985, when many conservation groups were bombarding the public with the message that a forest, once gone, is gone forever. "I was told donors couldn't handle both messages," Janzen scoffed. He ignored the warning, finished raising his money, and set about tackling the fires that were raging in the area.

Blazes had been frequent during the dry months of January to June, often ignited by people burning their fields and pastures in a centuries-old land management technique. Janzen allotted one-fifth of the ACG's budget to fire control, recruiting and paying local residents as caretakers and firefighters. Eager employees came from the former colonies of squatters, many of whom had invested the money Janzen paid them for their land in homes in small communities near the ACG. "I told them: no fires. You figure it out, and if you can't do it, we'll hire someone else," Janzen said. He also brought in cows, which he called "biotic mowing machines," to reduce the fuel load from the tall *jaragua*. He cultivated loyalty with paychecks and esprit de corps. "The biology of restricting fires became the sociology of having someone out watching for fires at 2:00 A.M. on Easter Sunday," he explained. He got funds for two fire lookout stations and two tractors with water tanks. By 2001, the ACG fire control program was putting out thirty to fifty fires per year, by Janzen's count.

Other ACG workers showed similar commitment to their jobs. Lucia Rios, a slender woman of thirty, bought her own house with savings from her salary after working for eight years as one of Janzen's parataxonomists, the assistants who help him gather specimens. It was a remarkable feat, considering that Rios was single and had only a sixth-grade education. But she clearly loved her work, and Janzen noted she had been the first to identify several caterpillar species. "We used to kill caterpillars before, on the farm," she said, smiling, "but now I think they're pretty."

Like many other investments in ecosystem assets, restoration of the ACG promised to yield some of its greatest benefits in the future, decades and even centuries away. Preoccupied with the project's

long-term security, Janzen has nurtured local loyalties with offers of
not only well-paying employment and job training for adults but also
"bioliteracy" courses for children. One of his first works as ACG foster parent was to design a curriculum that in 2001 was reaching all
2,500 children attending forty-two schools within some thirteen
miles of the ACG. A full one-fifth of the ACG budget is devoted to
the courses, including the salaries of eight teachers and the cost of
two buses for field trips. "We'll take fourth-, fifth-, and sixth-graders
out into the forest, put bandanas on their eyes, and have them identify ten sounds," he said. "Or we'll have them go out and find ten different fruits. It's natural history, not biology. When you're in the
fourth grade, you don't need to know about environmental legislation. You need to know what frogs do when it rains."

Karin Viquez, the nine-year-old daughter of a local hotel owner,
got the message. "We went to see the swamp, and saw crabs, and
learned about the life of a turtle," she said, climbing off a pink scooter
to talk. "We learned you have to take care of nature because in a few
years, if we don't, there may not be any animals around."

At the end of the two-day tour, Janzen returned to the small, hap-
hazardly converted storage building where he lives with Hallwachs
for six months of the year. Its determined humility suggests one reason he has managed to wield such influence for so long in his
adopted country. He owns no land himself, he says proudly, and
decided against building his own house in the ACG so as not to pro-
voke jealousy. He and Hallwachs live on about $22,000 of his
$100,000 annual salary from the University of Pennsylvania, spend-
ing the rest on the ACG. Their home amounts to about 400 square
feet, which Janzen said is shared with two species of bats and four
species of rodents, besides the dozens of varieties of ants, moths, spi-
ders, and mosquitoes claiming the space. Most of it is devoted to an
office crammed with the detritus of their shared obsessions. Scattered
across two desks was a blueprint for a field laboratory to study caterpillar guts, a receipt for tire repair, a glass bottle containing a broken
crocodile egg, and a small jar of fingernail polish for gluing small

insects to pins. Old credentials from scientific conventions and a half-used pack of Mini-Stix hamster snacks for Espinita, their pet porcupine, were pinned to clotheslines drooping from the ceiling. A black umbrella hung upside down at the top of one of the lines to catch a leak. "It's peaceful. We like it," Janzen murmured in the dim lamplight.

Janzen, as a rule, spends as little time brooding over the past as he does arranging creature comforts at home. "I've got so many things going that if one project tanks, I just move on to another one," he said. Even so, in early 2001 he was still mourning the failed promise of one of his favorites: the Del Oro deal, in shatters by then for more than a year. It had gotten the most acclaim and seemed so particularly full of promise, so articulate an example of the innovative multitasking Janzen champions. And its demise had been so brutal.

"It exploded in our face" was the way Mike Baker, Norman Warren's successor, explained it. Baker called the deal's birth "groundbreaking if not totally unique. From all points of view—ethical, environmental, from every point but the commercial battlefield point of view—it was a great thing to do." Yet in the grueling controversy that followed the initial hopeful press conference, Del Oro had been forced to pay about $100,000 in legal and public relations fees before it surrendered, withdrawing the contract in August 1999. At that point, the company replaced the biodegradation with a composting system, using the pulp on its own groves. The changeover cost $500,000 to set up and was expected to cost another $500,000 per year to operate.

Government environmental officials said they ultimately rejected ACG's disposal system because of a procedural problem: Costa Rica's Ministry of Natural Resources, Energy and Mines had failed to get the required approval of the comptroller general. But Alvaro Umaña, the former minister of environment and energy, agreed with Janzen that the real problem was rooted in commercial competition. "The science got lost in the noise," Umaña said. This version of events was disputed by TicoFrut's chief executive officer, Carlos Odio, who alleged that competition wasn't an issue. He said he'd made his complaint because Del Oro's "dumping" of pulp risked spreading disease to the country's citrus groves if transported by birds and trucks. All the same, two U.S. citrus experts consulted for the purpose of this chapter called such a threat minimal.

Reflecting on his ups and downs with Costa Rican officials over the past few decades, Janzen suggested that the orange pulp conflict illustrated the profound changes that most developing countries' societies must make to allow conservation to endure. He suggested the deeper problem was that the Del Oro scheme, and the ACG's success as a model for local development, challenged Costa Rica's very system of power—which is why, he suspected, officials never came to his aid.

"This is not an undeveloped country. It's a matter of how it's developed, who gets the benefits," he said. "This is like East Germany. Everything's state-run. It's an extremely bureaucratized state, a very, very centralized system. We want to move it into a democratic system, with power moving out into the countryside. But if we say we ought to have democratization, there'll be some people who'll want to retain the structure they have, the one putting their kids through school. If you want to take that away, it's extremely disruptive."

Warming to his topic, Janzen went on to indicate that some government officials viewed him personally as a threat. "When you're just out in the woods as a biologist studying monkeys, you're not as aggressive to them and them to you," he said. "But if you start messing with the system, you get into lawsuits, murders, accidents, and mothers-in-law. It's called starting a peasant revolution. And what do they do to people who start peasant revolutions? They burn them at the stake."

In reality, Janzen seemed in little danger of being executed anytime soon. Rather, he was cheerfully looking forward to the swearing in of a new national administration in May 2002. He was hopeful that any of the candidates would be more supportive of environmental innovation, as, indeed, officials had been in the past.

He said he even held out hope that the pulp experiment might someday be revived.

On a baking afternoon, he took visitors to the site of "Modulo One," the first biodegradation experiment. Looking out from under his bush hat with fatherly pride, he pointed past a field of whispering, six-foot tall *jaragua* to the small, dark patch of ground where five years earlier the pulp had started to restore the soil. To untutored eyes, it might not seem impressive. A single, tall, yellow-flowered *Cochlospermum* tree had staked out some ground, along with a few small shrub species. Yet Janzen was clearly envisioning the forest-to-be. "These seeds have been blown in by the wind. But there are thousands of other seeds, all in the guts of animals out there, in the magpie jays, woodpeckers, bats, and long-tailed grackles," he said. In a few years, or maybe decades, he expected, the dry-forest stalwarts would emerge: the *guanacaste,* the amber-producing *guapinol,* and the *chicle,* a source of chewing gum. Gradually, an image formed in the listener's mind of shady canopies full of whistling cicadas and jewel-colored birds above a forest floor rich with mammals and microbes. Never mind that it would take at least 200 years, perhaps 500, before the forest would truly resemble its untouched ancestors. Janzen had the determination, if not the life span, to wait.

As night fell, Janzen sat in a rocking chair on the terrace of a hotel near his home, watching orange-fronted parakeets, lovely green birds with long pointed tails, dart across the violet and orange sky. He was laying out his case that the best thing to do with one's life was to "choose a big lump of biodiversity" and defend it. Even though so many factors that had led to his triumphs in Costa Rica were unique, he insisted it was possible elsewhere in the Tropics to find creative ways to fund forest restoration and maintenance, and that in any case, it was urgent to try. "I've really wondered why no one else seems to be doing what Winnie and I are doing. People say there's only one Dan Janzen, but that's bullshit," he said. "Governments should start advertising. Like Guatemala. It could say, 'We have this area, the Petén, and we need help.' It could try to flush people out of the woodwork, scientists looking for the most useful thing to do. It wouldn't be turning the area over to anyone: it would be a friendly partner. There are lots of big lumps that need help: consider Honduras, Mexico, Madagascar. . . ."

He looked out across the dry landscape, toward the darkening deep green forests clinging to the volcanoes looming far ahead. "Down the line, face it, you're going to have just a few lumps left in an ocean of Sacramento Valleys," Janzen said, referring to central California's flat, featureless agricultural region. "Those lumps need someone to invest in them and figure out how they can be loved by society around them. Those lumps need tender loving care."

Teresópolis: The Spinning Motor

"No problem can be solved from the same
consciousness that created it."

—*Albert Einstein*

THE SMALL WHITE VAN swung along the curves of the
Teresópolis–Friburgo road, 4,000 feet above the sweltering valley of
Rio de Janeiro. From a window in the back, Dan Nepstad gazed out
at the stark, cylindrical mountain peaks known as the Dedos de
Deus, "God's fingers," rising from a coastal forest brightened by deep
purple bougainvillea and yellow-blooming *canafista* trees. The highway to the mountain resort towns was newly paved, the Southern
Hemisphere autumn air fresh, and the scenery postcard quality. Yet
barely an hour earlier, the van had passed by some of the continent's
ugliest slums, the stinking, unpaved shantytowns of northern Rio.

Nepstad was well versed in Brazil's sharp contrasts. A tall, taciturn
ecologist who divided his time between the Woods Hole Research
Center in Massachusetts and Brazil's Environmental Research Institute of the Amazon, he'd been spending an average of half of every
year since 1984 in the port city of Belém. On that late March morning in 2001, he was traveling to the Serra do Mar coastal range above

189

Teresópolis to attend the third international meeting of the Katoomba Group. He had argued for it to be held in Brazil because he wanted his colleagues to understand the dilemmas he dealt with every day. The country had long confused visitors with its two contrary faces: the charming, modern, tame one, witnessed mostly by tourists and a small fraction of its 160 million citizens, and the flip side, a frantic rush from poverty that was corrupting its cities and destroying its tropical wilderness.

Nowhere was this second, desperate face more evident than in Brazil's Amazon region, where Nepstad worked and where the hunger for advancement was leading to the yearly loss of nearly 5 million acres of the planet's largest rain forest. As custodian of the bulk of that resource, Brazil was under pressure to preserve what much of the rest of the world viewed as a global treasure for maintaining biodiversity and climate stability. Yet in dramatic contrast to official attitudes in Costa Rica, where Dan Janzen had been able to launch his innovative schemes for conservation, successive Brazilian governments had failed to share that perspective. More than 20 million people were already living in the Amazon region, which for Brazil was a kind of American West in the days of Manifest Destiny.

Even President Fernando Henrique Cardoso, a former diplomat who was still extremely sensitive to international opinion, had made it clear that Brazil wouldn't treat the forest as a sanctuary. To the contrary, that year the government was proceeding with a major new road-building project known as Avança Brasil. The implications for the Amazon were grave. A Smithsonian Institution study released shortly before the Teresópolis meeting predicted that if the project were to go forward, associated development would destroy or damage as much as 42 percent of the forest by 2020, with pristine areas reduced to less than 5 percent. Nepstad, alarmed, had calculated that the carbon emissions released by potential resulting deforestation could equal as much as half of those that would be saved by the most faithful adherence to the targets set by the Kyoto Protocol. Yet much more powerful incentives than that ominous prediction would be needed to persuade Brazil to seek a more environmentally friendly course. And no one, so far, had found any to offer.

Nepstad knew that if all the theories so earnestly debated in Katoomba and on Vancouver Island were ever to be of real use in the world, they'd have to make a difference in places such as Brazil. He longed to see a major role for the market in saving the Amazon from flames. Yet as the van turned up a steep private road for the last mile of the journey, he admitted he didn't feel great confidence. The small token of his hope was a stack of documents he carried in his backpack, a plan he intended to present the next day.

The van, along with the rest of a small convoy carrying the three dozen conference members, pulled up at the polished wooden doorway of Rosa dos Ventos (Rose of the Winds), the five-star mountainside chalets where the group would stay for the next three days. Inside, white-jacketed waiters were setting tables for a traditional Brazilian slave feast of black beans, pork parts, and collard greens, known as *feijoada,* and *caipirinhas,* the national rum cocktail.

Michael Jenkins, director of Forest Trends, had chosen the resort for several reasons. It was close to Rio, yet it provided a sense of isolation. It met the standards of comfort to which the few business executives attending were accustomed. Symbolically, also, it was potent for its location in the Atlantic rain forest, the Mata Atlantica, which was even more endangered than the Amazon. Half a millennium ago, the forest covered the eastern edge of much of South America, reaching from northeastern Brazil down to Paraguay and Argentina. But as the first point of entry for the Portuguese settlers, it endured the earliest sharp blows of progress until less than 7 percent of it remained. Through the large windows of the conference room where the group gathered after lunch, past some ornamental nonnative eucalyptus and pine trees, a denuded hill could be seen with a few withered logs strewn on the ground. For those in the group with the Amazon on their minds, it looked like the Ghost of Christmas Future.

In all these ways, the Rosa dos Ventos was well chosen. Yet a few of those who came—particularly those whose work focused on the poor—couldn't help but feel awkward in the face of so sumptuous a setting for the first Katoomba Group meeting to deal head-on with poverty. Not that they would have preferred camping out, but at this stage, nearly one year after the effort had been launched, they'd become uneasy about how much had been invested and how little produced. Jenkins' original call for a "skunk works" project had not taken shape. Instead, while pioneers such as Ron Sims and Dan Janzen were out closing deals, the Katoomba Group had turned into more of a traveling university, enriching the knowledge and projects of its individual members but failing to reach a common goal or even, in fact, to define that goal. Once again, most of the attendees in Teresópolis were scientists and would-be sellers of environmental services, with just a few insurance executives and analysts from socially responsible investment firms who might conceivably be buyers at some point in the future. They had not come close at all to designing the environmental services mutual fund Jenkins had imagined back in Australia. The group's only concrete products were Adam Davis' unfinished trading game—the fruit of his early dream of a Conservation Exchange—an unpublished paper on innovative approaches to managing watersheds, and a collection of baseball caps with the group's logo, which Jenkins passed out to raise morale.

"There's a motor that's spinning," Ian Powell, a former Shell forester who'd since been hired by Forest Trends, declared by way of welcome. "Now we need to find a clutch mechanism to engage and move forward."

Making things more difficult was that the world in general had turned cooler to the Katoomba Group's visions of markets in conservation than it had seemed back in 2000. The stock markets that had soared then were now plunging. Each day brought new reports of a possible recession. Investor sentiment had flip-flopped from a giddy openness to financial experiments to a frightened retreat to bonds. President George W. Bush was winding up his third month in office, making clear that environmental conservation wasn't a major priority of his administration. Most painful of all was the stalemate, since the previous fall, in the Kyoto Protocol negotiations, which had held such promise for stimulating new markets in environmental services.

Anxiety about where things were headed united the guests at the Rosa dos Ventos and occasionally broke through in their conversations. "I'm convinced we're going to need a lot more technology—for food, energy, and everything else—when we get to 10 billion people on this earth," an agroforester mused to a think-tank analyst over brandy late one night. "Yeah, that and a few strychnine Mars bars," the analyst responded.

At the same time, people were looking for reasons for hope, and they even found a few. During one presentation, the director of a British economics think tank showed a chart classifying 137 ecosystem services projects already being financed around the world. Most were still small and all were highly speculative, but their variety was impressive: projects including debt-for-Nature swaps, bioprospecting rights, and carbon sequestration deals were being arranged in Brazil, Canada, France, and even Uganda. And, as the director pointed out, increasing numbers of consumers were also paying for environmental services when buying ecotourism trips, salmon-safe food, shade-grown coffee, and certified wood, so his chart showed just a small part of the progress.

The group also learned of some new, pragmatic reasons for paying attention to the mostly impoverished people who lived in areas rich in environmental services. Forest Trends had prepared a study showing a recent massive transfer of land tenure, all over the world, to indigenous people. Some 70 percent of Mexican forests, for instance, had come to be controlled by *ejidos,* communal farms, whose land claims had been strengthened by Mexico's move toward more democracy. Ethnic groups were claiming a similar share of forests in Indonesia, and governments in Canada, Colombia, Brazil, Peru, and the Philippines were starting to recognize indigenous claims. Increasingly, local communities were becoming landlords of the world's dwindling forests—and not only in the eyes of the communities' own governments. In a potentially powerful trend, some international forestry certification programs, which put green labels on timber and other forest products that met their specifications, had started requiring that timber operations be approved by those living in or near the areas where they were located.

Sara Scherr, the agroforester from Maryland whose research focused on the needs of impoverished farmers, smiled at hearing this news. Her main concern with the Katoomba Group had been its scant attention, until then, to the millions of families who happened to be living in the ecosystems it aimed to protect. These mostly uneducated, mostly destitute people were at an enormous disadvantage in making markets work for them, a fact that increased the likelihood that the financial techniques being discussed would only make them more marginalized while enriching the elite. Scherr had seen too many cases in which governments branded forest dwellers as trespassers, eliminating the chance of giving the settlers incentives to switch from being despoilers of the land to protectors. Before markets could work their magic, governments simply had to take up the simple, routine business of giving titles to land.

Even then, to be sure, Scherr wondered how much profit could reasonably be derived from projects whose first goals were to protect ecosystems and raise living standards of people living in them. The presentation she liked best, judging it as the most focused on practical approaches, was by Patricia Moles, who worked for Terra Capital, a Brazilian venture capital firm specializing in biodiversity. Moles described several small businesses that were receiving support from her $15 million fund, most of which involved development of nontimber tropical products. All were as small in size as their promise was great. One such venture, for instance, was the sale of babassu oil, a refined oil from a native palm that can be harvested sustainably and has industrial uses. The fund's investors included the Inter-American Development Bank and the Swiss government. Their goal was to achieve 20 percent returns, which Moles called "philanthropic investment" because investors could probably find more profitable alternatives.

Sitting across from Scherr, Ken Newcombe was thinking along the same lines but on a much grander scale. Newcombe managed the World Bank's $150 million Prototype Carbon Fund, launched three months earlier. The fund allowed government and corporate investors to buy carbon credits—even though, at that point at least, there was still no legal way of claiming value from them. Like Scherr, Newcombe had focused his career on trying to help the estimated 1.2 billion people in the world who live on less than $1 per day. He was thrilled by the idea that investors might buy carbon credits to confront climate change and at the same time fight poverty. Whereas more pessimistic sorts envisioned carbon regulations as a squeeze on the global economy—yet another expense to deal with—Newcombe saw the promise of channeling what could be enormous amounts of private capital into improving people's lives.

His hopes hinged on the success of the Kyoto Protocol and its potential to launch a market in carbon sinks on farmers' soil. He imagined farmers in developing countries being trained in sink management—restoring and protecting forests and their carbon-holding capacity on land not suited to industrialized agriculture—as the AES Corporation was doing in Guatemala. Money, in this vision, would pour in to raise millions of families' living standards and keep them living on their land. It was a wild hope, he conceded, especially given all the doubt surrounding the Kyoto negotiations and the still large numbers of landless people, in spite of recent grants of land tenure. But in Teresópolis, Newcombe was surrounded by people sharing his eagerness to build palaces on Kyoto's wobbly foundation.

Dan Nepstad was as eager as any of them, and no less audacious. At his instigation, the Katoomba Group from its first meeting had been debating ways to use market mechanisms to address Amazon burning. Finally, he believed, he had come up with a plan. He described the idea to the group, presenting slides showing pictures of the fires and citing statistics as to the extent of their damage.

It was urgent, he explained, to come up with a response to Brazil's planned road-building program, particularly a new highway, BR-163, that was to run right through the Amazon River basin in the states of Mato Grosso—the name means "thick woods"—and Pará. With most of the highway already paved, government ministries had recently approved the pouring of asphalt to complete the last 700 miles. Powerful soy exporters had lobbied for this development because it would mean they could ship their wares overseas from the port of Santarém, at considerable savings. But Nepstad feared the road would cut through some of the rain forest's most vulnerable areas, opening them to settlers and, inevitably, to fires.

Historically, 75 percent of deforestation in Brazil had occurred within about forty miles of paved roads. These poorly policed areas had encouraged wasteful use of forest resources. The main cause of Amazon deforestation—conversion of forest to cattle pasture—provided little profit to landowners, Nepstad and his colleagues had discovered, whereas sustainable forestry, with selective timber harvests, usually involved more jobs, less damage to forests, and, most important, lowered risk of fire.

The risk of increased fires in the Amazon haunted Nepstad because he knew it threatened no less than to transform the region's climate. With the release of great amounts of smoke into the atmosphere, fire reduces rainfall and thereby raises the danger of more fires. An aerial photograph Nepstad often used in presentations told the story with chilling eloquence. It showed a sweeping view of a landscape that had been burned and cleared of most of its forest. Just a few clouds still hung over the area—each one perched above a remaining patch of forest.

There was one source of hope: as of 1995, Brazilian law prohibited owners of large properties from clearing more than 20 percent of their land. The law had not been well enforced, however, in part for lack of enforcement officials and equipment to put out fires. What Nepstad proposed was that foreign investors pay into a fund, managed by a local nongovernmental organization, that would help

local officials do a better job. In return, the investors would get carbon credits based on all the greenhouse gas emissions that would be
avoided by the reduction in fires. "We'd say we'd keep 80 percent of
the forests standing for twenty years," he explained. "Otherwise,
based on historical patterns, it's certain 40 percent would be deforested. Perhaps every five years we'd have satellite analysis to ensure
compliance."

Nepstad outlined his plan's advantages. At that stage, he believed,
there was no more point in fighting the road paving. Since it was
bound to go ahead, it was better that local scientists cooperate from
the start, providing information to the builders and local fire officials
that would spare the environment as much as possible. The strategy
was also a way to work with the limitations of the politically charged
Amazon. Carbon sequestration projects of the type The Nature
Conservancy had been involved in elsewhere in Brazil were virtually
impossible in that region—they'd be looked at as "tree cemeteries,"
offering no source of livelihood to Brazilians—and, indeed, none had
been attempted.

Still, there were obvious problems with what Nepstad called the
"green road" idea. Nothing like it had been tried before, and the
details of how it would work were still sketchy. As one economist in
the group remarked, the idea of paying Brazilians to enforce their
own laws seemed to raise some ethical problems. But the biggest pitfall was doubt that the plan's backers would ever be able to entice
investors to sign up. Although the Kyoto Protocol appeared likely to
allow some credits for carbon sinks, it looked much less certain that
carbon credits would ever be awarded for "avoided deforestation"—
unfortunately so, given that deforestation worldwide made up about
one-quarter of annual greenhouse gas emissions. As people in the
group raised these questions, Nepstad shrugged. The carbon contained in the Amazon trees still standing was as much as human
beings had released globally in the previous decade of activities such
as driving cars, running factories, and clearing land. *Something* had to
be done.

Privately, however, Nepstad was already wondering whether there were any role at all for private investors in developing countries such as Brazil. Certainly, most of the work that needed to be done to ensure some minimum of environmental protection involved simply strengthening the government's regulatory and enforcement capacity and educating its people. His uncertainty was reinforced by the presentation that followed his own, a real estate pitch from a developed country—Australia—that seemed a much surer bet to grab investors with both money and the environment on their minds.

Backed by State Forests of New South Wales, the pioneering quasi-governmental trading group in which David Brand had made his mark, a wildlife expert from Kansas named Jim Shields was going ahead with three ventures, essentially sales of environmental services. "I'm interested in defining a biodiversity credit and selling it," said the curly-haired Shields, who described his approach as a mixture of "Kansas-too-stupid-to-quit and Australian-let's-get-into-it-now." Where Nepstad's plan had been rough in its details, however, Shields' was clear. He was ready to sell contracts and even asked whether anyone in the group were interested in "bargains," including a twenty-year license, for $3.2 million, on 4,000 acres of prime rain forest and undisturbed old-growth forest in Doyles River State Forest. That land, about 200 miles north of Sydney, was inhabited by spotted-tailed quolls, fruit pigeons, parrots, and a spectacular variety of plants, from giant strangler figs to iridescent fungi. Shields said State Forests was "managing it for maximum biodiversity," meaning that threatened species would be actively protected and invasive species actively suppressed, with no timber harvests allowed in the most sensitive areas. But whoever bought the license could develop ecotourism and even build a hotel on the land, providing it didn't interfere with those goals. As for chances to make money on the deal, "You'd have to be interested in the triple bottom line," Shields said, "not only profits but [also] social and environmental benefits."

Listening to Shields, Nepstad couldn't help reflecting that saving that piece of land in Australia, however extraordinary it might be, just couldn't compare with slowing deforestation in even a small part of the Amazon in terms of solving the planet's biodiversity and greenhouse gas emissions problems went. Yet Shields' project was obviously more likely to succeed in the world the Katoomba Group was envisioning. That didn't mean it wasn't worth pursuing, of course: every little bit helped. But Nepstad found himself dwelling on questions that would come to worry other group members over the next couple of days. Would the sum of all their efforts amount to just a bunch of these little bits? Or did they really have a chance to make a difference, accomplishing something that would count on a global scale?

These questions, and the mounting impatience to put talk aside and start working on deals, led a few of the participants, including Nepstad and Scherr, to bow out when the group entered into a rematch of Adam Davis' trading game. Nepstad thought he wasn't learning anything more from it, and Scherr was tired of interrupting conversations to help plot her team's strategy. Others, however, were still committed to refining the rules and trying to get the game in shape to be of use to a wider audience. In fact, a war games expert from the U.S. Department of State who was attending the Katoomba Group meetings for the first time said he'd recommend it as an exercise for USDA Forest Service members.

If Adam Davis was feeling any doubts at that point, he didn't betray them. Sunburned and wearing khaki shorts, with his sunglasses dangling from his T-shirt collar, he looked confident as ever, which was more of a feat than usual. Natural Strategies, his consulting firm back in California, was going through, as he bravely put it, challenging times. In a marketing coup the previous year, Davis had contracted with Lowe's Home Improvement Warehouse, a major chain, to help the firm phase out its purchases of timber from threatened forests. But with the economy slowing, Lowe's had put the deal on hold, causing such a serious shortfall in revenues that Davis and his two partners had to consider laying off some of their recent hires. Instead, they had chosen to suspend their own salaries, and it had now been two months since Davis had been paid. Meanwhile, his Conservation Exchange was still no more than a domain name—that and this role-playing exercise remained leagues away from making money of any kind. The Beanie Babies–type fortune he'd dreamed of on Vancouver Island wasn't about to materialize anytime soon. Yet Davis spoke of the ConEx, as he called it, with seemingly fresh zeal. "Most people still don't know what ecosystem services are," he said. "Our whole point is to expose people to the concept, to give some experience trading in environmental services."

Davis, Ian Powell, and a few other Katoomba Group faithfuls had been working on the rules in the months since the Vancouver conference and had changed the game substantially. The site was no longer Australia but the imaginary "hitherto beautiful forested landscape" of Katland (Katoomba Landscape), set in a watershed of Brazil's highly threatened Mata Atlantica. The workshop members were assigned to six farming families, each owning about 500 acres with differing patterns of land use and access to credit. As before, the goal was to make a series of land-use decisions that would ultimately earn the most money. The families, for instance, could convert secondary forest to dairy land, ranchland, or non-native eucalyptus plantations. But certain rules applied: land originally assigned to primary forest could not be changed at all, and farmland converted to eucalyptus plantations could not be converted back to farmland. Any decision had to stick for five years, until the next round of conversions.

The scheme was still complicated, but less so than it had been in Vancouver. A computer program now calculated the costs and revenue changes involved in changing one land use to another, providing instant feedback. But just as in real life, as the players discovered, the game was rigged. One farm group, called Agrinvest, began with lots of credit, whereas another, Saladas de la Tierra, was described as previously landless peasants granted tenure to farm, but without credit and in danger of losing their land. The Katoomba Group members bent over their score sheets, haggling over whether to trade beef cattle land for dairy, for nearly an hour before Jenkins called for the next formal presentation.

The next morning, the group heard the results of round one. As in Vancouver, they were ominous. The computer image of Katland, projected on a screen at the front of the room, showed the effects of the first land-use decisions. There'd been an explosion of profitable eucalyptus planting and some clearing of secondary forest in favor of grazing land for dairy cattle. The river running down the middle of the region had stopped flowing, partly as a result of all the thirsty new trees. The families were chasing profits with environmentally harmful decisions, yet even so, few were growing rich.

In round two, as in Vancouver, the game-masters introduced buyers for environmental services. A team of conservationists would offer payments to maintain biodiversity, and municipal officials and hydropower firms would pay to guarantee the quality and quantity of water flow. Members of the group were assigned to the different roles and started meeting to plan strategies. One of the game-masters then announced that an extremely endangered frog, once thought extinct, had been found on land claimed by the Saladas de la Tierra. An economist, playing the role of one of the landless farmers, immediately announced: "We're wondering if it's edible. We're living on the edge, you know."

That was Sunday, the last full day in Teresópolis, and late in the afternoon most of the group took a hike. For about forty minutes they trudged straight up a steep hill, struggling for breath while continuing to chat about land tenure and biodiversity credits and techniques of measuring carbon sequestration. The talk barely paused at the top, where they all stood for a few moments to gaze at the panoramic view of jagged peaks and bare valleys. Pamphlets back at the hotel alleged that rare parakeets, woodnymphs, and thornbirds could be found in the scraps of surrounding forest, but none appeared—perhaps because of environmental degradation or perhaps a result of the stomping of boots and conversation.

That evening, the group heard the final results of the game. By determined negotiating, the biodiversity buyers had been able to save the endangered frog, but the hydropower buyers were in trouble because the river had definitely stopped. There were six new white patches on the computer image, denoting fallow land. More tinkering was needed, the group resolved, to create the right incentives for buyers of environmental services. Of course, that was just the point in the world outside Rosa dos Ventos. Yet the realization didn't seem to dampen people's spirits.

Sara Scherr, packing up for an extra day in Rio before flying home to her husband and children in Maryland, conceded that she felt some "disconnect between dreaming and reality." She wanted to see some clearer strategies and products from the group; it really seemed that time enough had gone by. Yet like so many others in the group, Scherr was a determined optimist. She had faith that all truly important change evolved slowly, and one just had to keep plugging.

Davis, as usual, pronounced himself electrified. As the workshops were winding down that Monday morning, he could be seen writing "FOLLOWUP" at the top of his yellow legal pad, with a list of phone calls and trips he'd have to make back home. In two months, he would fly to New York for a meeting with Mitsubishi Motors, perhaps followed by a trip to Brazil to work with Terra Capital. In all, he could count five potential deals from his networking in Teresópolis.

Michael Jenkins was also hopeful, if exhausted, as he climbed into one of the vans to return to Rio and then Washington, D.C. Jenkins had gotten married just a few months before, yet he had been on the road almost constantly since then. The Katoomba Group meetings were just one of Forest Trends' projects; he was going to China in another week to raise awareness of environmental services in Far Eastern forests. Besides, the conferences were a lot of work to pull off; he believed he had to keep things humming to maintain the group's attention. They were all overcommitted people; it struck him as a small miracle that they kept turning up at all.

Still, he felt confident of the momentum. The game was coming along, providing a tangible way to communicate ideas. Moreover, he still thought a mutual fund was possible. Jenkins was sure he'd have more ideas by the next reunion, scheduled for the following October in London—and even though he'd always thought that London would be the last of it, he had started considering future Katoomba Group meetings in Costa Rica and Japan.

Even Dan Nepstad left the meeting feeling energized. He'd talked to an economist who was working with Richard Sandor on efforts to launch the Chicago Climate Exchange and heard that they were looking for investments in the Amazon. And in a broader sense, even though Nepstad knew the Amazon was facing unprecedented threats, he believed that Brazil had more resources than ever to confront them. Cardoso's government, embarrassed by international criticism, had cracked down on fires the previous year, in a massive program with World Bank funds, and had succeeded in greatly reducing the burning. Technology to monitor compliance, such as satellite imagery, had become more sophisticated and effective. Perhaps most important, Brazilians themselves seemed to be growing more concerned about acting while there was still time to save the forest. Nepstad was impressed at the growth in committed nongovernmental organizations and local officials. In the Amazon state of Acre, a forester named Jorge Viana had become governor and even called his mandate "the government of the forest." He was putting together his own plans to engage foreign investors in "green road" projects and waiting to see whether he could offer them carbon credits. If the climate negotiations moved forward, there was still hope that large-scale improvements could be made.

That *if* got a lot iffier just two days later, however. On March 28, 2001, one day after most of the Katoomba Group returned home on overnight flights, President Bush announced his absolute rejection of the Kyoto climate process, which had given so much hope to the group's members, not to mention a large part of the rest of the world. If the United States, which accounted for a full one-quarter of the globe's yearly greenhouse gas emissions, pulled out of the negotiations, the whole effort was likely to fail. That in turn would be a crushing blow for all the foresters, farmers, and brokers who were counting on the cap-and-trade markets that it might create to transform their fortunes. Yet that's what appeared to be happening. "The idea of placing caps on CO_2 does not make economic sense for America," Bush said. "First things first are the people who live in America."

The Birds, the Bees,
and the Biodiversity Crisis

"When people do finally hear of the biodiversity crisis, too often it sounds as though it is
happening far away, in some exotic rainforest,
and not in our own suburban backyards, our
neighborhoods, our vegetable gardens, our
agricultural croplands, in our supermarket produce department or at the local fast food
burger, taco or pizza joint."

—Stephen L. Buchmann
and Gary Paul Nabhan

IN A NORTHERN CALIFORNIA farmer's field, Claire Kremen sits motionless, watching a green-eyed brown bee with red
antennae approach a watermelon blossom. The summer sun beats
down on Kremen's straw hat and intensifies the aroma of basil and
lavender from the patchwork of plots around her. A solitary figure in
a faded T-shirt and muddy tennis shoes, the Stanford University ecologist is seeking answers for questions as pressing as the quality and
cost of humanity's next meal.

The U.S. commercial food industry, an $800 billion concern, relies to an enormous degree on a twenty-first-century array of chemical fertilizers, pesticides, and genetic technology. Yet to an extent that might surprise most Americans, people's diets, and health, depend on insects. Bees and other winged life, sometimes including birds and bats, help plants reproduce via the matchmaking dance of pollination. And if farmers seek to use fewer pesticides, to reduce the toxic residues on food and in the soil, they must rely on certain insects to fight still other insects that would otherwise prey on our crops. In short, there are few more direct appeals to our self-interest in a new economy of Nature than the call to value these tiny stalwarts.

Yet despite the proven usefulness of insects, we still have much to learn about the complicated ways in which they help sustain our lives and what *they* need in order to keep doing their vital work. We do, however, know enough today to understand they're in trouble—as are we, if current trends continue. Wild plants that give helpful insects food and shelter are vanishing at an accelerating rate, under the steady advance of human settlement. And the continuing use of toxic chemicals on farms is wiping out the good bugs with the bad. Scientists, increasingly, are sounding alarms. They warn that we simply cannot continue producing food the way we do today without incurring costly losses. Claire Kremen, immersed in unprecedented research to find out more about wild bees, is one of a small group of researchers racing to fill in the blanks in our knowledge while we still have time to switch to more sustainable methods of food production. She and others are convinced that an important first step is to determine the economic value of the subsidies provided by insects and, indirectly, by their habitats.

"CAN I PARASITIZE some of your tuna salad?"

Mud-specked from her morning in the field, Kremen turns from the open refrigerator in Robert Bugg's kitchen, a periodic hangout for insect researchers from Palo Alto, California, to Beijing. Bugg, engaged in conversation at a table a few feet away, smiles and nods with distracted pride. The salad is a tangy delicacy, the tuna nearly overwhelmed by pungent herbs—lemon verbena, fennel, basil, even lavender—all grown just outside his patio door.

A prominent entomologist ("I figured my name would be an asset"), Bugg lives near Davis, California, in a colorless, treeless development. Yet his quarter-acre backyard is a lively oasis. Lush and fragrant, it teems and twitters with insects and birds drawn by the brilliant colors and scents. "I see it as a celebration of native plants," he says, waving an arm toward the California goldenrod, heliotrope, nodding needlegrass, and milkweed absent from most other gardens. Alongside his cook's garden of herbs, he cultivates more than a dozen plants that are favored homes for several species of bees, caterpillars, gnats, and wasps. He eagerly welcomes creatures other gardeners might see as pests because he knows they are actually beneficial.

Native plants are where Bugg's and Kremen's passions converge. Bugg's day job, at the Sustainable Agriculture Research and Education Program of the University of California, Davis, is counseling farmers who want to make their land more productive—both now and in the future. By teaching the art of hospitality to beneficial insects, using native plants, he helps his listeners step down from what some farmers call the pesticide treadmill. In his spare time, he receives delegations of scientists and government officials from as far away as Tasmania, and he has co-edited a major book on his expertise, a subject drawing increasing interest throughout the world with the rapid rise in popularity of organically grown food.

The organic juggernaut took off following the 1962 publication of *Silent Spring,* Rachel Carson's groundbreaking investigation of the harm done by pesticides, and within a few decades had led to a $7.7 billion U.S. industry, growing at a steady rate of 20 percent per year through the 1990s. The industry is particularly strong in California, a major farming state and naturalist's mecca that in 2001 was producing one-third of all U.S. organic fruits and vegetables. Many of the state's 2,000 organic farmers are engaged to some degree in "farmscaping," in which crops and other plants are combined in the most sustainable patterns. But the tactic has made even greater inroads in Europe, particularly Great Britain, where farmers in the 1990s were reducing their pesticide expenses by growing "beetle banks," grassy mounds providing havens for predators of crop-chomping aphids and greenflies. The British banks' lively returns suggest—as do similar experiments—that organic farming methods, usually assumed to be more costly than conventional techniques, can occasionally save money.

Kremen is among Bugg's many scientific collaborators, but the true practitioners of his art are committed organic farmers such as Tim Mueller and Paul Muller in nearby Yolo County. Both are trying to coax helpful insects onto their crops and, in their hunger to know how they might do it better, have offered their fields for Kremen's studies.

"I look out in the fields and see ladybugs, a wonderful generalist predator," says Muller, owner of the Full Belly Farm, which sells its produce at farmer's markets in the San Francisco Bay Area. "I see them on certain plants at certain times, up in the hills. But how do we create a residual population? Is it the nearby creek or the dry abandoned fields that are drawing them? And what pollinators do we want in the field? It's incredibly complex. So we shoot from the hip."

The need for more information has grown especially urgent when it comes to the fragile, fundamental process of pollination. As with many ecosystem services, the financial value of this work is understandably assumed to be great, yet specifics are lacking.

As they go about their feeding and nesting routines, more than 100,000 species of insects, birds, and mammals inadvertently, but fortuitously, transfer powdery masses of pollen grains from the male part of one flower to the female part of another. By doing so, these litterbugs play a major role in what we eat and what it costs. In one widely cited estimate, bee expert Stephen L. Buchmann, coauthor of *The Forgotten Pollinators,* claims that as much as one in every three bites of food we eat comes to us with their support. It's actually fewer than one in three, given that Buchmann and coauthor Gary Paul

Nabhan didn't count the cereal crops that are global staples but are pollinated by wind. But other scientists, while calling for more research and more reliable estimates, agree that pollination has enormous economic worth. In the late 1980s, the value of insect- (that is, mostly bee-) pollinated crops in the United States was estimated as ranging between $4.6 billion and $18.9 billion, depending on various assumptions about what should be included and how the calculation should be made.

Not only is our understanding of the economics of pollination somewhat cloudy, but research also shows that many Americans aren't quite sure what pollination *is*. One survey, at the National Zoo in Washington, D.C., disclosed that three-fourths of visitors thought of pollen as an allergenic nuisance and were unaware, even in a vague way, that it is involved in plant reproduction. Most plants require pollinators to transfer pollen for them.

Were pollinators to vanish, we wouldn't starve. But our menus would most likely become more boring, more costly, and less healthful. Potatoes, almonds, soybeans, oranges, eggplants, peppers, and tea might become expensive luxuries, if available at all. Root crops such as garlic, onion, and carrots might also be lost because they, too, need insect visitors to make their seeds productive. "We'd be culturally and nutritionally impoverished," says Kremen. No one knows whether that day will come soon or at all. Yet the evidence at hand is prompting fear. Breeding and feeding habitat for pollinators is declining rapidly as the last bits of seminatural vegetation are cleared in farming landscapes and as pesticide use continues to climb. Insects once common are vanishing. "Serious problems for world food supply, security, and trade could be in the offing if current declines in pollinator abundance, diversity, and availability are not reversed," warned the on-line journal *Conservation Ecology* in 2001.

Kremen's vigils in the California fields are inspired by these concerns. An earnest, soft-spoken woman of forty who decided to be a biologist when she was in the ninth grade, she keeps the global pollination crisis in mind even as her work comes down to tracking one bee and one blossom at a time. On Tim Mueller's family-run River-dog Farm, she traps one of the green-eyed brown bees, identifies it as a *Melissodes* species, and puts it in a tiny cage. Next, she lifts a piece of bridal veil that covers a virgin female flower—one never visited by any insect. The thin net has more than symbolic importance: it keeps out would-be visitors Kremen doesn't wish to study. The blossom has just opened, and now Kremen inserts it in the cage. For a few minutes, the *Melissodes* flies about, distracted, as Kremen patiently waits for it to calm down and sip some nectar.

The bee's legs bulge like Popeye's arms, packed with pollen it has already gathered to take back to feed its offspring, helpless larvae waiting in a nearby nest. Some of the pollen inevitably falls behind. Kremen will later take the flower to her laboratory to measure the grains deposited on the female flower's reproductive parts. She believes that only two or three visits by this particularly productive bee species will leave behind enough pollen to meet the blossom's heavy demands and produce a large, delicious melon.

"You might think transferring one pollen grain would be enough to get a nice, big watermelon," she explains. "But actually, you need about 1,000 grains to get something marketable." If the blossom receives substantially less pollen, the plant will abort its fruit. A little more but still below the 1,000-grain threshold, and the resulting melon will be small, misshapen, and less tasty. That's because a plant will expend the photosynthetic energy needed to make a melon big and sweet—and attractive to birds and mammals that will disperse its seeds—only on a fruit with enough seeds to merit all that effort. Complicating matters is that all that pollen has to be transferred in the space of just one day, the window of time that each flower is open.

Little is known about the daily lives of native bees such as the *Melissodes* species, despite all their hard work. What array of plants provide the nectar and pollen they require? Where do they live? To what degree are they succumbing to the pesticide blitz on conventional farms? We've never taken the time to find out because we've never felt much need to know. Beginning as early as the 1620s, American colonists brought honeybees with them from Europe, and since that time, U.S. agriculture has turned its back on natives while becoming increasingly dependent on millions of the tiny migrant workers.

A modern mainstay on U.S. farms, the honeybee *Apis mellifera* is both an efficient pollen distributor for many different crops and a "social" bee, living in hives and thus easy to manage and transport. Its convenience and reliability got farmers used to paying for its services, despite what can sometimes be hefty bills—as much as $40 per acre for almonds. "No conventional farmers I know of use native bees," says John Foster, who manages 7,000 honeybee hives near Riverdog Farm. "They have so much invested in their crops that they just can't take the chance. You really need to saturate your crop to get the best results, and honeybees are the only bees that can guarantee you the numbers you need to do that."

Still, the days when *Apis mellifera* meant dependability may already be over. A biblical assortment of plagues, including a tracheal mite that smothers bees by lodging in their throats, and the steady northward migration of the Africanized honeybee, which breeds with managed bees and makes their offspring too mean to handle, has threatened the U.S. beekeeping industry with collapse. The number of managed honeybees in the United States has dwindled from a peak of 5.9 million colonies in 1947 to 2.63 million in 2000. (In California, there's so much demand for managed honeybees that almond growers import them from as far away as North Dakota.) Scientists believe the number of wild honeybees has fallen even more sharply—by as much as 70 percent since 1990, by one estimate—a phenomenon noted by many backyard gardeners who've resorted to buying mail-order bees to pollinate their plots.

The decline of the honeybee represents a turning point in global farming history. For nearly as long as human beings have raised crops, they've relied on the honeybees' labor. The Egyptians were avid beekeepers who floated small barges with apiaries up and down the Nile

River as different crops came into bloom. The pharaoh made his royal symbol the bee. And the history of shortfalls of pollinating insects is almost equally as long. Scholars record that date palms had to be pollinated by hand in Mesopotamia 3,000 years ago. Still, today's problems potentially are dramatically greater in scope than any before them, in part because of how dependent our extensive croplands have become on managed honeybees.

The current economic effect of the honeybee crisis remains unmeasured. There are no reliable, up-to-date, and comprehensive data about whether or how much the gradual loss of these buzzing agricultural workers may already be costing consumers. Yet in a growing chorus of warnings, scientists and farmers alike project serious future costs from pollinator declines.

Kremen, who shares these worries, believes the native bees she's been studying since 1999 may offer a solution—a kind of insurance policy should the managed-honeybee technique finally fail. A big point in the natives' favor is that they can't mate with Africanized honeybees—an advantage that will doubtless grow in importance as the Africanized bees inexorably extend their range. Africanized bees arrived in Texas in 1990, having migrated steadily north since 1956, when African bees escaped from a geneticist's lab in Brazil and interbred with local European honeybees. The scientist had hoped the African bees would perform better in tropical conditions than the European bees, which evolved in a milder climate. But the aggressive Africanized bees have been taking a toll ever since, with swarms occasionally attacking and even sometimes killing people and animals.

Another major advantage to the use of native bees is that some of the estimated 20,000 species are more efficient pollinators of certain plants. Blue orchard bees (*Osmia lignaria*), for instance, skillfully disperse the pollen of apple, pear, and almond trees, with the added benefit that they're less aggressive with people than are honeybees, Africanized or no.

"Native bees can do the job!" Kremen boldly concluded in a draft paper on her work in 2001. Kremen's research has shown that native bees in Yolo County, in areas where they are sufficiently abundant, can provide all the pollination necessary for watermelon crops. Her work has also shown, however, that the bees are sufficiently abundant only on organic farms close to wild habitat. Conventional farms or organic farms far from wild habitat simply don't host enough native bees to provide the pollination services they need—therefore, they have to import honeybees. But throughout the United States, there are great doubts as to how native bees are faring; the general assumption is that they're in even worse shape than honeybees.

Pesticides, despite all the bad press they've received, continue to be staples on most farms. Cornell University entomologist David Pimentel has estimated that U.S. farmers use 700 million pounds of pesticides per year. That includes some toxins, such as malathion, that are more deadly to bees than DDT. Wild bees are much more vulnerable to these pesticides than are managed honeybees, whose hives are routinely whisked away before areas are sprayed.

In addition, the natives have serious food and shelter problems. They must compete for pollen and nectar with the abundant honeybee immigrants, and they're losing nesting places at an unprecedented rate as subdivisions and farms cut into their homes. They're also caught in a vicious circle. As their numbers decline for various reasons, so does their habitat because the bees pollinate some of the same plants they need to live. Without bees to carry out pollination, the plants leave no progeny and gradually die off. As these relationships, developed over the ages, break down, fewer bees means fewer plants, which in turn means fewer bees.

The obvious first step to build back native bee numbers would be to ensure that their basic needs are met. But first, scientists have to get a better notion of what those needs are. This mission was made to order for Kremen. On a research trip in the 1980s to Costa Rica, where she saw habitat being destroyed at a startling rate, she became convinced she'd never be comfortable isolated in a laboratory. "It just started to seem like a luxury to do basic research when it looked as if all the organisms you planned to study were going to disappear," she recalled. So she joined the field of conservation biology—an emerging area of study that challenged traditional disciplines with its determined focus on real-world problems. In the 1990s, while on staff at the Wildlife Conservation Society, she oversaw a team that created a new national park in Madagascar. Part of her work was justifying the project's economic value, specifically trying to show that the local benefits of watershed conservation and nontimber forest products in areas outside the park, along with the global benefits of carbon sequestration, outweighed the strong national incentives to let large logging companies operate freely.

Kremen had been back home for about two years when she opened an issue of the magazine *Conservation Biology* that featured an article by Buchmann and Nabhan, authors of *Forgotten Pollinators*. She read it as a research agenda. "It said, this is what we need to know," she recalls. With funds from the National Fish and Wildlife Foundation and other groups, she embarked on a three-year project, studying native bees on thirty-five farms in Yolo and Solano Counties, some of the world's most productive land.

The bulk of the area's agriculture takes place on flat, spacious mass-market fields to which truckloads of honeybee hives are periodically delivered. But Kremen spends an equal amount of time on organic farms such as Riverdog, whose seventy acres are tucked into foothills bordered by a creek and surrounded by thickets and oak groves. Owner Tim Mueller doesn't hire hives because he doesn't need to. As Kremen's research confirms, he's in an ideal spot to attract native bees: close to wildland areas and reasonably far from farms that use pesticides. His crops buzz with locally supported life, including bumblebees that fly back to their hives in abandoned rodent's nests and solitary bees that make their homes in holes in fallen logs or in the ground beneath the thickets. Outside the growing season, when the farm crops don't support them, the bees feed on a sequence of blooming herbs, shrubs, and trees, from wild manzanita blooms in January to flowering toyon shrubs in June.

"We're just hoping it works," says Mueller, a former anthropology student who wears a ponytail under his cap. So far, so good: Kremen has detected nearly thirty species of native, mostly solitary, bees working away on such farms. On Riverdog, they support a colorful harvest of four different types of watermelon, five of cantaloupe, eight of sweet pepper, and sixty of tomato.

With help from half a dozen undergraduates, Kremen spends many hours each day watching the native bees visit flowers and then analyzing what they've left behind. She focuses on watermelons for two main reasons: their complete dependence on insects to pollinate them and their heavy pollination requirements. If the local bee community is healthy enough to fulfill a watermelon's needs, it can probably also take care of other, less demanding crops. In the field, little red flags mark locations of virgin female blossoms, waiting underneath their bridal veils.

On a day-to-day basis, the fieldwork has often been frustrating. Kremen continually has had to chase off stray honeybees to give the native bees she wants to study access to the flowers. She has spent several months collecting a tiny data set because of the difficulty of getting bees to behave naturally inside their little cages. Only one in ten bumblebees will visit flowers when confined. Recently, however, one of her researchers came up with a solution: an "interview stick," a long pole with a flower attached, which Kremen and her associates can hold out as an irresistible temptation to the bee of choice. Since then, the data have been coming in fast and furious.

Kremen, who left Stanford for Princeton University in 2001 while continuing her California research, wanted to refine her data in the third year of her study and was counting on help from a particular native bee, the bumblebee *Bombus vosnesenskii*. Like the honeybee, *Bombus* is social, living in colonies that can be easily managed and tracked. Kremen's idea was to place bumblebee colonies on various farms and then keep track of the residents on their routine returns, marking their survival rate and the kinds of pollen they were collecting. "*Bombus* is an ideal environmental probe," Kremen says.

The bumblebee is also drawing interest elsewhere as more commercially motivated scientists try to come up with a stand-in for the increasingly besieged honeybee. Bumblebees have already proven effective in pollinating hothouse tomatoes and other vegetables. Nor are they the only ones auditioning for the honeybees' starring role. The U.S. Department of Agriculture has been investigating the potential of native specialists such as the blue orchard bee and the blueberry bee *Osmia ribifloris,* and the tiny alfalfa leafcutter bee *Megachile rotundata,* imported from Europe in 1935. The idea is that if these bees prove adept as generalists, they might be bred and managed by the millions of hives, just as honeybees are now.

Still, as far as is known, no one to date has come up with a bolder scheme for honeybee replacement than William Harper, a former computer network administrator in Washington State. In 1998, Harper began taking out patents to market "designer pollinators"—genetically modified, mass-marketed, disposable insects he claims will "dramatically change the face of agriculture worldwide." The idea is to design and breed, in vitro, insects with characteristics—such as size, body shape, and flight patterns—suitable for specific crops. The pollinators could be produced and deployed at a fraction of the expense of the honeybees because they'd die after serving their matchmaking function, thus dispensing with the cost of retrieval. (They'd also allow farmers to use pesticides without fear of harming valuable managed bees, as Harper points out.) The "keepers" of these bees would launch them into fields using explosive-gas mortars, thus replacing the age-old mobile-hive technique, which Harper dismisses as "an awkward lash-up of an ancient handicraft created to produce honey."

Harper describes himself as a "deep-green environmentalist," yet his entrepreneurial enthusiasm is sufficiently fierce as to give even the likes of Adam Davis the willies. "In an underdeveloped technology like pollination, the landscape is target-rich," Harper has written, comparing the situation to the Oklahoma land rush, when people raced to place claims on critical positions such as water sources and road passes. Late in the year 2001, Harper was still refining his inventions and had not yet contracted to market them, but he was already contemplating ways to make the pitch, including demonstrating his explosive-gas mortars at county fairs. "It sure beats passing out literature from a booth," he says.

Harper's extreme ambitions highlight a growing sense of financial potential in the overall beneficial-bug industry, no doubt related to the hefty recent increase in spending on organic food and sustainable farms. Farmers aiming for the organic market, and ready to abandon pesticides, are eagerly seeking alternative pest management techniques. Even some conventional farmers have become more receptive since 1966, when the United States Congress approved new restrictions on pesticides, outlawing some of the harshest toxins and making others less easy to buy. Many in the produce industry are turning to a philosophy of integrated pest management—combining some pesticide use with strategic releases of beneficial insects. Helpful warriors include *Trichogramma* wasps, which lay eggs inside the eggs of crop predators, destroying the offsprings' chance of survival, and beneficial nematodes—microscopic worms that attack soil-dwelling and wood-boring insects. An increasing number of home gardeners averse to spraying their vegetables and roses with insecticides have also joined the trend, buying packages of aphid-eating lady beetles (widely known as ladybugs) and other beneficial insects from firms such as the Los Angeles–based Orcon, which promises "the right bug for the right job."

Beneficial Insectary, based in Redding, California, is one of the largest U.S. suppliers to farmers and gardeners alike, selling an array of "natural enemies" that include not only wasps and beetles but also microbials—fungi and bacteria—authorized for use by organic farmers. The company's owner, Sinthya Penn, past president of the Association of Natural Bio-control Producers, surveyed the industry and, in 2001, estimated total worldwide sales at around $500 million. That's still just a small fraction of the global pesticide industry, which has revenues of several billion dollars per year, but Penn says the natural-enemy business has had far greater annual growth, by as much as 16 percent in the 1990s. The industry is also becoming more efficient. Recently, for instance, a technique was developed by which beneficial-insect eggs could be sprayed onto plants, much like chemicals.

Even as increasing numbers of U.S. farmers and gardeners deploy the tiny warriors, they may be handicapped by ignorance of what they might do to induce helpful insects, including native pollinators, to stick around. In this endeavor, farmscaping, arranging environments to make best use of insects, can provide several benefits at once. Certain plants, arranged in hedgerows or ground cover, can offer food and nesting sites to insects that farmers want to make welcome. Others provide weed control through competition, or windbreaks that help shield both the good bugs and the crops. Finally, the way crops themselves are planted can help reduce pests. As most farmers know or are learning, patchwork fields, like the ones on Tim Mueller's Riverdog Farm, are best, with crops varied to keep specific pests from simply chomping their way through while building up ever larger numbers.

Farmscaping is actually quite an ancient art. For more than 1,700 years, Chinese citrus growers have placed colonies of predaceous ants in their trees and built moats around the roots so that the guardians can't escape. The ants attack large pests that threaten the trees but leave smaller, beneficial ones alone. One recent study found that orchards employing this technique had a more than 60 percent reduction in fruit damage compared with those in which chemical pesticides were used.

On Full Belly Farm, Paul Muller experiments with "growing insects" alongside his watermelon, corn, eggplant, and other crops. Muller became a fan of biological control—the term used for insect warfare—after his squash-bug problems were solved by a fly, *Tricopoda pennipes,* recommended by researchers at the University of California, Davis. "We had just about given up on growing winter squash," he says, biting into a sweet white corncob in his pine-ceilinged kitchen. "But now we've got a battleground out there."

Since that first experiment, Muller has released hundreds of thousands of *Trichogramma* wasps, lacewings, and lady beetles onto his crops. He's also working on making the insects feel at home. He plants hedgerows with native trees and shrubs including toyon, whose flowers attract both bees and beneficial lacewings. His fields and orchards are bordered by several varieties of flowers that wave in the wind. "The key is to have something around all the time that's blooming, so you have pollen and nectar," he says. "Beyond that, there are lots of uncertainties."

Muller worries—with good reason, say even farmscaping devotees—that by making things comfortable for beneficial insects, he might also be cultivating the bugs they're supposed to eliminate. It's easy in farmscaping to make other innocent mistakes as well. Mugwort, for instance, a plant used as a medicine by Native Americans, attracts solitary bees and lady beetles but also harbors a pathogen that causes Pierce's disease, which weakens and kills grapevines. Muller frets that he's farming by trial and error. Farmscaping has been studied far less than the chemical alternatives, no doubt at least partly because it's simply not as profitable to sell seeds as it is to sell gallons of chemicals. There's hardly any scientific information available to answer the questions farmers such as Muller most urgently ask—like, for example, what percentage of their land should be devoted to habitat in order to render the maximum net benefit per acre. "We're used to looking at a bottle of pesticide that says 'Apply three ounces per acre' and just going out and spraying it," he says. "This is a far cry from that, and that's the real challenge. What we're doing is just touching the tip of the iceberg. There are so many research needs at this basic level of agriculture. And still too much emphasis on quick fixes."

This conviction has made Muller an activist. He's on the board of the Yolo Land Trust, which buys up development rights to keep farmland farming. The newsletter he sends out to subscribers who receive monthly baskets of Full Belly produce is filled with his conservation ethic, along with recipes for dishes such as Heirloom

Tomato Soup. Meanwhile, he, Tim Mueller, and other farmers persist with their shot-in-the-dark land management while scientists such as Bugg and Kremen hurry to provide them with more biological and economic understanding.

For the time being, Kremen is certain that farmers seeking to maximize their subsidies from insects can benefit from a few rules. First, protect any natural habitat where native bees and other beneficial bugs can thrive. Avoid fragmentation, which means leaving enough wildland to provide a functioning habitat. Ideally, buffer these important areas from pesticides by making sure they're surrounded by organic farms. On the crops themselves, which should always be mixed, maintain weedy borders, ground cover, and hedgerows. Aim for sequential flowering so that there will be nectar and pollen to go around all year.

Bugg takes a broader view, saying that these kinds of farm investments must be supported by basic reforms in the marketing of food. "Food in the United States is much cheaper than it should be, and that's very destructive," he says. The problem, he says, is that not only the work of pollinators but also many other hidden subsidies, such as those that keep the price of water low, still aren't brought into the price calculation.

With many of our natural subsidies starting to run out, this reality may soon change. Somehow, maybe soon, we'll have to pay more to maintain the environment around our farms. Whatever designer replacements may be waiting in the wings, we still have no good reason to trust that technology can take the place of the birds and the bees.

E p i l o g u e

The Revolution in the Wings

"This is not rocket science. It's way more complicated than that."

—*University of British Columbia conservation
biologist Fred Bunnell, on sustainability*

ADAM DAVIS' FONDEST DREAM remained unfulfilled
twenty-one months after he had traveled so hopefully to the first
Katoomba Group meeting in Australia. By the start of 2002, he'd put
aside his vision of fathering the world's first Conservation Exchange
in favor of projects that helped feed his family. In a season sobered by
an economic recession, the September terrorist attacks on New York
City and Washington, D.C., and the ensuing war in Afghanistan,
Americans were feeling much less brave about investing at all, never
mind putting money into imaginative new "green" commodities.
Bowing to this new reality, the Hancock Natural Resource Group
had delayed the U.S. launch, which had been planned for the previous October, of its new carbon-credit investment fund. And Michael
Jenkins had regretfully postponed the Katoomba Group reunion in
London scheduled for that month.

As judged in the context of that dark season, history had disappointed the Katoomba visionaries. Dan Nepstad, the scientist from Woods Hole Research Center, was frustrated that no market-based solution had emerged to stop the fiery destruction of the Amazon rain forest. Sara Scherr, the agroforestry expert, was vexed by the continuing lack of large-scale private investment in environmentally sustainable development that would also improve the lives of the poor. And everyone in the group was depressed by watching how the U.S. government's rejection of the Kyoto Protocol deflated the promise of that process to funnel huge new investments into forests.

In a particular disappointment, far off in Australia, John Wamsley had reason to ponder Andrew Beattie's warnings about the "gales that rock economics." In January 2002, Earth Sanctuaries announced that its financial returns weren't keeping up with its achievements in conservation. It began a "major restructuring" that included offering its sanctuaries for sale.

Seen in the long-term context, however, these setbacks didn't seem quite so gloomy. Every revolution has its fits and starts, and the great number of frustrations actually reflected the great number of experiments being launched. Progress *was* taking place, even if it was erratic, hard-won, and easily pushed off the newspapers' front pages. Much too slowly, yet unmistakably, the world was moving forward with a widening array of efforts to make environmental conservation economically profitable.

The most sweeping instance of this progress was the rescue of the Kyoto Protocol in July 2001, in a pivotal meeting of international environmental negotiators in Bonn, Germany. As the United States stayed on the sidelines, per President George W. Bush's decision, three dozen other industrialized nations agreed on rules that, for the first time, would require them to cut emissions of gases linked to global warming. The industrialized countries also pledged to contribute more than $450 million per year to help developing countries adapt to climate change and make a transition to cleaner, more efficient technologies. In a giant step forward in the art of creating incentives for conservation, the Bonn negotiators established the outlines of the first global system for buying and selling credits earned by reducing greenhouse gas emissions. They also approved of giving credits for carbon sinks—the storing of carbon in vegetation and soils. Although U.S. participation would, of course, have strengthened this system—as would have stricter targets and enforcement measures—it was nonetheless a huge leap forward that such a system was now in place, with the chance that the rest could follow, in time. (In a follow-up meeting in Marrakesh, Morocco, four months later, delegates moved the pact closer to ratification by several nations, including Japan and Russia, whose approval would be essential for it to gain legal force. David Doniger, director of climate programs for the Natural Resources Defense Council, called the document "by far the strongest environmental treaty that's ever been drafted.")

In at least two countries, meanwhile, national governments were taking the lead in pioneering some remarkable experiments to integrate the work of Nature into the formal economy. Costa Rica was continuing and strengthening its program of payments to farmers who preserved ecosystem assets on their land, with compensation based on the ecosystem services provided (as described in chapter 8). And Australia, in an effort to confront its farmland salinity crisis, was sponsoring the Murray-Darling Basin Initiative, which officials boasted was the world's largest effort to manage a river basin. The plan, involving an investment of U.S.$1.4 billion over its first three years plus a major tree-planting program, involves six governments, responsible for an area of more than 360,000 square miles that accounts for more than 40 percent of the country's agricultural production. A key feature of the initiative was the establishment of salinity targets—"caps" on the amount of salt that can leave individual river valleys—according to factors such as the vulnerability of crops and roads, both of which can be harmed by salt, and the drinking water quality needs of rural towns and cities.

Even in Washington, D.C., there were some signals that the tactic of assigning financial value to the work of Nature was moving into the mainstream. The debate over the 2002 farm bill featured unprecedented support in the United States Senate and in the White House for higher levels and new kinds of cash payments to support a broad range of environmentally beneficial land management practices. In a sign of the times, midwestern senators could be heard stumping for new aid for "land stewardship" practices that would preserve and produce ecosystem services, including flood control, water quality improvement, and greenhouse gas reduction.

On a more local scale, all the projects described in this book were enduring, and some were actually prospering. Napa's flood protection program and New York's watershed scheme were overcoming their various financial challenges, with the caveat that Napa had yet to be tested by major winter storms. Ron Sims was counting on a third term as he ran unopposed for reelection in King County, Washington, while negotiating new development-rights swaps to protect thousands of acres of forests and open space. And David Brand kept his faith in carbon-credit markets, designing one scheme after another. His latest was a unique life insurance policy that would invest in new forests planted to store carbon. The new forests theoretically would mitigate the policyholder's responsibility for fossil fuel emissions over his or her lifetime.

Even Adam Davis, despite his setbacks, had discovered a way to earn income with his new expertise in marketing the work of Nature, something he maintained wouldn't have been possible back when the Katoomba Group began. He'd recently joined the Eco-Solutions team of the Electric Power Research Institute (EPRI), a wealthy think tank in California's Silicon Valley serving hundreds of energy firms all over the world, which had begun to market a cutting-edge service. The team was offering audits of EPRI's clients, many of whom were big landowners, that would list all the ecological assets held on their properties. Those assets included endangered species habitat, carbon-sequestering forests, wetlands, and watersheds, and they were adding to property values under both new and potentially forthcoming local, national, and international government rules. About half a dozen firms had signed up for the audit by early 2002. One of them, Allegheny Power, managed to establish a higher value for a tract of land in West Virginia that was particularly rich in ecological assets. It then sold the property to the federal government at previous, and lower, appraised value, but was able to claim a $16 million tax write-off.

The EPRI project represented one of the world's most advanced efforts to calculate concrete values for environmental services that for so long had been taken for granted. It was also another sign of how a hitherto radical notion—treating ecosystems as vital capital assets—was becoming more broadly accepted. (That fall, even Christine Todd Whitman, former Republican governor of New Jersey and then head of the United States Environmental Protection Agency, said that progress in solving the dawning freshwater crisis "demands the adoption of a watershed-based approach," elaborating how communities must take responsibility for controlling all kinds of pollution in such areas. "We all live downstream," Whitman added.)

The growing acceptance of this new way of thinking owed more than anything to a renewed sense of urgency. As the world's population continued to climb, it was dawning on people that the extent of overconsumption in the most affluent countries, combined with increasing consumption in the poorer ones, meant we have only limited time to rescue the planet's life-support systems. Steadily growing adverse human effects had been unsteadying Earth's natural systems to the point that those systems' past patterns of tolerance were not reliable guides to the future. Lakes in the U.S. Midwest, for instance, can absorb manure-laden runoff from farms for long periods with no visible damage until a threshold is reached, at which point the lake shifts abruptly from clear to turbid. As the new millennium began, scientists were discovering similar dynamics in other ecosystem assets, such as grasslands, rain forests, coral reefs, and oceanic fisheries. They could all be exploited, with no obvious harm, up to a threshold, beyond which they were suddenly badly degraded and difficult to restore. "Gradual changes in vulnerability accumulate," says Wisconsin ecologist Steve Carpenter, "and eventually you get a shock to the system—a flood or a drought—and, boom! You're into a degraded state."

Many scientists worried that the whole planet was being pushed toward a threshold of catastrophic climate change by the gradual buildup of greenhouse gases. Extrapolating from past trends, Harvard University physicist John Holdren, a prominent energy expert, said that global energy consumption was likely to triple from the year 2000 to 2050, with carbon emissions increasing by more than two and one-half times. Yet Holdren also offered a more reassuring scenario—assuming that societies could induce a transition to cleaner energy technologies—in which the level of energy consumption would plateau at about twice that of the year 2000, with a slight, and temporary, increase in carbon emissions.

To help speed this type of transition, as Adam Davis and his fellow pioneers knew, their isolated efforts had to be greatly expanded and multiplied. They naturally felt frustrated at the slow pace of change and the idiosyncratic, trial-and-error nature of their projects. Yet they recognized that they had to start somewhere. As Davis said, referring specifically to the Kyoto Protocol, "It's not like no deal is better than a bad deal. You've got to start with *a* deal. We're now leaving theory-land and moving into the ugly, messy world of practice."

In that world, with all its complexities and contradictions, it's worth noting that every project described in this book has something in common. In each case, the proponents have followed three basic steps in producing their innovative schemes.

The first of these steps is to identify options—a point of departure requiring great creativity and a willingness to break with convention. With New York City planners, the spark came when they first seriously considered paying upstate farmers to be stewards of the city's natural water purification system. David Brand's insight was envisioning forests not simply as sources of commodities but as hospitals, offering several valuable services with revenue streams. One of Dan Janzen's many inspirations was realizing how a degraded, fire-prone pasture might provide valuable waste disposal services in a process that would also hasten the restoration of forest. Not surprisingly, the people behind each of the projects described in this book share a streak of unconventionality. Yet all are also pragmatic. In identifying options, they've been able not only to take leaps into unfamiliar territory but also to visualize all the incremental moves needed thereafter to nudge innovative ideas into being.

The second basic step in incorporating the values of Nature into decision making is to identify the implications of each alternative being considered. This can be an enormous task because the implications can be so sweeping and varied. What is gained, and what is lost—in terms of farmers' income, public health, and scenic beauty in rural countrysides—when those farmers rely on native pollinators and beneficial insects instead of their technological substitutes, managed European honeybees and pesticides? What are the pros and cons of forest conservation in the Amazon for Brazilians living there today, as well as for the climate and biodiversity to be inherited by future generations across the planet? The novelty in these questions is the focus on ecosystem capital, and on the potential effects of alternative options on its value to society.

Finally, one must *compare* the alternatives. This is the truly tricky part because it invariably means comparing apples and oranges and even passion fruit. Some gains and losses might be easily expressed in dollars, whereas others are less tangible and often subjective. How much, after all, is a numbat really worth? How much are we personally enriched by helping to ensure a safer future for our children? These questions are ever present, if often hidden. They confront residents of Napa and New York as they evaluate the success of their approaches to flood control and water purification. They confront farmers in California who are choosing between conventional and organic farming methods and the various intermediate options. In some cases, purely economic factors are decisive; in others, moral impulses play a part.

In the end—and fortunately—these kinds of comparisons needn't require pinpoint precision. It didn't really matter, for instance, that the costs of protecting New York City's watershed weren't dead certain. Planners knew that the watershed option would cost much less, and confer many more benefits, than the next cheapest alternative, that of building a water filtration plant. At the same time, the very process of *considering* a natural-asset approach in these early efforts has been worthwhile because it has drawn in a much greater variety of people, information, ideas, and values than is normally the case in planning development. Consider the cases of New York and Napa. Once a commitment was made to give attention to environmental services, it became necessary to involve people who would normally be left out, such as upstate farmers in New York and steelhead trout experts in Napa. This point of departure meant that the final shape of the projects much more genuinely reflected the values—often hard to quantify in dollars—of people whose lives would be most directly affected.

On the other hand, one great difficulty has hindered this kind of decision-making process: each of the three basic steps relies on a tremendous amount of scientific understanding, which too often is simply unavailable. It's the kind of information that might help insurance officials such as Will Romero determine the difference in financial payoff between two or three kinds of flood protection strategy or might aid local officials such as Ron Sims in judging which of two land parcels available for protection might render more salmon habitat, drinking water quality, or carbon sequestration. It's information that's in much too short supply when a farmer such as Paul Muller tries to figure out more precisely how much, and which, land he needs to set aside as habitat so that his crops will benefit from pollination by local bees and protection by other beneficial insects.

A better understanding of ecosystems would also help potential investors consider the inevitable trade-offs between the types of work the ecosystems do. Eucalyptus and Monterey pine, for instance, are native to only a few parts of the world yet are some of the planet's fastest-growing trees. If planted in place of native trees, they will store a lot of carbon but will also compete with native plants and either add nothing to or reduce the habitat for local wildlife. Although some of these choices will be easy to make, given their context, government officials and entrepreneurs will eventually need much more scientific understanding to target investments in natural capital in order to take advantage of the greatest possible mix of resulting benefits—from water quality to flood protection to carbon sequestration to pollination services, and others.

In recent years, scientists themselves have grown more concerned by the lack of such information. Marine ecologist Jane Lubchenco, while president of the American Association for the Advancement of Science, urged her colleagues to devote the same energy and skill that had been enlisted in helping win World War II (with the Manhattan Project), and in wiping out scourges such as polio, to confronting the modern-day dilemma of how societies can rearrange their activities in a way that will no longer destroy the earthly resources on which we depend.

In fact, efforts to meet Lubchenco's challenge were gathering force as the new millennium got under way. Most notable among them was the Millennium Ecosystem Assessment, an unprecedented project to report the status and value of Earth's ecosystem capital to help governments, corporations, economic institutions, local communities, and others use it wisely. The United Nations–sponsored assessment, expected to cost $25 million and take four years to complete, officially began with an April 2001 meeting in The Netherlands. Over four gray days, in a chandeliered government conference hall in the small city of Bilthoven, ninety-five leading scientists from all over the world—including experts on everything from climate and ecosystems to economies and social change—met to design the broad outlines of the assessment. Stanford University biologist Hal Mooney, a cochair of the conference, called the meeting "the first Big Think."

In its structure and scope, the project was envisioned to be similar to the Intergovernmental Panel on Climate Change (IPCC), whose reports provided the inspiration and urgency behind the international negotiations that led to the Kyoto Protocol. As with the IPCC, the Millennium Ecosystem Assessment would draw mostly on existing research, pulling together information from ongoing smaller assessments of the world's biodiversity, forests, and water supplies. It even had the same director, Robert Watson, a veteran atmospheric scientist turned diplomat. Watson had confidence in the power of science to sway policy makers, as long as the findings are solid and presented without prejudice. He'd seen it happen decisively many years earlier when he directed his first international assessment, on ozone depletion. That effort resulted in the groundbreaking 1987 Montreal Protocol on Substances That Deplete the Ozone Layer, in which leading nations agreed to cooperate to abolish such harmful chemicals.

In the ozone assessment, Watson said, there was "a direct path from science to policy. And the reason it was such an incredible success was one of the scariest words in the English language: cancer. And white people get it." With the climate change panel, the path to policy had been less direct and the progress somewhat less satisfying. Unlike the situation with the Montreal Protocol, which was geared to protect people living at the time, politicians struggling over what to do about global warming had to be convinced to invite sacrifice for the sake of generations to come. Yet the climate scientists also held a key tactical advantage in getting their point across. They had a single familiar point of entry into their complex of issues, something that everyone talks about: the weather. People could relate.

There was no such single focus for the issues of the Millennium Ecosystem Assessment. Its scope would be broad, and unlike the situation with the ozone assessment, there'd be no single scary word for the harm humanity faced from the general deterioration of ecosystems. Nonetheless, Watson was convinced that he and his colleagues could capture the public's imagination by making a case for the specific economic value of Nature's besieged assets: the coral reefs, watersheds, floodplains, and forests that provide such essential services for human—indeed, all—life, and that would be so hard to replace.

Making that case would be only the first step, of course, in establishing a truly new economy of Nature. As Watson and everyone else involved in the Millennium Ecosystem Assessment knew, much more would be needed, from both institutions and individuals.

Government support would be decisive—indeed, governments played a major part in each of the projects described in this book, from funding Napa's flood protection project to changing the Australian accounting laws. They've set limits, for example, through laws such as the Endangered Species Act and new obligatory reductions in sulfur dioxide emissions that have created financial value where none existed before, stimulating trade. They've also established the rules for the resulting new markets. In Costa Rica and Australia in particular, governments have given the world a vision of how experiments in valuing the work of Nature can be scaled up to involve large areas of land.

Still, just as important would be visionaries, to offer up inventions and push governments along. A Winston Churchill or two would certainly be welcome, but even more valuable would be leagues of aggressive community leaders like Ron Sims or corporate figures like David Brand who can achieve high-profile victories with unconventional approaches, attracting the attention of other decision makers and inspiring imitation. Many of these leaders would be pure idealists like Moira Johnston Block and Karen Rippey, but others, of necessity, might be just as driven by greenbacks as by greenery, since self-interest is what makes this approach self-sustaining. They could be entrepreneurs like Adam Davis, John Wamsley, and Daniel Janzen, working solo or via institutions, from Moira Johnston Block's Friends of the Napa River community group to John Browne's British Petroleum oil firm. They'd have in common not only exceptional powers of imagination and persuasion but also a wonk's grasp of the detailed economic and legal frameworks of their fields, details that are often overwhelming to outsiders, be they part of the Kyoto Protocol, the United States' Safe Drinking Water Act, or King County's zoning ordinances.

There is no single answer to the world's environmental dilemmas, and the progress to date toward capturing the economic value of environmental services has been so limited as to be almost symbolic. Still, what has happened so far illustrates an approach with great scope for improving the world. The goal is a planet where forests are being restored and protected and where farmland is being used more productively, for the sake of the systematic delivery of nontraditional "commodities" such as carbon sequestration, salinity control, and biodiversity. It's a world where Mother Nature at last receives fair compensation for her labor and recognition in our formal financial accounting. For any of these changes to be possible, of course, much more must be done to confront two formidable challenges: controlling population growth and consumption and raising the living standards of the poor. Also necessary will be new or improved institutions for effective global management of vital global resources such as the oceans and the atmosphere.

It all adds up to a total reordering of our world economy—"a complete transformation," as economist Geoffrey Heal has described it, "of the way our economic activities impinge on the natural world." And that, of course, would require a revolution more sweeping than any humanity has yet experienced. The pioneers whose stories are presented in this book have been good at working the system—pushing the limits of what is possible, given the laws and conventions of the day, to make relatively incremental changes. Perhaps more important, however, they are preparing us all for this kind of greater change, a change that grows more necessary every day. At this writing, at least (November 2001), the new danger from terror-ism seems to have quite forcefully done that as well, reminding world leaders in an abrupt and menacing way of the intimate connections between the United States and remote parts of the world, the array of risks involved in our heavy dependence on fossil fuels, and the urgency of confronting global problems with global cooperation.

"What gives me hope is that I know social systems are just as non-linear as the many biological systems I've been studying," says ecol-ogist Paul Ehrlich. "Just as there are thresholds in ecosystems, there are thresholds in human behavior, times when cultural evolution moves unexpectedly rapidly. We saw that in the dramatic progress in racial justice in the 1960s, the surprise decline of American birthrates in the early 1970s, and the utterly unexpected fall of the Berlin Wall and dissolution of the Soviet Union in the early 1990s. When the time is ripe, society can be transformed virtually overnight—and that could occur in our treatment of the environment in general and nat-ural capital in particular. Our challenge now is to find ways to ripen the time."

ACKNOWLEDGMENTS

We came to this endeavor from strikingly independent paths—one from journalism, the other from science—yet with some deeply shared convictions. Chief among these is the belief that even though trends in Earth's environmental problems are alarming, there's much we can still do to help reverse their direction. We also share a belief that the process of change will require new kinds of partnerships, often among people, such as ourselves, not particularly used to working together.

KATHERINE: From 1987 to 1999, I lived in two of the world's largest mega-cities: first Mexico City, then Rio de Janeiro, where I served as chief of bureaus for Knight Ridder Newspapers. In Mexico, I installed air filters in my home but still ended up with a chronic cough as I reported regularly on the desperate city's efforts to control its infamous air pollution. While based in Rio, I traveled several times to the Amazon jungle, where the world's largest remaining rain forest was steadily vanishing under an assault by loggers and settlers. The last story I wrote from Brazil described the single remaining member of a beautiful parrot species called Spix's macaw, hunted to assured extinction. At the end of my twelve years in Latin America, I moved back to the United States with my husband and two young sons, to settle in California, where I'd grown up.

What brought me back was a John S. Knight journalism fellowship at Stanford University and a chance to learn more about environmental issues and what could be done about them, a story that had become more compelling to me than any other. The Knight fellowship is a unique gift allowing midcareer journalists to indulge their intellectual passions. I found myself delving into the science and politics of climate change, the environmental issue that held my most dreadful fascination. Obviously, our way of doing business had to be changed dramatically. But what, besides fear, might provide the incentive? I was starting to look into that question on the morning Gretchen Daily gave a guest lecture in one of my classes.

Until then, the lectures in Introduction to Earth Systems had focused on the worst nightmare news for the planet: overpopulation, the ozone hole, the extinction of birds and other animals. Gretchen's lecture didn't stint on depressing news. Yet she also spoke of hope—specifically the hope that new ways of thinking about valuing the environment might lead decision makers to include environmental harm and benefits in their regular cost accounting. This, in turn, would provide a major incentive for environmental conservation. Three years earlier, Gretchen had edited *Nature's Services,* a groundbreaking collection of academic essays elucidating the economic value of forests, marine systems, pollinators, and other aspects of Nature. She was still giving a lot of lectures on the topic and working hard to draw business executives, as well as other scientists, into thinking in those terms.

At the end of the class, I approached Gretchen with a question about climate change. She politely ignored it, peering intently at me as if she'd possibly discovered a new butterfly species. Out of the blue, she started telling me about what she called a broad campaign to spread the word about these new ways of valuing Nature; she said that as part of it she wanted to present the ideas in *Nature's Services* in a new book, directed at a general audience. Maybe I could help. Before the fellowship had ended, we'd become friends, and she had given me an intriguing new lens with which to look at the world.

GRETCHEN: I came to environmental science at a young age. In the name of adventure, my dad had left his successful San Francisco Bay Area medical practice to join the U.S. Army's 97th General Hospital in Frankfurt, West Germany, with his family in tow. It was 1977, and I was twelve years old, when I woke up to a turbulent world of street demonstrations against environmental devastation I could hardly fathom. The protesters said acid was falling from the sky and that no one was doing anything about it. Back in California, I had never seen mass protests over anything. And as a twelve-year-old kid, I was stunned to learn that acid—*acid*—might be falling from the sky, killing beautiful lakes and forests.

A few years later, I heard an announcement on Armed Forces Network radio of a high school science competition. With the encouragement of a dream chemistry teacher, Mr. Holmquist, I signed up. He thought acid rain was a bit too ambitious a topic, but he helped me launch a study of the pollution in a nearby river, whereby I discovered my passion for scientific research.

Although I could spend lifetimes exploring the wonders of the universe for sheer pleasure, like Katherine I find I cannot take my mind off the big issues confronting society. Most of all, I wonder whether human ingenuity will be up to the task of bringing our ever intensifying activities into balance with what the planet can sustain. In considering how society might address such issues, it's clear that scientific understanding is but one of a complex of interacting factors shaping the future. Science *alone* will get us nowhere.

When I met Katherine, I held a wonderful research position designed to foster new, integrated approaches to environmental issues. The funding for my position came from Peter Bing, former chairman of Stanford's Board of Trustees, and his wife, Helen; the

Winslow Foundation paid for much of my actual research. This generosity allowed me to invest time in building a background in economics, law, and other key academic disciplines and in cultivating a network of people far removed from academia who shared a sense of urgency about the state of the environment.

When I first ventured outside the natural sciences, I feared I would be checking my sense of ethics at the door and entering a narrow realm of cost-benefit analysis and legalese. I rapidly discovered, however, that many economists, legal scholars, and others have studied ethical issues in much greater depth than have many critics of their disciplines. I still worry that a rushed embrace of economic incentives for conservation might take us all down a slippery slope, in which the drive for short-term profits would lead to mistakes. But these days, I worry more that neglecting the potential of economic approaches would be the greatest blunder of all.

My dealings with this integrated group of experts has helped me arrive at new ways of thinking about the environment, revealing the wealth of opportunities to make conservation both practical and profitable. *Nature's Services* was aimed at synthesizing the *scientific* basis for managing Earth's life-support systems. We still need a lot more scientific understanding to proceed effectively, yet our greatest challenge now lies in the social realm, including efforts to scale up and replicate the small models of success to date.

NEITHER ONE OF US could have produced this book alone. Each of our very different professional backgrounds has its own culture and its own peculiar strengths and weaknesses. Gretchen had never done investigative reporting nor tried to capture the dramatic human element in a story; Katherine was still relatively new to reporting on hard science. Yet by the project's end, though we were still far from experts in each other's domains, Gretchen was comfortably discussing "ledes" and "grafs" and Katherine was asking more informed questions of our experts and reading their technical publications.

Our collaboration has blessed us both with learning, friendship, and hope.

Gretchen early on came up with the general idea of a book that would tell the human stories of some of the most remarkable experiments in finding incentives to conserve Nature. Together we developed a list of case studies from around the world and an outline of how we might present them. Next, we traveled to Australia, Vancouver, Costa Rica, Los Angeles, New York, and The Netherlands to report on some of the stories and Katoomba Group meetings. Katherine traveled alone to Brazil, Chicago, Napa, and Seattle, and Gretchen to Stockholm, to cover others. Katherine then supplemented the reporting and wrote the first drafts of each chapter while spinning off related feature articles for publications including *Fortune, Worth,* and *Latin Trade* magazines and the *Philadelphia Inquirer,* the *Detroit Free Press,* the *San Jose Mercury News,* and the *Los Angeles Times.* After that, we toiled jointly over the drafts of each chapter, responding to the invaluable suggestions offered by generous, and numerous, reviewers.

TOGETHER, we owe our greatest debt to those who have shown us the way and encouraged us as we explored our own directions. No one stands out more in this regard than Paul Ehrlich, a constant source of support, wisdom, and friendship. For many years of support and inspiration, Gretchen also especially thanks Peter and Helen Bing, John Holdren, Jane Lubchenco, Hal Mooney, Steve Schneider, Brian Walker, and Kelsey, Tim, and Wren Wirth.

We are fortunate to have a wonderful set of colleagues, to whom we are also deeply indebted. They somehow always find the patience and good humor to offer all manner of help, from sharpening our understanding to suggesting new contacts, refining strategy, and generally making work productive and fun. In addition to those just named, we thank Paul Armsworth, Ken Arrow, Sallie-Anne Bailey, Patty Balvanera, Ricardo Bayon, Carl Binning, Carol Boggs, Steve

Buchmann, Steve Carpenter, Gerardo Ceballos, Steve Cork, Partha Dasgupta, Adam Davis, Tom Davis, Josh Eagle, Anne Ehrlich, Wally Falcon, Marc Feldman, Chris Field, Carl Folke, Madhav Gadgil, Larry Goulder, Liz Hadly, Geoff Heal, Jessica Hellmann, Jen Hughes, Don Kennedy, Richard Klein, Jeff Koseff, Claire Kremen, Simon Levin, Tony McMichael, Pam Matson, Norman Myers, Roz Naylor, Dan Nepstad, Henrique Pereira, Sandi Postel, Paul Raeburn, Peter Raven, Walt Reid, Taylor Ricketts, Karl-Henrik Robèrt, Terry Root, Joan Roughgarden, Osvaldo Sala, Jim Salzman, Arturo Sánchez-Azofeifa, José Sarukhan, Çagan Sekercîoglu, Karen Seto, David Starrett, Buzz Thompson, Alvaro Umaña, Peter Vitousek, Mathis Wackernagel, and others at Stanford University and at the Beijer International Institute of Ecological Economics of the Royal Swedish Academy of Sciences. Many of the ideas presented in the book were inspired and nurtured by these colleagues, although, of course, the responsibility for any errors rests with us.

Without funding, our partnership and this project would not have been possible. We are very grateful for financial support from Peter and Helen Bing, the David and Lucile Packard Foundation, the W. Alton Jones Foundation, the Flora L. Thornton Foundation, and the Winslow Foundation. We appreciate the faith put in us by the Bings, Pete Myers, Jeanne Sedgwick, and Laney Thornton.

We have drawn from the work of many people, not least those farmers, ranchers, foresters, other businesspeople, and public servants who in many cases were testing the new approaches we describe before academics caught on to them. We owe a huge debt to the pioneers whose lives and work we describe in our chapters, all of whom were gracious in the face of our relentless pestering. They include Arthur Ashendorff, Moira Johnston Block, David Brand, Robert Bugg, Linda Coady, Adam Davis, Daniel Janzen, Michael Jenkins, Robert F. Kennedy Jr., Claire Kremen, Hilary Meltzer, Tim Mueller, Paul Muller, Karen Rippey, Richard Sandor, Ron Sims, John Wamsley, and Robert Watson. Many other people played, and continue to play, critical roles in the efforts described in this book. We are indebted to all of them—for taking the time to share their stories with us and for the creativity and optimism they inspire in others.

Enormous thanks go to our reviewers. Paul Armsworth, Paul Ehrlich, and Mark Seibel read the manuscript from end to end, and with a nice blend of wit and criticism provided invaluable suggestions for improving the book. We subjected many people to parts of the book and received wonderful help from Chetan Agarwal, Andy Beattie, Kathy Blair, Cathleen Breen, David Burley, Mark Dangerfield, Partha Dasgupta, Dave Dickson, Gene Duvernoy, Josh Eagle, Mark Edwards, R. "Fuzzy" Fletcher, Larry Goulder, Lori Grant, Geoff Heal, Michael Jenkins, Gary Luck, Katie Mandes, Hilary Meltzer, Sinthya Penn, Daniele Perrot-Maître, Charles Pickett, Michael Principe, Ethan Raup, Don Regan, Walt Reid, Jim Salzman, Arturo Sánchez-Azofeifa, Sara Scherr, Steve Schneider, Eric Schroff, Lynnaire Sheridan, Dan Simberloff, Mark Sollitto, Heather Stanton, Ira Stern, Brian Walker, and Marc Yaggi.

We also owe great thanks for all the logistical help we received to keep our little show on the road. Carol Boggs, Pat Browne, Jan Curtis, Jenny Manson, Steve Masley, Jill Otto, Bettye Price, Pat Ramirez, Joan Schwan, and Peggy Vas Dias came to the rescue on more occasions than they might care to remember. Katherine sends a special thanks to Jim Risser and Jim Bettinger, the former and current chiefs of the John S. Knight Fellowships for Professional Journalists, and to the newspaper and magazine editors who took interest in this work and published related articles, including John Koten, Clifton Leaf, William Nottingham, Barbara Plumb, Bert Robinson, Mike Sante, Paul Schweizer, Steve Spalding, Darlene Stinson, and Mike Zellner.

Those at Island Press have been a pleasure to work with from start to finish. Most of all, we owe a debt of gratitude to our wise and patient editor, Jonathan Cobb, who saw us through from initial hand-scrawled notes about how this project might develop to its final publication, and who in many instances knew better than we did what we really meant to say. We are also thankful to Jan Curtis, Kristy Manning, and especially Chuck Savitt. We're particularly indebted to

Pat Harris for her brilliant, resourceful, and unfailingly good-humored copyediting.

Thanks beyond what words can convey go to Gideon Yoffe and Jack Epstein—so suffice it to say that we'll continue to treat them like kings. As for others in the realm of domestic and friendly support, Gretchen thanks Chuck and Suzanne Daily, Scott Daily, Kirsten and Kurt Ziegenhagen, and, in addition to the friends named earlier, Susan Alexander and Fred Watson, Ellyn Bush, Andrea Butter, David Goehring, Ana Herra, Kalon and Becky Holdbrook, Karen Myers and Rob Hall, and Amir Najmi. Katherine thanks Ellis and Bernice Ellison, David Ellison and James Ellison and Jean Milofsky, and Carl Blomgren, Nancy Boughey, Michelle Bullard, Katia Conceição, Arturo Garcia, Robin Giantassio-Malle, Jane Hall, Leslie Harari, Pascal Liope, Karel Sidorjak, and Ana Souza for all kinds of indispensable moral and logistic aid.

Here follows a somewhat idiosyncratic list of books, papers, and Internet sites on the topics we've presented. It is offered as a guide to relevant literature but is by no means comprehensive.

On the Relationship between Human Well-Being and the Environment

Diamond, Jared M. *Guns, Germs, and Steel: The Fates of Human Societies.* New York: Norton, 1997.

Ehrlich, Paul R., and Anne H. Ehrlich. *Betrayal of Science and Reason: How Anti-Environmental Rhetoric Threatens Our Future.* Washington, D.C.: Island Press, 1996.

Ehrlich, Paul R., Anne H. Ehrlich, and John P. Holdren. *Ecoscience: Population, Resources, Environment.* San Francisco: Freeman, 1977.

Helvarg, David. *Blue Frontier: Saving America's Living Seas.* New York: Freeman, 2001.

Hollowell, Victoria C., ed. *Managing Human-Dominated Ecosystems.* St. Louis: Missouri Botanical Garden Press, 2001.

Vitousek, Peter M., Harold A. Mooney, Jane Lubchenco, and Jerry M. Melillo. "Human Domination of Earth's Ecosystems." *Science* 277 (1997): 494–499.

Wackernagel, Mathis, and William Rees. *Our Ecological Footprint: Reducing Human Impact on the Earth.* Gabriola Island, B.C., Canada: New Society Publishers, 1996.

On Biodiversity and Ecosystems and Their Services

Allen, William. *Green Phoenix: Restoring the Tropical Forests of Guanacaste, Costa Rica.* New York: Oxford University Press, 2001.

Australian efforts to invest in ecosystem capital: "The Nature and Value of Australia's Ecosystem Services," on-line at http://www.dwe.csiro.au/ecoservices/, and "Murray-Darling Basin Initiative," on-line at http://www.mdbc.gov.au.

Baskin, Yvonne. *The Work of Nature: How the Diversity of Life Sustains Us.* Washington, D.C.: Island Press, 1997.

Beattie, Andrew, and Paul R. Ehrlich. *Wild Solutions: How Biodiversity Is Money in the Bank.* New Haven, Conn.: Yale University Press, 2001.

Buchmann, Stephen L., and Gary Paul Nabhan. *The Forgotten Pollinators.* Washington, D.C.: Island Press, Shearwater Books, 1996.

Cocks, Doug. *Use with Care: Managing Australia's Natural Resources in the Twenty-First Century.* Canberra: New South Wales University Press, 1999.

Daily, Gretchen C., ed. *Nature's Services: Societal Dependence on Natural Ecosystems.* Washington, D.C.: Island Press, 1997.

Earth Sanctuaries: on-line at http://www.esl.com.au.

Heal, Geoffrey. *Nature and the Marketplace: Capturing the Value of Ecosystem Services.* Washington, D.C.: Island Press, 2000.

Janzen, Daniel H. "Costa Rica's Area de Conservación Guanacaste: A Long March to Survival through Non-damaging Biodevelopment." *Biodiversity* 1, no. 2 (2000): 7–20.

Janzen, Daniel H.: on-line at http://janzen.sas.upenn.edu/.

Levin, Simon. *Fragile Dominion: Complexity and the Commons.* Reading, Mass.: Perseus Books, 1999.

Myers, Norman. *A Wealth of Wild Species: Storehouse for Human Welfare.* Boulder, Colo.: Westview Press, 1983.

Pickett, Charles, and Robert Bugg, eds. *Enhancing Biological Control: Habitat Management to Promote Natural Enemies of Agricultural Pests.* Berkeley and Los Angeles: University of California Press, 1998.

Pollan, Michael. *The Botany of Desire: A Plant's-Eye View of the World.* New York: Random House, 2001.

Simberloff, Daniel, Don C. Schmitz, and Tom C. Brown, eds. *Strangers in*

Paradise: Impact and Management of Nonindigenous Species in Florida. Washington, D.C.: Island Press, 1997.

Stein, Bruce A., Lynn S. Kutner, and Jonathan S. Adams, eds. *Precious Heritage: The Status of Biodiversity in the United States.* New York: Oxford University Press, 2000.

Terborgh, John. *Requiem for Nature.* Washington, D.C.: Island Press, Shearwater Books, 1999.

Western Shield program: on-line at http://www.calm.wa.gov.au/projects/west_shield.html.

Wilson, Edward O. *The Diversity of Life.* Cambridge, Mass.: Harvard University Press, 1992.

On Climate Change

Barnes, Peter. *Who Owns the Sky? Our Common Assets and the Future of Capitalism.* Washington, D.C.: Island Press, 2001.

Gelbspan, Ross. *The Heat Is On.* Reading, Mass.: Perseus Books, 1995.

Leggett, Jeremy. *The Carbon War: Global Warming and the End of the Oil Era.* New York: Routledge, 2001.

Schneider, Stephen H. *Laboratory Earth: The Planetary Gamble We Can't Afford to Lose.* New York: Basic Books, 1997.

Woods Hole Research Center, "The Warming of the Earth," on-line at http://www.whrc.org/globalwarming/warmingearth.htm.

On Water Quality and Flood Protection

American Water Works Association. *Infrastructure Needs for the Public Water Supply Sector.* Washington, D.C.: American Water Works Association, 1998.

Cronin, John, and Robert F. Kennedy Jr. *The Riverkeepers: Two Activists Fight to Reclaim Our Environment As a Basic Human Right.* New York: Scribner, 1999.

Koeppel, Gerard T. *Water for Gotham: A History.* Princeton, N.J.: Princeton University Press, 2000.

Mount, Jeffrey F. *California Rivers and Streams: The Conflict between Fluvial Process and Land Use.* Berkeley and Los Angeles: University of California Press, 1995.

New York City Department of Environmental Protection: on-line at http://www.ci.nyc.ny.us/html/dep.

Riley, Ann L. *Restoring Streams in Cities: A Guide for Planners, Policymakers, and Citizens.* Washington, D.C.: Island Press, 1998.

United States Environmental Protection Agency, Office of Water: on-line at http://www.epa.gov/safewater/.

Vaux, Henry J. *Watershed Management for Potable Water Supply: Assessing the New York City Strategy.* Washington, D.C.: National Research Council, 2000.

On Ecological Economics

Arrow, Kenneth, Bert Bolin, Robert Costanza, Partha Dasgupta, Carl Folke, Crawford S. Holling, Bengt-Owe Jansson, Simon Levin, Karl-Göran Mäler, and Charles Perrings. "Economic Growth, Carrying Capacity, and the Environment." *Science* 268 (1995): 520–521.

Costanza, Robert, Charles Perrings, and Cutler Cleveland. *The Development of Ecological Economics.* Cheltenham, England: Elgar Press, 1997.

Daily, Gretchen C., Tore Söderqvist, Sara Aniyar, Kenneth Arrow, Partha Dasgupta, Paul R. Ehrlich, Carl Folke, AnnMari Jansson, Bengt-Owe Jansson, Nils Kautsky, Simon Levin, Jane Lubchenco, Karl-Göran Mäler, David Simpson, David Starrett, David Tilman, and Brian Walker. "The Value of Nature and the Nature of Value." *Science* 289 (2000): 395–396.

Dasgupta, Partha. *An Inquiry into Well-Being and Destitution.* Oxford, England: Clarendon Press, 1993.

Davidson, Eric. *You Can't Eat GNP: Economics As If Ecology Mattered.* Cambridge, Mass.: Perseus Publishing, 2000.

Hawken, Paul, Amory Lovins, and Hunter Lovins. *Natural Capitalism: Creating the Next Industrial Revolution.* Boston: Little, Brown, 1999.

Heal, Geoffrey. "Valuing Ecosystem Services." *Ecosystems* 3 (2000): 24–30.

Jansson, AnnMari, Monica Hammer, Carl Folke, and Robert Costanza. *Investing in Natural Capital: The Ecological Economics Approach to Sustainability.* Washington, D.C.: Island Press, 1994.

Myers, Norman, and Jennifer Kent. *Perverse Subsidies: How Misused Tax Dollars Harm the Environment and the Economy.* Washington, D.C.: Island Press, 2001.

Repetto, Robert, and Duncan Austin. *Pure Profit: The Financial Implications of Environmental Performance*. Washington, D.C.: World Resources Institute, 2000.

Schmidheiny, Stephan, and the Business Council for Sustainable Development. *Changing Course: A Global Business Perspective on Development and the Environment*. Cambridge, Mass.: MIT Press, 1992.

Smart, Bruce, ed. *Beyond Compliance: A New Industry View of the Environment*. Washington, D.C.: World Resources Institute, 1992.